The Teachings of Jesus Unplugged

The New Wine

Christopher John Joseph

Copyright © 2026 by Christopher John Joseph

All rights reserved.

Cover Images by Vecteezy.com

Design by Christopher John Joseph

Published by Christopher John Joseph

Other Titles by author. The Gospels of Jesus Unplugged.

ISBN 978-1-7637703-1-7

Printed by Ingram Spark

First edition 2026

Available from: various outlets

Contact Author: jcinfocus@gmail.com

Gospel texts compiled from, The Gospels of Jesus Unplugged, Assorted Bibles, Interlinear Greek Translations and the Author's own Understanding of Jesus as Seen Through His Words.

No portion of this book may be reproduced in any form without written permission from the publisher or author, except as permitted for educational purposes or for quoting in written articles or books.

Contents

Introduction	1
1. The New Wine Corrections	4
2. Our Loving Spiritual Creator	19
3. Why Jesus Taught Spiritual Teachings	30
4. Jesus Teaches We Have Two Bodies in One	39
5. Powerful Two Body Events Called Miracles	62
6. Disciples Don't Understand Jesus	71
7. Greatest Demonstration of Two Bodies in One	82
8. Jesus Was a Pacifist Are You?	99
9. Pacifist Teaching of Jesus Destroyed	114
10. Two Different Gods	131
11. Two Identities	148
12. Identity of Light or Identity of Shadow	160
13. Equanimity	179
14. Forgiveness	185
15. Judge Not Condemn Not	192

16.	Divine Spiritual Law of Reaping What We Sow	197
17.	Spiritual Awakening	212
18.	Manifesting Spiritual Love in a Material World	218
19.	Commit to Being Spiritual	227
20.	Always Be Ready To Die and Live	237
21.	His Words Will Save You Not His Blood	245
22.	The Kingdom of Heaven is Within	256
23.	Our Characteristics as Spiritual Children	267
24.	Jesus Rose from the Dead Yes and No	286
25.	The Revelation Ruse	321
26.	Apocalyptic Overlays Put Onto Jesus	332
27.	Spiritual Analogies	354
28.	Conclusion	369
29.	GOD IS LOVE LOVE IS LIFE	371

Introduction

Jesus of Nazareth was a pacifist Spiritual Teacher of Peace and Universal Love. His Teachings provide a Spiritual path and Way of life to follow that lead us to a Spiritual awakening and inner transformation. He taught we all have another Spiritual body with us right now that is only empowered by a Loving Spiritual Life-force from a pure source of Love belonging to a Divine Loving Spiritual Creator in a Heavenly Spiritual World. He calls this 'The Treasure Hidden in the Field of Our Flesh,' that we all must seek and find to become at one with while here on Earth.

He Teaches that our Spiritual body and identity is Eternal and is singular in the way we view all of life through a Soul mind of only Love. He Teaches our bodies of flesh are temporary, die and return to the earth from which they are formed and are dualistic by nature and must be brought into alignment with our Spiritual body and Soul mind of Love to manifest this Heavenly Spiritual Love on Earth that empowers our Spiritual bodies and Soul mind.

The main purpose of His Teachings and Spiritual Way of Love and Non-violence is to awaken us to our True Spiritual Eternal identity and Heavenly Life empowered only by this Loving Spiritual Life-force and arise from the temporary flesh into Eternal Spiritual Life in a Heavenly Spiritual World of Love. We only need to understand and follow His Teachings and Spiritual Way of Love to awaken our True identity as Spiritual children of a Spiritual Loving Creator in a Heavenly Spiritual World.

In order to reveal a clearer understanding of the Spiritual Way of Love that Jesus taught and how you and I can become at one with it as He did, we must unplug Him from the dualistic Jewish religion which worshipped two opposing Gods both called Yahweh. A brutal, murdering War God and a God of Peace and Love. Two different Godheads making it dualistic on a monotheistic body called Yahweh. Jesus cut the Godhead of War from the body of Yahweh leaving only a singular Godhead of Divine Love which is not dualistic. This is what He meant when He said, "If your eye or mind is single, your whole body will be filled with Light. But if you are divided, you will be filled with darkness."

This book was written to help remove the Old Wine Jewish overlays placed onto Jesus and our Loving Spiritual Creator that are distorting His original Universal Spiritual Teachings of Love and Non-violence and the source of Divine Love. I have met many Christians who have left the Jewish/Christian churches because of the Jewish Old Testament distorting our Loving Creator and Jesus but they also left behind the wonderous Spiritual Teachings and Way of Jesus as well. I left the Jewish/Christian Catholic church over 50 years ago because of this same reason but I took Jesus and His beautiful Spiritual Words of Love and Non-violence and the Way to the Heavenly Spiritual World with me. My understanding of what He taught was never poisoned by the Jewish War God Yahweh because I rejected it just as Jesus did as being a false God and nothing to do with Jesus and His Way of Love.

Jesus warned His followers to never mix His New Wine understanding of the Loving Spiritual Creator in with the Old Wine two headed God Yahweh of the Jews, but the early Christian leaders mixed the two wines together perverting the identity of our Loving Spiritual Creator and distorting the Way of Love of Jesus.

I hope this book will help restore the connection to Jesus and the One True Spiritual source of our Spiritual Life through freeing the words of Jesus and their meanings from the distortions of the Jewish overlays that have held them captive for over 1700 years and inspire children to believe in the Heavenly Spiritual World and His Spiritual Way of Love to enter this Spiritual World.

INTRODUCTION

Daily Prayer to Center Your Spirit

As I rest upon the Earth,
the Holy One will give birth to who I really am.
Awakening me from clay and sand,
a Spiritual child of the Divine,
with only Her (His) Love that fills my mind.
To every creature I will be kind,
in every single land.
For this is truly who I am.
A Spiritual child of the Loving Spiritual Creator
in the Heavenly Spiritual World.
Born out of the Earth,
to bring Her (His) Love to children in need
and help guide them home to Heaven,
as She has guided me.
Through the Spiritual Way and Teachings
that Jesus gave us to be just as He.
A Spiritual child of Love on Earth.

I use the pronoun 'She' but most use the traditional 'He'.
Our Spiritual Creator is beyond gender.

Chapter One

The New Wine Corrections

The following is a short summary of the main points and corrections concerning the New Wine understanding that Jesus taught about our Spiritual identity and Eternal Life, our temporary body of flesh, our Loving Spiritual Creator and the Way to the Heavenly Spiritual World.

Never Mix the New Wine with the Old Wine

This following one Truth is extremely important to see and understand as it will help you remove the distortions that have been placed onto Jesus, our Loving Spiritual Creator in the Heavenly Spiritual World and the Way of Love that will definitely lead you to the Heavenly Spiritual World after your Spiritual body separates from your body of temporary flesh after passing through the death experience of your body of flesh.

Jesus said, "A man should never put new wine into old wineskins, for if he does the new wine will burst the skins, and the new wine will be lost, and the old wineskins will be destroyed; but new wine must be put into new wineskins. And no man used to drinking old wine desires new wine, for he only knows the old wine and thinks it is good enough."

Thomas Gospel: Jesus said, "A person cannot mount two horses or bend two bows, just as a servant cannot serve two Lords or Gods. That servant would respect one and offend the other. No person drinks aged wine and immediately wants to drink new wine. New wine is not poured into old wineskins for the skins may break and aged wine is not poured into new wineskins for the wine may spoil.

No one tears a piece of cloth from a new garment and sews it onto an old garment; if he does, the patch will not match the old and it will lift away from it, the new from the old, and a worse split or schism is made between the two"

These are the warnings Jesus gave to His followers about the Old Jewish religion and His New Spiritual awakening to the True source of our Spiritual Life and all Christians have to wake up and also understand what Jesus understood. The Jewish religion is not a monotheistic religion with only one God but a dualistic religion with two very different opposite Godheads on one body called Yahweh. A Godhead of War, murder and thieving called Yahweh 1 and a Godhead of Love and Peace called Yahweh 2. Once you realise this obvious Truth you will see Jesus and the Loving Spiritual Creator of Jesus in a New Way and Light. It is extremely important that all Jewish/Christian churches in the world stop teaching this lie that there is only one God in the whole Bible. Yahweh 2 is a God of Love and Peace. But now that the Jewish War God Yahweh 1 is on full display in the West bank and Gaza in 2025, if you don't wake up to this Truth now you never will.

Yahweh 1 is a Godhead of brutal revenge, war, murder, stealing and lies. This is the Satanic Godhead of War Jesus was referring to when He said to the Jews who followed it, "Why don't you understand My words. It is because you cannot bear to hear My message. For you are children of your father Satan and you want to carry out his desires. He was a murderer from the beginning and dose not abide in the Truth because there is no Truth in him. When he speaks a lie, he speaks from his own resources; for he is a liar and the father of it."

The best example of the Jews worshipping this Satanic Godhead of War Yahweh 1 can be seen in the book of Joshua at the slaughter and genocide of Jericho committed by the Jews who were directed by this Satanic Yahweh 1 to go and do it. They murdered every man, woman, child, sheep and donkey by the sword and stole the gold, silver and bronze treasures to take back to their God of War Yahweh 1 Temple and burned the whole city to the ground and stole all their lands.

These are the same modern-day Zionists who are committing murder and genocide in Gaza and the west bank because they say their Godhead of War Yahweh 1 has promised the land of the Palestinians to them. So, they are going to drive them out or wipe them out, try to obliterate Gaza and the west bank and steal it from them. Jericho all over again. This is the Satanic Godhead of War that Jesus cut off from Yahweh's body leaving only the Godhead of Love, but as Jesus said Himself the Jews did not want to let it go and they still don't.

We must remember Jesus risked being stoned to death every day for speaking out against the War God Yahweh 1 and He had to use parables or words that indirectly pointed to and condemned the evil Yahweh 1 without directly stating it was Yahweh. And He was in a bind because He could not easily say it was Yahweh because the cunning Jews also called their God of Love and Peace Yahweh as well.

He referred to the two different Yahweh's condemning the evil War God Yahweh while praising the God of Love in ways like this when He taught, "You have heard it said of old to 'Love your neighbour and hate your enemy.' But I say to you, love your enemy, pray for those who persecute you and despitefully misuse you so that you may be children of your Loving Spiritual Creator in Heaven. For Her sun rises for the evil and the good and Her rain falls for the just and the unjust. If you wish to be Her Spiritual children, your Love must be as perfect as Her Love." Here He is obviously calling out the War God of the old dualistic Jewish religion as being a false God while leading them into the singularity of the One True Loving Spiritual Creator of our Spiritual bodies and Soul minds of Love.

Yahweh 2 is a Godhead of Love that could lead to the Universal Loving Spiritual Creator that Jesus was at one with and we all could be. The simplest example is found in Leviticus, Yahweh 2 says, "If a foreigner resides amongst you in your land, do not mistreat them. You must treat them as a Jew and love them as yourself." This is the Universal message of Love that Jesus taught that we are all Spiritual children of our Loving Spiritual Creator, and we should all recognise this in everyone we meet regardless of superficial differences. Many Zionists ignore Yahweh 2 to worship Yahweh 1 instead but use Yahweh 2 to love other Jews while they slaughter other foreigners and steal their land as in the West bank in 2025 using Yahweh 1 as a pathetic excuse. A schizophrenic religion built on a lie that these very two different opposing Godheads are the same one God called Yahweh.

This is what Jesus is saying when He stated they cannot ride two horses at the same time or bend two bows at the same time or serve two Lords or different Gods at the same time. If they kill and murder foreigners in the name of their War Godhead Yahweh 1 then they offend their Godhead of Love Yahweh 2. And if they love foreigners in the name of their Godhead of Love Yahweh 2 then they offend their War Godhead of dominance, murder and thieving Yahweh 1. As Christians we must never believe the lie that Yahweh is One God and the same Loving Spiritual Creator of us all that Jesus became an awakened Spiritual child of while here on Earth in the flesh. We must only turn to our Loving Spiritual Creator who gives True Life and can never harm anyone.

He also was clearly referring to the old two headed God of the Jews and the One True Loving Creator when saying that the garment or identity of this new Spiritual Loving Creator does not match the garment or identity of the old two headed Yahweh God. And if anyone tries to tear a piece of the new One Spiritual Loving Creator and try to sew it onto the old two headed Yahweh God it will lift off because they do not match. And you will make things a lot more confusing and complicated to understand the Truth about your Spiritual identity as Her children. And the schism between you and our One True Spiritual Loving Creator will be made worse and more confusing.

Again, we see Jesus using clever analogies to indirectly condemn the War God Yahweh 1 so as not to be stoned to death for directly blaspheming the War God Yahweh. The Divine Spiritual source of Life that Jesus found and became a Living Spiritual child of is not the two headed God Yahweh. This is why Jesus could never use the word Yahweh to refer to Her/Him because Yahweh refers to two Gods not One. But nearly all the Jewish/Christian churches do exactly what Jesus said not to do and teach Yahweh is the one God of Jesus. They must stop doing this today.

Is it any wonder many intelligent Jewish/Christian church children have walked out on their churches as a direct result of all those dualistic churches teaching this lie and distortion about Jesus and our Loving Spiritual Creator causing confusion and disillusionment. Once you realise this simple Truth it will help 'Set you free,' from the Jewish distortions overlayed onto Jesus and open up your Spirit to really come alive empowered only by the Loving Spiritual Life-force of our Loving Spiritual Creator in the Heavenly Spiritual World. The Loving Spiritual Creator only heals, restores and gives True Spiritual Eternal Life to all who wish to receive it and can hurt no one as Her whole being is only empowered by pure Love. And it is the purity of Her Spiritual Love untainted by any Evil that is the real power we all need to join with right now while our heart is still beating.

The Jewish Yahweh is a divided God within itself and is therefore filled with darkness. Jesus said, "If your eye or mind, is single your whole body will be filled with Light." Thomas Gospel: "When anyone should come to be whole, they will be filled with Light, when however they come to be divided, they will be filled with darkness." Wake up, this is a new day to understand the

Truth that Jesus was really teaching and become a Living Spiritual child of our Loving Spiritual Creator in the Heavenly Spiritual World while you are still in the body of flesh. Cut yourself free from the tentacles of the Jewish Yahweh 1 War Godhead and stay with the Divine Loving Spiritual Creator of Jesus which Yahweh 2 was moving towards.

We All Have Two Bodies with Us Now

In the chapters ahead we will see how many times Jesus actually taught this Truth. He explains they are made of different life-forces one being Earthly and one being Spiritual. All our Earthly bodies of flesh are only empowered by Earthly material things such as potatoes, water, gases and other material elements and die and return to the earth just as His did. But He teaches we also have an Eternal Spiritual body with us when He taught, "The Kingdom of Heaven is within you." Our Spiritual body is only empowered by the Loving Spiritual Life-force of our Loving Spiritual Creator. Jesus spoke of this when He taught, "I am in our Loving Creator's Spiritual Life-force and our Loving Creator's Spiritual Life-force is in Me." If we just understand His words and follow and practice them, they will awaken our Spiritual bodies and they will become our primary body on earth and beyond after our body of flesh dies. As Jesus said, "Flesh only gives birth to flesh. Spirit only gives birth to Spirit. Marvel not that I tell you, you must be born again from above."

The Importance of Being a Pacifist Christian

In these chapters we will see how the early church leaders were corrupted by Emperor Constantine in the fourth century and converted True pacifist Christians, following faithfully to the Spiritual Way of Love and Non-violence that Jesus taught, back into being Jewish/Christians so they could murder the enemy like the Jews. A total disgrace that this filthy lie is still being preached by most Jewish/Christians today slandering Jesus and our Loving Spiritual Creator. As Jesus said, "Do not be afraid of those who can kill your body of flesh but can never kill your Soul and Spirit but rather be concerned about your Spirit and Soul being destroyed by corruption preventing you from entering the Heavenly Spiritual World of Love." Jesus let go of His body of flesh and so must we one day. Get ready by becoming Spiritually alive now.

The Identity of Light or Shadow

In these chapters we will see how we can become our True Spiritual Eternal identity of Light now or create a false shadow identity from our own imagination by turning our back on the Light and Love of our Loving Spiritual Creator. No evil of any kind can come forth from an awakened Spiritual child of Light empowered only by our Loving Creator's Spiritual Life-force. Only Love, Compassion, Forgiveness, Non-violence, Equanimity, Generosity, Honesty, Spiritual Truth and care for others can be manifested. However, all Evil can only come forth from a false, lying, dark shadow identity created by a narcissistic, egotistical, self-serving state of mind. They project an identity onto themselves to live out of produced from a figment of their own imagination to dominate others, to steal, enslave and even murder empowered only by the body of the flesh. There is no Spiritual Life-force involved in their actions or thoughts so consequently their Spirit grows weak and is covered in their own darkness cut off from Heaven and the source of real Life.

Mother Teresa, Mahatma Gandhi, Martin Luther King and many other beautiful children lived out of their True Spiritual identities of Light to a great degree. Buddha and Jesus perfected the Spiritual Light within themselves and became fully enlightened children of our Loving Spiritual Creator on Earth, and they both said we can all be just as fully enlightened as they were.

On the other hand, all the warmongers of the world including those in 2025 are false shadow identities and living a lie while they slaughter and rob children of our Loving Creator. They have become the children of the Satanic war god and as they give out suffering to other children of our Loving Creator they will eventually all receive that same suffering back upon themselves unless they repent for their evil before their body of flesh dies. We must feel outraged at their Satanic actions and do our best to try and stop them but sorry they are all heading for a Hellish experience after death. There is no need to kill their bodies of flesh as one day they will all die anyway and reap what they have sown.

The Spiritual Law of Reaping What We Sow

In these chapters we will see that Jesus clearly taught there is life after the death of our body of flesh, but we must be careful because we will all reap as we have sown. Our Loving Spiritual Creator and Jesus do not cause any suffering to anyone. If we end up in a place of 'Burning Realisations' cut off from Heaven, where we have to undergo cleansing of our Souls and Spirits then we are the ones who created it by ourselves. Our Loving Creator and Jesus will do all they can to stop us creating a living Hell for ourselves after we die to fall into, but they must allow us free will to choose.

All the beautiful children of the Light who only bring Love into the lives of others will receive that same Love after their body of flesh dies when their Soul and Spirit leaves and enters into a Spiritual World beyond all suffering empowered only by Love. We are all under the Spiritual Law of Reaping as we Sow for how could there be a more perfect justice. Instead of our Loving Spiritual Creator and Jesus being our judges as many Jewish/Christians wrongly teach, it is we ourselves who pass judgement upon our own life by planting seeds while alive to reap the fruits of after we die. Evil seeds we plant while alive in the flesh can produce many various fruits of bitter sufferings we must later consume. Seeds of Love can only produce fruits of Love. As Jesus and Buddha both taught, "With what measure you give out, it will be measured back to you." Karmic consequences really do happen.

Characteristics of a Spiritual Child on Earth

Jesus describes our True Spiritual identity and the Spiritual characteristics that form our Spiritual identity as, "The New Covenant." The Greek word translated as 'covenant' more correctly means our new disposition or new character. His own awakened Spiritual life displayed these qualities to us. These mainly include, Love, Compassion, Forgiveness, Non-violence, Equanimity, Generosity, Honesty, Spiritual Truth and caring for those in need whether in physical or Spiritual need. Jesus provides numerous parables and direct Teachings to help us understand and focus on these important living Spiritual aspects we all must integrate into our Earthly lives to awaken our True Eternal Spiritual body and Soul mind of Love.

These Spiritual qualities are all empowered by our Loving Spiritual Creator's Life-force and all of them are necessary for us to become whole or singular in Light. They are like the wedges of a circle that are all needed to come together in order to form a full circle window for the Light to shine through. And every single child on earth only has to become at one with these characteristics and they will become an awakened Heavenly Spiritual child on Earth. But they must not have any of the dark counter forces in with them or they will become divided and be in darkness

Regardless of having religion or no religion or belief in Heaven or not or in a Loving Creator or not with these characteristics making up who you are we will automatically all be brothers and sisters and Loving Spiritual children of Heaven on Earth.

His Words Save Us Not His Blood

Jesus is recorded saying approximately seventeen times that it is His words that clean you and save you if you listen to them, understand them and become awakened or transformed by them. Nearly all the Jewish/Christian churches wrongly teach that it is His blood on the cross that cleans you of sin and saves you. But this is another one of the Jewish overlays placed onto Jesus seeing Him through a very strong Jewish lens making Him out to be a sacrificial lamb who dies for our sins. This is an incorrect understanding based on the Old Testament Yahweh 1 War Godhead who demanded sacrifices of innocent animals to gain his favour. We see it in the sacrifice of an innocent lamb and its blood being placed over the doors of the Jews in Egypt to protect them from sickness, killing innocent animals in the Yahweh 1 and 2 temple to atone for their sins and in the red heifer sacrifice where an innocent unblemished cow was slaughtered and burnt and the ashes are used to cleanse you of sin. Bad luck if you're a vegetarian and can't be involved.

Only once in the Gospel of Matthew is it recorded that Jesus said at the last supper "Take this cup and drink from it for this is my blood of the new covenant poured out for many (for the forgiveness of sins.) This ending was added by Matthew and is not in the other Gospels. In John's Gospel Chapter 15:3 Jesus at the last supper actually said this is what makes you clean of sin, "You are already clean because of the words I have spoken to you." And many times, He stated, "My words they are Spirit and they are Life. He who listens to My words and understands them, will never taste death." His blood on the cross tells us we all have another body that is Spiritual and eternal, but it is His words that save us by bringing us alive to who we really are. Spiritual children of a Loving Spiritual Creator in a Heavenly Spiritual World of Love.

Manifesting Spiritual Love in a Material World

Once we understand His Teachings and we awaken to become Spiritual children we then must manifest this Heavenly Love through our body of flesh for all children we meet. Jesus makes this very clear in His teachings that once awoken to our Spirit we are to serve others and help them in any way we can. It is our awakened Spiritual identity that then uses our Earthly body of flesh to manifest the Loving Spiritual Life-force that empowers our Spiritual body here in this material world. Without our Earthly body of flesh, we could not easily manifest Spiritual Love for other children in this material world. Jesus teaches that our two bodies must be at one in purpose when He says, "The inner will be like the outer." The Spiritual body of water in the vase and the Earthly vase body containing the water become one dynamic manifestation of Heavenly Love on Earth.

All Christian charities in this world manifesting Heavenly Love for all without discrimination come forth from the Teachings of Jesus. They are seen in His Teaching about the sheep and the goats. When the sheep come into the presence of our Loving Spiritual Creator after passing through our death experience the children of Love and Light will hear Her say, "When I was hungry you fed me. When I was thirsty you gave me to drink. When I was naked you clothed me. When I was a stranger, you took me in. When I was sick you cared for me and when I was in prison you visited me." And they will say, "But when did we ever see you in such need Loving Creator and do these things for you?" And She will answer, "When you did it to the least of my children, you did it to Me. Enter into the Heavenly Spiritual World of Love."

And the Goats are those who refused to help her children in such need and are not allowed to enter the Heavenly Spiritual World and are dismissed and must undergo cleansing and further learning and reap the consequences of their heartless, greedy actions.

Apocalyptic Jewish Overlays Placed onto Jesus

All the sayings in the Gospels about Jesus returning one day on the clouds to personally usher in a massive destructive Apocalypse upon the earth are all false. Jesus never said any of these even those directly put into His mouth mostly by Matthew. Matthew is well known as the Jewish Gospel with numerous Jewish overlays placed onto Jesus for the benefit of the Jewish people to try to make Jesus more acceptable to the Jews and persuade them to follow His new understanding of our Loving Spiritual Creator. But Matthew often distorts the Teachings of Jesus and links Jesus back to the two headed Yahweh God of the Jews and especially the book of Daniel

I have shown clear examples of how Matthew deliberately perverted a saying of Jesus from the original found in the Gospel of Thomas about awakening Spiritually to your True Spiritual identity into a segway to attach an Apocalyptic ramble of his own making. He shifts other sayings around also to produce this same distortion perverting the real Spiritual meaning of the words of Jesus. Jesus was never an apocalyptic Jew. It has all been fabricated and overlayed onto Him. Jesus is not coming back. He wants you to wake up to your True Spiritual identity and follow Him to the Heavenly Spiritual World beyond all suffering where He is waiting to greet you.

Jesus Rose from the Dead Yes and No

Here we will look at the Truth that the body of flesh of Jesus did die and did not rise again just as Jesus Himself taught using His own words. We will also see quite clearly, He repeatedly taught that our Spiritual body would leave our body of flesh and reap as it has sown. We then sift through the red herrings placed in the Gospels to cover up this Truth but also the clues left to reveal the

Truth that He did indeed rise in a body of Spirit, not flesh. The best two examples are found in John who provided a very strong red herring but also the most telling Truth about Jesus now being in a perfect Spiritual body.

John's red herring is the doubting Thomas episode where Thomas was not present when Jesus appeared to the disciples. And John drops it in to the storyline and gives graphic details about the wounds on the hands, side and feet of Jesus from the crucifixion. But it does not appear in any other Gospel and in fact the Truth is found in the Gospel of Luke stating that Thomas was actually present when Jesus appeared.

John's obvious and best confirmation that Jesus rose in a fully Spiritual body is when He appears to Mary Magdelene at the tomb in John's Gospel. Mary goes to hug Jesus after she recognises it is Him, but Jesus says to Mary, "Do not try to hold Me Mary for I have not yet ascended to our Loving Spiritual Creator." It is put this way to cover the simple fact that Jesus was now only in His Spiritual body while Mary was still in her body of flesh and could not hold the Spiritual body of Jesus as they are two different life-forces. John was a very close disciple of Jesus and while covering up the Truth to save the Teachings He also hid the clues in amongst his writings for those who have eyes to see and ears to hear.

Revelation Ruse

Here we will see how the Book of Revelation is a cunning ruse to destroy the Teachings of Jesus and slander Him and our True Loving Spiritual Creator while converting Christians back into being Jewish/Christians to worship the two headed God Yahweh of the Jews. It was placed in to tie Jesus into the Old Testament book of Daniel and the false Apocalyptic accounts in the Gospels attributed to Him. The Apocalypse belief was adopted from the Zoroastrians by the Jews, and the Old Testament book of Daniel is the real Apocalyptic book. The fake Revelation Book is just a regurgitated Daniel and a load of rubbish to slander Jesus and our Loving Spiritual Creator, confuse and distract followers of Jesus and sever your connection with our Loving Creator and Heaven while destroying your True Spiritual identity. I personally advise every single Christian to rip it out and burn it. The only thing it is useful for is to start a fire.

These Are Some of the New Wine Truths

The above topics represent some of the much-needed corrected understandings about the Life and Spiritual Way and Teachings that Jesus gave. It is extremely important that all the distortions and perversions still being taught to children about Jesus and the True Divine Loving Source of His Life and ours are brought to an end right now by all the Jewish/Christian churches. The Bible must be cut into two separate Books. The Old wine Jewish two headed God Yahweh religion and the New Wine One Loving Spiritual Creator religion that Jesus founded. Rip out the book of Revelation and burn it. I have explained as best as I can the Truth amongst the lies to help free Jesus and our Loving Spiritual Creator from the chains of Jewish overlays that have been poisoning the beautiful Universal Spiritual Way and Teachings of Jesus for over 1700 years. And I hope it helps free confused children from the distortions as well.

I have been a gardener and close to nature all my life on Earth. And I have always seen Jesus and our Loving Creator since a very young child as Love and Non-violence. I have never been polluted or poisoned by being brainwashed with the Jewish overlays which has given me a seemingly unusual, but I believe clearer understanding about Jesus and His Teachings compared to Jewish/Christians. I hope my own beliefs are of some help to others on their own journey to awaken Spiritually and make their Way home to the Heavenly Spiritual World of Love.

GOD IS LOVE LOVE IS LIFE

Love your Way to Heaven

Bring Heaven's Love to Earth.

We need you to help this happen.

There is no one else who can be you.

Help increase the power of Love on Earth

by becoming a Spiritual child of Heaven on Earth.

Chapter Two

Our Loving Spiritual Creator

Our Loving Spiritual Creator is beyond gender. I personally choose to refer to our Loving Creator as She, but you may feel more comfortable replacing my female pronoun with the male pronoun He as you read this book. I prefer the pronoun She as it is our Earthly mothers who give birth to our biological bodies, so it is reasonable to also call our Divine Spiritual Creator She, as She gives birth to my Spiritual body and Life. Also, in this Earthly world it seems a common satanic sickness that mostly males start wars not females, so to align the Divine Loving Creator with females is quite in accordance with the more Spiritual and intelligent gender on Earth.

Another interesting coincidence in the English language is that the pronoun 'He' only represents the male identity. Whereas the pronoun 'She' has both male and female pronouns in the one word. Therefore, using the pronoun She covers the identity of our Divine Loving Spiritual Creator more fully. But She is not dualistic and beyond gender.

Our Loving Creator has placed a perfect Spiritual body and Soul mind of Love in every single human being on Earth to find, become at one with and enter the Heavenly Spiritual World of Love after our body of flesh dies and returns to the earth. Our Loving Creator holds every single child as being equally precious whether saint or sinner and does everything in Her power to guide them all home to safety in Heaven. She only heals, restores, forgives and lifts you up when you fall down. She can never hurt any of Her children.

This is a dangerous material world, filled with dark forces, traps and temptations to make you go astray along with simple physical dangers and sufferings, and we need the Loving Spiritual Teachings and Way given to us by an awakened child of Hers like Jesus or Buddha to navigate safely through this challenging world. They are our Spiritual shepherds who only protect us.

It is true that we all need a good Spiritual Teacher of Love and Non-violence to help guide us to awaken and become Spiritual before our body of flesh dies and naturally, we honour those Loving Teachers and give great thanks for their kindness to care about us. But it is incorrect to say that only followers of Jesus will enter the Heavenly Spiritual world but rather to say only those who know the Way of Love and Non-violence and become at one with it that Jesus and other great Spiritual Teachers like Buddha taught will enter the Spiritual Heavenly World of Love or Nirvana. It is not just the person Jesus who saves you but His words explaining the Way that awakens your Spirit and leads you to Heaven. These Truths are universal and found throughout many religions and philosophies to varying degrees.

I believe Jesus had a complete understanding of the Spiritual Way after His inner experience of enlightenment and had a fully opened connection through His awakened Spirit with our Loving Spiritual Creator in the Heavenly Spiritual World. His Teachings when seen correctly will transform anyone into becoming a living Spiritual child of Heaven on Earth transcending this material world and becoming a bridge between the Heavenly Spiritual World and the Earth material world to bring Heavenly Love to all other children. Our Loving Creator has inspired many children from different cultures and religions over the centuries to search for Her and the Heavenly Spiritual World and the Way of Love to get there. They all Teach the same Way of Love.

She is Only Love. Matthew 5:43-48. Luke 6:35.

Our Loving Spiritual Creator's identity and very existence is only formed from a Loving Heavenly Spiritual Life-force and mind of Pure Love. She can harm no one. She Loves and cares for every living thing. And She has created a Spiritual world of Love for us to come to if we just choose to be Her Spiritual children of Love on Earth now. It is a free will decision we must all make ourselves. Jesus clearly states that the source of our Spiritual Life comes forth from a Divine Spiritual Being of Perfect Love.

Jesus describes our Loving Spiritual Creator and Her perfect, Loving mind and nature when He taught, "You have been wrongly taught of old, 'You shall Love your neighbour and hate your enemy.' But I say to you, Love your enemies, bless those who curse you, do good to those who hate you, pray for those who spitefully use you and persecute you, so that you may be Spiritual children of our Loving Creator in the Heavenly Spiritual World. For She causes Her sun to rise on the evil and the good and sends rain on the just and the unjust. She is kind to the ungrateful and the evil and forgiving to all who come to Her in Truth and in Spirit.

If you love them who love you, what degree of Spiritual Life is that. Do not even sinners, thieves and tax collectors do the same. And if you greet your fellow brethren only with respect, what more are you doing than others who are little in Spirit. But I say to you, Love your enemies do good and lend, hoping for nothing in return and your Spiritual Life will increase.

If you only Love some but not others, you are divided within yourself and cannot be called Her Spiritual children. In everything treat others the same way you want them to treat you. Therefore, if you wish to be Her Spiritual child on Earth and later enter the Heavenly Spiritual World, your Love now must be as perfect as Her Love towards all of Her children on Earth."

This is why one of the most important Spiritual attributes we must have as children of our Loving Creator and as followers of the Way of Jesus is to be a pacifist just as He was in order to awaken, establish and strengthen our Heavenly Spiritual body and mind of Love to be ready to enter into an entirely new Spiritual World and existence in our Spiritual body after the death of our Earthly body of flesh.

She is a Loving Spiritual Being. John 4:23-24

Jesus said, "The hour is coming and now is, when the True worshippers will adore the Loving Spiritual Creator in Spirit and Truth; for such are those who the Loving Creator seeks to be Her children. The Divine Loving Creator is Spirit, and those who wish to adore Her and be with Her must come to Her in Spirit and in Truth."

It is difficult at first for us to understand that this perfect Spiritual Being of Love really exists due to be being born in a temporary body of flesh in a dualistic material world of Love and Hate, Pleasure and Pain, War and Peace, Birth and Death. Our Earthly physical senses cannot easily detect Her presence in our life however, She does exist but is a Spiritual Being not physical. Which is why we need to awaken our Spiritual Body and Soul mind of Love to be able to connect with Her and feel Her presence working in our Life.

She places our Spiritual body in our body of flesh and helps us awaken Spiritually through Her children who have already awakened Spiritually like Jesus and Buddha who give us the Teachings of the Spiritual Way so we may also awaken. Then we will be able to feel Her presence being always with us before we die and be guided by Her to Heaven. This is the treasure hidden in the field of the flesh that Jesus spoke about. Our Spiritual identity must be alive, and because it is our ultimate True identity then we can enter into Her Spiritual World of Love in 'Spirit and in Truth' as Jesus taught.

Jesus was a fully awakened Spiritual child of the Loving Spiritual Creator filled with Her Love on Earth which He then manifested through His physical actions and words to help us all be raised from the life and death of the flesh into the Eternal Life of the Spirit. If we follow His Way we will also become awakened Spiritual children of our Loving Creator as He did. For as He said we must come into the presence of the Divine Spiritual Creator in our body of Living Spirit not body of dead flesh.

She is Wholly Good. Mark 10:18

Jesus said, "Only the Divine Loving Spiritual Creator is wholly good." Clearly Jesus is telling us that Her entire being and nature is truly perfect in Love and goodness. And like gold, cannot be tarnished by anything evil such as killing or throwing children into Hell and suffering.

That would be a characteristic of the two headed God of the Jews with the Godhead of War and the Godhead of Limited Love on one body called Yahweh, not the Divine Loving Creator of Jesus. She is perfectly good and only Love and we can be Her Spiritual children of Love on Earth if we choose to believe in Her and Her Spiritual Way.

Jesus teaches that our Loving Spiritual Creator can only give us Life because Her very nature is Eternal Spiritual Life itself. And all the things we need to have that Spiritual Life are given freely to us by Her if we just choose to accept them. Jesus reveals Her nature and character through His own Life on Earth and says if we understand and know Him, we will understand and come to know Her and then know our True selves as Her children.

His Spiritual Life of Love, compassion, forgiveness, non-violence, equanimity, honesty, generosity, and caring for those who have fallen down seen throughout His Life on Earth is the very essence of our Loving Spiritual Creator in the Heavenly Spiritual World of Love. Jesus displays all the necessary characteristics we must become at one with to awaken our Spiritual bodies and Life to enter the Heavenly Spiritual World of Love.

She Never Harms Her Children. Matthew 18:12

Jesus teaches that our Loving Spiritual Creator never destroys any of Her lost children but only Loves them to Heaven by lifting them out of the darkness of their own making. Jesus taught "If a man has a hundred sheep, and one of them has gone astray, does he not leave the ninety-nine who are safe on the mountain and go and search for the one that has strayed into danger? And when he finds it, truly I say to you, he rejoices over this lost one being found than over the ninety-nine who never went astray. Likewise, it is the will of our Loving Spiritual Creator that not even one of the least of these that has gone astray should ever perish or be destroyed."

Neither Jesus nor our Loving Spiritual Creator can ever harm any of us because their whole being is only empowered by their Loving Spiritual Life-force which is Eternal. There is no suffering in Heaven at all. They will do all they can to help bring us out of any dark dangers we may have fallen into and been captured by or inspire us to overcome disbelief and complacency to help awaken our Spirits by shining their Light of Truth and Love upon us to guide us into becoming Spiritual, and be ready to have a new Life in the Heavenly Eternal Spiritual World after the death of our body of flesh. They will reach into the darkest places to bring us out because no darkness can overcome their Light.

However, Jesus also teaches we must all cross over the River of the Spiritual Law of Reaping as We Sow or River of Karma to reach Heaven's shore. Those alive in Spirit with Love will just walk across like Jesus did on the water. Those who have covered their Spirits in evil filth will sink into the river and undergo the cleansing experiences of burning realisations of their own wrongdoings. Only we can harm our Spirits by committing evil through free will decisions. If a physical sickness or pain affects our behaviour in a bad way our Spirit is not tarnished as it is not a free will decision but an external interference.

She Only Gives Us Good Things. Matthew 7:11.

Jesus explains our Divine Loving Creator who is perfect Love can only give us Loving good things. Jesus said, "If you, being imperfect, know how to give good gifts to your children, how much more will your Loving Spiritual Creator in Heaven give what is good to all Her Spiritual children who ask Her."

At all times we are Spiritual children of our Loving Creator whether we know it or not. Only the degree of awakening into our Spiritual identity differs between all children. Some of course become dark shadow figures as beasts of the flesh like the war mongers murdering, stealing and causing great death and suffering to other children with very little Spiritual Life-force left in their Spirits. While other children are selflessly helping and Loving all other children they meet and are filled with Her loving Spiritual Life-force. But for both groups She will only give good things to support their Spiritual Life and Spiritual needs. How each child receives Her support will depend on their situation and state of Spiritual awakening but her intention is always to help wake them up to becoming a child of Love and Non-violence so they can enter the Heavenly Spiritual World.

Her Spirit Gives Us True Life. John 6:63

Jesus said we are given True Life by Our Loving Spiritual Creator through Her Spiritual Life-force to become Her Spiritual children. Jesus teaches, "It is the Spirit who gives Life; the flesh profits nothing." and "Man does not live by bread alone but by every word that comes forth from our Loving Spiritual Creator."

All bodies of flesh die, disintegrate and perish leaving no trace of their existence. No matter how much food we have all our bodies of flesh will still die one day and return to the Earth. We must shift our primary identity from a physical being to a Spiritual being while we have time to do so. As Jesus taught, we must all be born again into our Spirit to have our ultimate True Life and become Spiritual children in the Heavenly Spiritual World She has created for all Her Spiritual children to come to after our body of flesh dies. And it is Her words given to us through Jesus and other great Spiritual teachers that make us aware of who we really are beneath the covering of flesh and bones. She is Spirit and gives us True Life if we wish to accept it now.

She Only Helps Us Reach Heaven. Luke 12:32

Jesus states this is the only intention of our Loving Spiritual Creator. Jesus allays the fears of children by telling them, "Do not be afraid little flock about your life on Earth, for it is your Loving Spiritual Creator's good pleasure to give you all Spiritual Life in the Heavenly Spiritual World." Jesus is always explaining that our Loving Creator can only Love us and never hurt us while trying to awaken us to become at one with our True Spiritual identity to be ready when our body of flesh dies to enter Her Heavenly Spiritual World of Love beyond all suffering.

She is Omniscient. Luke 8:17

She is omniscient and the reason She knows all about us is because we all have a Spiritual body that is enlivened by Her Loving Spiritual Life-force connected to Her within our body of flesh. Nothing we do, say or think can be hidden from Her. Jesus talks about Her omniscient mind when He said, "For there is nothing concealed that will not be revealed or hidden from view that will not be known, or anything secret that will not come to Light." And in Luke 16:15, Jesus said, "You are those who justify yourselves in the sight of men, but the Loving Spiritual Creator knows the truth of your hearts."

Often in life we may feel abandoned, misunderstood and alone but She knows the real you and She can always see you, so we are never really alone Spiritually. And that is a very good thing because you can talk to Her about anything that is happening in your life be it good or bad because She is always watching over you. Jesus said when we talk with our Loving Creator about the needs for our life, She already knows all about them before we even ask Her for help.

Jesus tells us to pray in a personal way to our Loving Creator in Matthew 6:6-8, "When you pray, go into the room of your inner Spiritual Soul to talk with our Loving Creator. And our Loving Creator hearing all you say will respond by sending Her Heavenly Love into your life often in an unexpected way to help you." While others may not understand you, She always does.

Even if we commit some dark actions we only have to come to Her in Spirit and Truth and apologise for dirtying our beautiful Spiritual Life She gave us and She will wash our Spirits clean with Her Love and is always full of joy to receive us back into Her Loving Spiritual Life-force and see us get back on the Spiritual Path that leads to Heaven's shore. Knowing that Heaven can see you all day and night is a comforting and good thing providing of course you are Good.

She Sees Our Good Works. Matthew 6:2-4

Jesus tells us to perform our Spiritual good works naturally and simply without wanting acknowledgement from others, for our Loving Spiritual Creator can always see us doing them and She Loves us all the more for doing so. Jesus teaches, "When you give to the poor, do not sound a trumpet before you. But when you give to the poor, do not let your left hand know what your right hand is doing, so your giving is in secret and your Loving Creator seeing you do this without wanting any praise will fill you with Her Spiritual Love." Of course, if we were to steal from someone, She would also see that and you would spill out and lose some of Her Loving Spiritual Life-force from your Spirit.

She is With Us in Life and In Death. Luke 12:6-7

Jesus said, "Two sparrows are sold for a copper coin. But not one of them falls to the ground and dies without our Loving Spiritual Creator being with them. And our Loving Creator even knows the number of hairs on your head. Therefore, do not fear to die to your flesh, you are of more value than many sparrows and our Loving Creator will be with you even at that time." She is always with us throughout our whole life on Earth even unto the end. But the question is are we with her?

We must be aware that Heaven and our Loving Creator can see us all the time even though we cannot see them for they are fully in Spirit while we still perceive things through our senses and eyes of flesh. But if we become Spiritual, we can perceive and feel their presence being with us and working in our life. We connect with them through our Spirit by simply talking to them about our daily life as we would to an old, close friend.

They always listen to us and never turn away from us, and we can imagine them sitting beside us in their beautiful Spiritual bodies with thoughts of Love and support for us joining in with our own Spiritual journey. They may even give us ideas that arise unexpectedly in our Spiritual mind and thoughts to guide us in the Way we must proceed.

I personally see Jesus as my great, loyal friend and Spiritual Teacher just sitting sometimes beside me on a park bench while I chat with Him. At other times I talk directly to our Loving Spiritual Creator who created my Spiritual Life for me or sometimes to loved ones who have gone to the Heavenly Spiritual World before me. I stay connected to Heaven in this simple Way and Spiritual practice of acknowledging the reality of the Spiritual Heavenly World, our Loving Spiritual Creator and all the children who are already there.

GOD IS LOVE LOVE IS LIFE

Heaven can always see us.

We can look towards them with our Spirit.

If we still our busy Earthly minds, we may hear them.

Lovingly and gently guiding and encouraging us onwards.

Towards our destination. The Heavenly Spiritual World of Love.

Chapter Three

Why Jesus Taught Spiritual Teachings

The first reason Jesus spent the last few years of His life on Earth giving Spiritual Teachings was so we could all be transformed into Spiritual children of our Loving Spiritual Creator, just as He was, through understanding His Teachings and Spiritual Way. And then we could all come out of this material, dualistic world of suffering and enter into the Heavenly Spiritual World of Love when our two bodies of flesh and Spirit separate at the time of death. But we must become alive or awoken to our Spirit before we leave. If we follow and understand His words correctly, they can bring those dead to their Spirit back to True Spiritual Life before they die. He Loves us to Heaven by bringing us into the singularity of Heavenly Love of our Loving Spiritual Creator in the Heavenly Spiritual World that we can find within ourselves if we search for this hidden Treasure by following His Teachings.

The second reason was to enable the singular Spiritual Love and Loving Life-force of our Loving Creator and Heaven to come into this material, dualistic world of suffering through each child's awoken Spiritual identity, body and Soul. For this is what empowers the manifestation of all good Loving actions and works we may perform in this world for the benefit of other children of our Loving Creator.

It is His Teaching parable about the sheep and the goats that speaks directly to this important Spiritual dynamic we must all be involved in as Living Spiritual children of our Loving Creator on Earth. And this is one of His most powerful Teachings that has been a massive driving force behind all the Christian charities in this world.

The Sheep and the Goats

Matthew 25:32-40

Jesus taught, "All children will come before their Spiritual Loving Creator, and they will be separated into two groups like sheep from the goats according to their works. And our Loving Creator will say to the warm hearted sheep, 'Come into the Heavenly Spiritual World I have created for you; for when I was hungry you gave Me to eat, I was thirsty and you gave Me to drink, I was a stranger and you welcomed Me in, I was naked and you clothed Me, I was sick and you cared for Me, I was in prison and you came to Me.' And the sheep will answer Her, 'But when did we ever see you needing any of these things and give them to you our Loving Creator?' And She will reply, 'Whenever you did these things to one of the least of My children you did it to Me. Come and enter into the Heavenly Spiritual World filled with My Love.'

Then our Loving Creator will say to the cold-hearted goats, 'Depart from Me and go to another place for you are not ready to enter the Heavenly Spiritual World. For when I was hungry you gave Me no food, I was thirsty, but you gave Me no drink, I was a stranger and you did not take Me in, naked and you did not clothe Me, sick and you did not care about Me or visit Me when I was in prison.'

And the goats will say to our Loving Creator, 'But when did we ever see you needing any of these things Loving Creator?' And She will say to them, 'Whenever you did not do these things to one of the least of My children in need you did not do it to me. Begone away from here until you wake up to who you really are.'"

The third reason He taught children the Spiritual Way to Heaven was so that after He finished His time on Earth helping children to arise into their Spiritual body and True Heavenly Life, they would pass on His Spiritual Teachings and Way to other children coming into this world to bring them to Heaven also through His Teachings. And as long as His Teachings were understood correctly and continued to be taught correctly then everyone would be linked to the Heavenly Spiritual World through Him and His Teachings. As Jesus said, "My words they are Spirit, and they are Life."

Then we can all become a Living bridge between the two worlds for other children by having one foot in Heaven and one foot on Earth. This is like the beautiful story of St. Christopher's Spiritual awakening to follow Jesus. He became a living bridge by using his strong body to carry others safely across a dangerous river to yonder shore and saved their lives because many who tried to cross by themselves were drowning.

Jesus had to teach us a basic Spiritual Truth that our two bodies of flesh and Spirit can become directly opposed to each other if we are not careful. A Spiritual child will tend the wounds of another child injured in war. A child who becomes a beast of the flesh devoid of Spiritual Love creates the war. A child filled with the Loving Life-force of our Heavenly Creator using their intelligent brain can create a kidney dialysis machine for children with failed kidneys. A child with the same brain but devoid of this Spiritual Loving Life-force can create a bomb, a tank, a drone or missile to blow children's bodies to pieces.

One is a child of our Loving Spiritual Creator in Heaven in their True Spiritual identity worshipping Life, with both bodies at one in purpose to bring Love into this world, while the other is a beast of the flesh, a child of satan and Hell worshipping death devoid of Spiritual Life and Love living out of a false, empty, dark shadow identity. Their two bodies are divided in purpose, so they are filled with darkness. It is a free will choice. This is why Jesus was always giving Spiritual Teachings about the flesh versus the Spirit and the dangers to look out for while guiding us into the straight and narrow Way of singular Spiritual Life and Love that leads us to Heaven.

Jesus had to teach us that the Loving Spiritual Life-force from the Heavenly World is the ultimate medicine that we all need to awaken our Spirit and Live out of in this Earthly world to help reduce manmade suffering in all of its forms including war, poverty, starvation, racism and the destruction of the natural environment. Love is the only answer to all such evils.

For the Loving Life-force in our Spiritual body cannot be involved in creating suffering because it comes from a Spiritual Creative Being whose entire mind is only filled with Love. It counteracts any false beast of the flesh identity from arising from the dualistic mind of our body of flesh to indulge in selfishness or dominance and transforms us into selfless, caring and True Loving Spiritual children of our Loving Creator in the Heavenly Spiritual World.

Jesus had to teach us that we all have two different bodies with us right now. He discovered His own Spiritual body within Himself after being inspired and guided by our Loving Spiritual Creator in the Heavenly Spiritual World to seek it and find it. The main directive He used to find it was the power of Love. He had to teach us that She placed this beautiful Spiritual body and Soul in our body of flesh to provide us with a way to leave this material world of suffering and come into a Spiritual World of Love and Peace beyond all suffering and death. Jesus said, "Flesh only gives birth to flesh. Spirit only gives birth to Spirit. Marvel not that I tell you, you must be born again from above."

He also reveals this Truth in His Teaching about two women sitting in the same position grinding at one millstone and one body dies while one body is taken to be received near to our Loving Spiritual Creator in Heaven. The woman at the millstone, had two very different bodies like all of us. Jesus teaches that her body of flesh that died was nothing more than food for the vultures and the important one of Spirit lives on and rises up from her dead body of flesh into the Heavenly Eternal Spiritual World, if she is ready to enter.

This is the extraordinary, beautiful balance that Jesus was able to achieve in His Teachings explaining the interactions between the two different worlds of Spiritual Heaven and material Earth and the two different bodies we all have formed from each world that appear as one. Our Earthly body of flesh is a temporary, dualistic material body formed out of the earthly elements and life-forces which returns to the earth at the end of its life cycle. Our other body is an Eternal Spiritual body formed from the Spiritual Life-force of our Loving Spiritual Creator in the Heavenly Spiritual World only empowered by Her Loving Life-force and returning at the time of death to be in Her presence in Heaven, the source of our Spiritual body and True Life. Then we all reap as we have sown.

After Jesus draws our attention to the two different bodies that we have with us right now, He then teaches us how to unify them through Love. We are easily drawn into being dominated by our body of flesh to only find happiness through it, with all of its physical sensations, its dualistic mind and temptations to become a satisfied self-serving identity to varying degrees and intensities. This is an easy road to take, and Jesus warned that many go in that way, but it can lead to the destruction of their body of flesh and seriously damage their Spiritual body and Life as well.

So, Jesus teaches a counterbalance to us that will avoid that happening. We must bring our Spiritual body fully alive. And then through awakening to our Spiritual Life and body, we can bring both bodies into balance by being at one in purpose. Only then when the division between the two different bodies is brought into perfect alignment with our Spiritual Life and body becoming the primary identity to live out of, will we find True happiness and inner peace in this dualistic material world. Only our Spiritual mind is singular in Love and Light and no evil can exist in it or enter and disturb it, while the mind of the body of flesh is dualistic and is susceptible to infections, evil poisonous thoughts and beliefs and can be easily divided into Love and hate and this is how darkness enters into us.

Once we are fully awoken and arise into our Spiritual body and Soul then the body and minds of flesh and Spirit will become merged into being at one with Spiritual Love. Battles and challenges may still arise on our journey to maintain this oneness of Love, but a strong commitment to our Spiritual Life awakened through the words of Jesus will not be easily overcome. By following the Spiritual Teachings and Way of Jesus that awaken us to our True Spiritual identity we will be filled with the Light and Loving Life-force of our Loving Spiritual Creator. As Jesus taught, "If your eye or mind is single in Love your whole body will be filled with Light. But if you remain divided within yourself you will be filled with darkness."

Jesus teaches that once we become children of Light and Love in this material world, it is essential that we always make our Spiritual Body, mind and Soul our primary identity that we live out of until the day we leave. Then our temporary, biological body of flesh simply becomes our great companion that we travel with while here on Earth in this material world.

We need our Earthly body while here in a material world to be able to manifest good works empowered by the Spiritual Love in our Spiritual body that flows into us from the Heavenly Spiritual World. Jesus taught this will now become like, "A well of Living water springing up inside your Spiritual body, Soul and mind sustaining you now for all eternity."

So, we become like Spiritual riders on an earthly horse with us holding the reins directing our earthly bodies to take us wherever our Loving Creator's Spiritual Life-force in us is needed to share with other children. We are not our horse, and our horse is not us as our bodies are made of different substances and empowered by different Life-forces. But when we ride together as one in purpose, to bring Love to all children on Earth, we will find the perfect balance and harmony between being in our Earthly body of flesh as well as our Heavenly body of Spiritual Love at the same time. Then we will indeed be a bridge from Heaven to Earth.

And according to Jesus there is no greater achievement than that on Earth that we can attain to. We will become as He, a Living Spiritual child of our Loving Spiritual Creator in the Heavenly Spiritual World on Earth to bring Her Love to all children and help guide them home to Heaven as He has guided us.

All His other important general Spiritual Teachings, discussed later in the book, concerning such things as endless forgiveness, endless generosity, endless compassion and endless Love are things we must practice in order to bring our Spirit to Life. Just as a river is only a true living river when it is flowing, so also our Spiritual body is only a True Living body when our Loving Creator's life-force is flowing into and through us to other children. And we give this Living water of Love to all in need.

Then at the end of our journey here on Earth, when our two bodies separate, we will enter the Heavenly Spiritual World of Love beyond all suffering and be in the presence of our Loving Spiritual Creator whose beauty, perfection, kindness and Love is beyond all words. But over time distortions, slanders and misunderstandings have infiltrated the simple purity of the Spiritual Teachings and Way of Love that Jesus gave to us.

I hope this book may provide a clearer and fresher way to see Him and understand His Teachings more easily to help inspire and empower us to awaken to our True Spiritual identity and bring Heaven's Love to Earth. Humanity devoid of Spiritual Love is moving towards self-destruction and the countdown to zero is getting closer. But we can turn it around if we all come together in Spirit and in Love and every single individual is important and needed to achieve this, including you and me.

I will end with a simple, personal example of how understanding this important dynamic of having two bodies of Spirit and flesh at the same time, that Jesus Teaches us about, actually works to bring a unified Love from Heaven into this Earth world of suffering through the unification of both bodies at one in purpose. Love is the driving force behind all good actions.

One day after visiting my sister Joan I was driving back when I saw an elderly man with his dog trip on the gutter and hit the concrete path with his head. My Spiritual body and Soul mind immediately wanted to stop and go to him straight away to see if he was alright, but I could have caused a traffic accident. In that moment my Spiritual body was my primary body. But I needed my talented horse who was driving the van to carefully negotiate all the traffic and turn the van around safely to take my Spiritual body back to him. In that moment my body of flesh became my primary body in order to accomplish my Spiritual action of Love.

My Earthly companion body successfully did this and together we then tended his wounds, and then we dropped him home safely to his house. My two bodies were in perfect harmony inspired primarily by Spiritual Love from the Heavenly Spiritual World empowering my Spiritual body and manifesting it in this material world of suffering through my talented horse's body of flesh working together as One in the purpose of Love.

I will miss him when we part ways when I leave this world. But while I am here with him, I will take good care of him and thank him for staying with me until I had awoken to my Spiritual body and rode with him for a while in this Earth world to bring a little bit of Heaven's Love to children in need through him. I hope you do the same.

GOD IS LOVE LOVE IS LIFE

We all have Two bodies in One.

Our Spiritual body is primary and Eternal.

Our physical body is secondary and temporary.

All Love flows into our Spiritual body from Heaven.

This Love then flows out of us through our physical body.

And we can then bring Heaven's Love to all children in need.

Chapter Four

Jesus Teaches We Have Two Bodies in One

What did Jesus really teach about our life on Earth in a biological, dualistic, temporary body of flesh made from material earth elements such as water, gases and earthly foods and empowered by the intricate interaction of all these different elements, chemicals and body parts, which eventually ends in death?

He taught that we all have another hidden body within us which is Eternal, totally Spiritual in nature and singular in its identity. Empowered not by various temporary, finite Earthly elements but only by a Loving Spiritual Life-force from an Eternal Spiritual Loving Creator in a Heavenly Spiritual World of perfect Love. This is the treasure hidden in the field of our Earthly bodies that He spoke of and which our Loving Creator offers to all human children to bring us out of this material world of suffering into a world of Spiritual Love.

Jesus taught our True primary identity is our Eternal Spiritual body with a Soul mind of only Love. No matter how healthy our bodies of Earthly flesh may be, they all eventually disintegrate and die. But once our Spiritual body and Soul mind of Love is healthy and alive we will continue to exist after our body of Earthly flesh dies.

Two in a Single Bed

Luke 17:34-37

The following is one of the most important, overlooked and misunderstood Teachings of Jesus where He literally says we have two different bodies with us right now that will separate at death.

Jesus taught, "He who lives an Earthly life of only the flesh will lose it. But he who separates himself out from his life of flesh, by following My Spiritual Way and Teachings, will find his Eternal Spiritual Life.

There will be two bodies in a single bed. One is Spiritual, one is flesh. The one of Spirit will be taken to be near to our Loving Spiritual Creator. The one of flesh will no longer be of any use and being redundant will be sent forth.

There will be two women grinding at a millstone in the same position. One is Spiritual. One is flesh. The one of Spirit will be taken to be near to our Loving Spiritual Creator. The one of flesh will no longer be of any use and being redundant will be sent forth.

There will be two standing in a field. One is Spiritual. One is flesh. The one of Spirit will be taken to be near to our Loving Spiritual Creator. The one of flesh will no longer be of any use and being redundant will be sent forth."

Thomas Gospel: Jesus said, "Two will relax on a couch. One will die; one will live. If the flesh has come into being because of the Spirit, it is a wonder. However, if Spirit came into being because of the flesh, this is a wonder of wonders. But I am amazed at this, how such great richness of Spirit could be placed in such poverty of the flesh.

When you know your True selves, then you will be known and understand that you are Spiritual children of the Loving Spiritual Creator. But if you do not know your Spiritual self, then you live in poverty, and your flesh will embody that poverty."

The disciples then asked Jesus, "Where will they be Lord?" Jesus replied, "The dead body of flesh will be where the vultures gather." This next saying has been deliberately cut out, "The body of the Spirit will be where the eagles fly."

This very clear and important Teaching of Jesus can also be seen in one of His most, simple and profound sayings, "It is the Spirit who gives life, the flesh profits nothing."

The Greek translations clearly emphasise Jesus is saying that there are two bodies in a 'single' bed. Two people cannot be resting in a single bed made only for one. Women in each home ground their own flour on a small personal millstone which only had room for one person grinding at a time. Yet Jesus clearly emphasises again that there are two women grinding in the same position at the millstone. And there are two standing in a field and two will relax on a couch and in all cases, one is sent forth which means dies, and one lives on and is taken to be received near to someone. The Greek word 'taken' in all Gospels should correctly be translated as, 'Taken to be near to (someone).'

Jesus is firstly reminding us that the death experience can occur at any time during our ordinary daily or nightly activities so always be ready to leave in your Spiritual body. He is then saying at the time of our physical death our body of flesh is nothing more than food for the vultures. It has no life in it anymore. But the other body lives on and is lifted up above to be received near to someone not mentioned in the Greek translations of the Gospels because it has been deliberately cut out but clearly refers to our Loving Creator in the Heavenly Spiritual World. Jesus actually said, "One body (Our Spirit) is taken to be near to our Father in Heaven."

Jesus is stating that our Earthly body of flesh returns to the earth from which it was made, and our Spiritual body returns to the place and source of its creation which is the Heavenly Spiritual World and our Loving Spiritual Creator who made it for us. But this happens for everyone at the time of our death just as it did for

Jesus. He did not rise from His dead body of flesh in His Spiritual body three days later but the moment His heart stopped beating just as we all will.

And we will not rise in our reconstituted body of flesh during an apocalyptic day of judgement and massive suffering instigated by Jesus and our Loving Creator as nearly all Jewish/Christians wrongly teach and slander Jesus and our Loving Spiritual Creator. Lying and misleading children away from the Truth to suit their own Jewish/Christian beliefs in Yahweh the two headed God of the Jews. For this Truth spoken by Jesus Himself interferes with and contradicts the Jewish/Christian distorted overlays placed onto Jesus and our Loving Creator by the corrupted early Christian leaders and continued to be upheld by the current corrupted Jewish/Christian leaders of virtually all such churches.

Where the body of the Spirit goes is missing in all Bibles. It has been deliberately deleted because it upset the traditional status quo established in the meeting at Nicaea in 325 A.D. by the Jewish/Christian leaders. That is why 'The Gospels of Jesus Unplugged' has included the reference, "The body of the Spirit will be where the eagles fly," as a counterpoint to the vultures saying about our body of flesh and to replace the missing Truth that Jesus taught about our Spiritual body. For eagles glide high above the material world with wings outstretched lifted up by the wind amplifying the words of Jesus and their meaning. The word wind of course in Greek can also mean 'Spirit'. Another interesting point that strengthens this analogy is that vultures only feed on lifeless dead flesh. Eagles however mainly live on prey that is still full of life.

Our Loving Creator's Spiritual Life-force will sustain and carry our Spiritual body, mind and Soul through the last physical experience we all have to pass through. The death of our temporary body of flesh. This is how we are connected to the Heavenly Spiritual World from within ourselves, for the Loving Spiritual Life-force that sustains our Soul and Spiritual body comes from

Heaven not the Earth. This is the Living Eternal Spiritual body that Jesus spoke of that we need to become at one with and consolidate while here on Earth by manifesting the Spiritual Love in us through our temporary physical body and life. Jesus taught that if we can become Spiritual in a material, dualistic world, we have overcome the world and will enter the Heavenly Spiritual World just as He did when we die.

Most Jewish/Christians have not understood this very important Teaching, and many try to pervert it and link it to a belief in an apocalyptic rapture event involving two completely different people in the bed, field or at a millstone. Surprisingly and shockingly some Jewish/ Christian teachers even go so far as to say those who are 'taken to be received near to' are being thrown into Hell and those who remain will be saved. A complete misunderstanding and corruption of what Jesus was really saying.

Gain the World but Lose Your Soul

Matthew 16:26, Luke 9:25

Jesus teaches, "For what does it profit a man of flesh if he gains the whole material world but injures or destroys his True Spiritual body and Soul. Or what thing that is only earthly and material can a man exchange for his Spirit and Soul?"

Again, Jesus is pointing out our two different bodies are formed from very different sources and are not interchangeable. Even if you owned the entire Earthly world and all of its Earthly riches while in your body of flesh for a short while but have damaged or lost your Eternal Spiritual Life, you have gained absolutely nothing in the end. And our Spiritual Life cannot be bought with material things no matter how valuable they may be in the material Earth world.

Jesus often taught, "Rich people hardly ever find their Way to the Heavenly Spiritual World. You cannot worship material things and Our Loving Spiritual Creator at the same time."

Flesh is Born of Flesh Spirit is Born of Spirit

John 3:3-8

Jesus teaches this to Nicodemus saying, "Truly, truly, I say to you, unless one is born again from above, he cannot see the Kingdom of the Loving Spiritual Creator." Nicodemus said to Him, "How can a man be born again when he is old? Can he enter a second time into his mother's womb and be born?"

Jesus answered, "Truly I say to you, unless one is born of water and the Spirit, he cannot enter the Kingdom of the Loving Spiritual Creator in the Heavenly Spiritual World. That which is born of the flesh is flesh; and that which is born of the Spirit is Spirit. Do not be amazed that I tell, you must be born again from above. The wind blows where it wishes and although you hear the sound of it, you do not know from where it comes and where it is going. So, it is with all children who are born of the Spirit."

Nicodemus replied, "How can these things happen?" Jesus answered him, "Are you a teacher of Israel but do not know these things? Most assuredly I say to you, we speak of what we know and testify about what we have seen, but you do not accept or believe our witness. If I have told you about Earthly things and you do not believe they are true, how will you believe Me if I speak about Heavenly Spiritual things that you cannot see?"

Jesus is clearly stating that we all have two very different bodies. One is Earthly flesh which we can see with our earthly eyes. One is Spiritual but we cannot see it with our earthly eyes. As Jesus said to Nicodemus, "You do not see Spiritual children come or go just as you cannot see the wind for, they are born from the Heavenly Spiritual World above."

The Jews had no idea about this Truth of our two bodies in one and could not comprehend what Jesus was explaining. We see this clearly when Nicodemus who was a Jewish teacher asks if we have to climb back into our mother's physical body and womb to be reborn. Jesus had a difficult task to bring them out of the Old Wine understanding of a dualistic two headed God into the New Wine understanding of Spiritual Life and the One Loving Spiritual Creator that He was now a child of and teaching about. They must not be mixed together as Jesus warned otherwise you will lose the full understanding of His Spiritual Teachings and who our Loving Creator really is.

When any living creature or human on Earth is born, they are formed from the very substances of their mother's body. And every physical body can only give birth to another physical body. "Flesh only gives birth to flesh," as Jesus said. All earthly bodies are formed, created and sustained out of the substances of the Earth. All bodies of flesh are temporary and eventually die and disintegrate back into the earthly elements they were formed from and sustained by. The body of flesh as a complex unit no longer exists for us to live in and out of.

When any Spiritual Child is born, they are formed from the very substance of our Loving Spiritual Creator. And our Loving Spiritual Creator can only give birth to Spiritual bodies because Jesus told us She is a Spiritual Being. As Jesus said, "Spirit only gives birth to Spirit." All Spiritual bodies are sustained only by Her Spiritual Loving Life-force which will well up inside us like a fountain of water as Jesus taught. All our Spiritual bodies are born from above in the Heavenly Spiritual World and placed in our bodies of flesh at conception. All Spiritual bodies are Eternal and return to be in the presence of our Loving Creator who formed them for us to have True Spiritual Life in Heaven when we separate from our body of flesh when it dies. Our Spiritual bodies are one and whole and remain so.

Our body of flesh is dualistic, and we are automatically in it and under its power at birth. But Jesus reveals that we must choose through free will to move into and become at one with our Spiritual body and Spiritual mind of Love. We are not necessarily automatically at one with it until we choose to be so. Our Spiritual mind and body are singular and the experiences we can have as awakened Spiritual children are more beautiful and subtle than the physical sensations. But in this dualistic material world, sensations from our body of flesh can overpower our Spiritual body and mind experiences and rob us of those beautiful Spiritual states of being. Jesus clearly states that we need our Spirit to come alive, which has a body, in order to enter the Heavenly Spiritual World of our Loving Spiritual Creator and this is the most important body we have. He is also saying the body of flesh cannot enter the Heavenly Spiritual World of Love.

Just as we need blood to be circulating through our body of flesh for it to have Earthly life, likewise we need Her Loving Spiritual Life-force circulating through our Spiritual body to have Spiritual Life. This is the Living water Jesus speaks about that we need to receive in order to awaken, activate, empower and bring our Spiritual body and Soul alive. Without it they will remain present but dormant like a seed waiting to be watered to sprout, grow, come alive, flower and bear fruit. We must move into our Spirit now while we have the chance.

Do Not Fear Your Body Being Killed

Matthew 10:28

Jesus taught, "Do not fear those who can kill your body of flesh but can do no more to you but only fear sin that can lead your Spirit and Soul into outer darkness tormented by being separated by your own hand from your Loving Creator, Her Light, Her Love, Her Spiritual Life-force and Heaven."

Again, we see Jesus giving us the same message that our body of flesh can be totally destroyed but not to be frightened about losing it even if it is killed by someone. Instead, He draws our attention towards our inner Spiritual body and Soul that we have within us that will not die but separates out from our flesh after death. He knows this is far more important because you need it in good condition to enter the Heavenly Eternal Spiritual World beyond all pain and suffering.

But He strongly warns that it can also be damaged or injured like our body of flesh but only if we perform wrong doings that go against our Spiritual Life of Love and our Loving Spiritual Creator. So that is the thing to be most frightened of because Jesus taught, we reap as we sow. And all sin or wrong doings place a dark barrier between us and our Loving Spiritual Creator and cuts us off from Her and the Heavenly Spiritual World. And that is truly Hell.

Treasure Hidden in The Field

Mathew 13:44-46

Jesus taught, "The Kingdom of the Heavenly Spiritual World is like a treasure hidden in a field of earth which a man found and concealed again and in great joy at finding it, he sells all his Earthly possessions and buys that field."

Thomas Gospel: Jesus taught, "The Kingdom of the Spiritual Heavenly World is like a person who had a treasure hidden in a field, but he did not know it. He went plowing through the field and discovered the treasure and shared the treasure with whomever he pleased receiving interest for doing so." Here, Jesus explains in more detail that the man who had the field only discovered the treasure after turning over the earth by plowing and looking under its surface. And then he shares this treasure to whomever he pleases and receives interest, so it never runs out.

The Treasure Jesus speaks about is our Eternal Spiritual body, mind and Soul of Love hidden within our temporary Earthly body of flesh that we cannot see with our physical eyes. This is because it is a Spiritual body and not material. Our body of Earthly flesh is the field. The person had to plow or turn over the field of earth to find the Treasure. Plowing here indicates he had to search within himself under the surface of his earthly physical identity and life to find his Spiritual Life with a body, mind and Soul which is His True Eternal Heavenly identity. This searching is done by understanding and following the words of Jesus who leads you to find your Spiritual identity and Life within and help you awaken and become at one with it to connect to Heaven and our Loving Spiritual Creator.

In the first version Jesus says the man concealed his new Spiritual identity for a while until he sold all his material possessions to own the field. You have to own something to have full control over what you will do with it. He now chose to no longer have any interest in collecting temporary material things or wealth for physical pleasures and let go of them as they could not compare in value to his Spiritual Body and Soul. What he had found within himself will eventually enable him to enter the Heavenly Spiritual World after the death of his body or field. Here Jesus is saying his previous priorities in his earthly life that he was living out of, based on believing he only had one body of flesh, have seriously shifted as he now realises he has an Eternal Spiritual body as well.

The man had now switched the positions of his two bodies. Instead of his physical identity being his primary outer identity with his Spirit hidden within, he now had his Spiritual identity on display as his primary outer identity with his physical secondary identity merging with it to manifest his Spiritual Love which he shared with other children. The two bodies were now at one in purpose despite being made from different life-forces.

It is no wonder he was filled with great joy after discovering he had another Spiritual body that was Eternal which meant he did not have to worry about his body of flesh dying anymore. And this Spiritual Loving Life-force he had found within his Spirit he could share with everyone, and it would never run out because the more he gave the more he received from our Loving Spiritual Creator in Heaven. That is the interest Jesus refers to.

At death we all have to let go of our material identities made of earth and leave in our Spiritual identities. That is why Jesus kept teaching that we must get ready to leave this world in our Spiritual body of Love while bringing Love into this world through our body of flesh until we leave.

Walking on Water with Two Bodies

Matthew 14:22-33

Immediately Jesus made the disciples get into the boat and go ahead of Him to the other side, while He sent the crowds away. After He had sent the crowds away, He went up on the mountain by Himself to pray into the evening.

The disciple's boat was already a long distance from the land, battered by the waves; for the wind was blustery. And in the fourth watch of the night, He came to them walking on the water. When the disciples saw Him walking on the surface of the sea, they were terrified and cried out in fear, "It is a ghost, a Spirit!" But Jesus immediately spoke to them to allay their fear saying, "It is I; do not be afraid."

Peter said to Him, "Lord, if it is really You, command me to come to You on the water?" Jesus said, "Come." And Peter got out of the boat and began to walk on the water and came towards Jesus. But Peter's attention on Jesus wavered and was turned towards the power of the blustering wind and waves surrounding him and he became frightened thinking he would drown and so began to sink. He then cried out to Jesus, "Lord save me."

Immediately Jesus stretched out His hand and took hold of him and said to him, "You of little Spiritual faith, why did you doubt?" When they got into the boat the blustery winds stopped. And those in the boat honoured Him saying, "You are truly a Spiritual child of the Loving Spiritual Creator."

Here is a living example of having two bodies in one that Jesus clearly demonstrated when He walked on the water and defied the material laws of gravity that impact our physical body of flesh but not our Spiritual body empowered by the Spiritual Life-force of our Loving Creator. We must always remember that the Spiritual Life-force of Love of our Creator is much more powerful than any material law.

In this recorded event Jesus had switched His inner Spiritual body, which was fully alive, with His outer physical body so that His Spiritual body became the outer and His physical body became the inner. Then He could easily carry His physical body across the water without sinking.

Even with our Spiritual body fully alive in our body of flesh there are physical laws that must still be dominant over our body of Spirit during our stay on Earth. Such as the material fact that all bodies of flesh eventually die and fall apart including the body of flesh of Jesus. But He could easily carry it across water with the power of His Spiritual Life-force in His Spiritual body as the air does not hinder the movement of our physical bodies on Earth, but His physical body could not pass through a physical wall.

Peter confirms this when we see what happened when he tried to walk on the water to Jesus. The first important thing to note is that when the disciples in the boat first saw Jesus walking on the water, they thought He was a ghost or a Spirit. Of course, they were right without knowing it because the primary, ultimate Spiritual body of Jesus was now fully awakened for them to see on the outside of His body of flesh.

When Jesus calls Peter to come to Him on the water, Peter's full attention is fixed only on Jesus his Spiritual Teacher in whom he has total trust and faith. Based solely on his faith in Jesus and His direction to come to Him, he is willing to risk confronting and ignoring the material laws of this world that he knows so well as a fisherman by believing in Jesus more than them. In order to do this Peter has to overcome the fear of death of his physical Earthly body by sinking and drowning.

So, without Peter realising it Jesus is challenging him to shift through faith into his Spiritual body even though he does not yet know that he has one. But as long as he stays fixated on his

JESUS TEACHES WE HAVE TWO BODIES IN ONE

Teacher Jesus who is clearly standing safely on the water and given him the instruction to also walk on the water, he has the belief and confidence that he can do it. And he does do it as long as he stays connected to Jesus and ignores the material law of gravity. He has been awakened now into his Spiritual body, and it has become the outer body he is in which is carrying his inner physical body.

But then he becomes distracted by the blustering wind and waves, takes his eyes of Jesus and he begins to shift out of his Spiritual mind and body and back into his physical body and earthly mind of logic that tells him no one can walk on water. The connection with Jesus and his own Spirit breaks down as he concedes more power to the Earthly laws and decreases belief in the Spiritual laws. Then he feels himself sinking and the fear that he will drown takes hold of his mind of the flesh, so he calls out to Jesus for help to save him from drowning. He is now only aware of his body of flesh again and has lost belief he has a Spiritual body that cannot die. Considering it was the first time Peter was challenged at such a high level of Spiritual belief, he did pretty well.

Jesus sums up the problem quite simply by saying to him, "You of little Spiritual faith, why did you doubt?" The beautiful thing about this story is how Peter is a perfect model for all of us as we face the same challenge that he did. To overcome fear of the death of our body of flesh by bringing our Eternal body of Spirit and Love to Life through the Spiritual Teachings and Way of Jesus and making that our primary identity on Earth as well as in Heaven later. Only through this personal inner transformation and awakening in all of us will we be able to enter the Heavenly Spiritual World and bring peace on Earth while here.

It is the Loving Spiritual Life-force empowering the Spiritually awakened body and mind of Jesus that allows Him to perform miracles. He even states, "It is the Loving Spiritual Life-force of our Loving Creator in Me that does the works, of myself alone I can do nothing." And because the Loving Spiritual Life-force is pure, we must keep our Spirits clean to be able to receive it fully and use it to help others.

Bodies Like Angels in Heaven

Mark 12:24-27, Luke 34-38

Jesus said, "The children of this Earthly material world marry and are given in marriage. But those who are ready to arise and live in Spirit from their dead body of flesh and enter the Heavenly Spiritual World, they are no longer married or given in marriage as on Earth for they now have beautiful Spiritual bodies like Angels. And they have become the Spiritual children of our Loving Creator, being children of the Spiritual resurrection from the flesh and they cannot experience death anymore being now in their Spiritual bodies. Now concerning the belief that the dead body of flesh awakens again, our Loving Spiritual Creator is not a Creator of dead bodies of flesh but of those who are alive in their Spiritual body."

Jesus is teaching that we have Living Spiritual bodies in Heaven, and they will be like the beautiful Spiritual bodies of Angels after our bodies of flesh die and have no life in them anymore. He states the biological function of reproduction of couples in the flesh is no longer necessary and cannot happen anyway as we have different bodies. He then further confirms this by correcting the misunderstanding the Jews had about life after death by saying our Loving Spiritual Creator is only the Creator of those who are alive in their Spiritual body not of dead lifeless bodies of flesh. This is a repeat of another shorter saying, "It is the Spirit who gives Life, the flesh profits nothing."

Yet unfortunately all the Jewish/Christians teach the opposite of this to children misleading them by saying our dead lifeless body of flesh will come back to life and that our material body of flesh will go to Heaven instead of our Spiritual body as Jesus correctly teaches. My sister Joan and I agreed before she passed through her death experience that there is no toilet paper in Heaven as we no longer need it in our beautiful Spiritual bodies.

The Living Water at the Well Teaching

John 4:5-14

Jesus came to a city of Samaria called Sychar, near the parcel of ground that Jacob gave to his son Joseph and Jacob's well was there. So, Jesus being weary from His journey sat down by the well. There came a woman of Samaria to draw water from the well. Jesus said to her, "Please may I have a drink?" For His disciples had gone away into the city to buy food.

The Samaritan woman said to Him, "How is it that You, being a Jew, ask me a Samaritan woman for a drink?" For Jews looked down on Samaritans and had no dealings with them. Jesus answered and said to her, "If you knew the gift of our Loving Creator and who it is who says to you, 'Please give me a drink,' you would have asked Him and He would have given you Living water."

She said to Him, "Sir, you have nothing to draw the water with, and the well is deep; where then do You get this Living water?" Jesus answered her, "Everyone who drinks of this earthly water their physical bodies will be in need of it again but whoever drinks of the Spiritual water that I shall give him shall never thirst again. For the Spiritual water that I shall give him will become in him a well of Living water springing up to Eternal Spiritual Life."

Once again, Jesus draws a contrast between our temporary physical body of flesh and its needs which have to be continually replenished by earthly elements to have life, or it will die. As opposed to our Spiritual body and Soul which once it is connected to the Loving Spiritual Life-force or Living waters of our Loving Spiritual Creator, it not only comes to Life but will be sustained eternally from within from a perpetual Spiritual wellspring. And as Eternal Life is in the Heavenly Spiritual World, not the Earth world, we need this Living water now to bring our Spiritual body alive to be able to enter that world.

The water Jesus refers to is given to us in the form of His words and through hearing His words and understanding them our Spirit comes to Life and is strengthened by them. We must drink them in and be nourished by them Spiritually. This awakens us to our True Spiritual identity and then we will begin to realise who we really are as Spiritual children of our Loving Spiritual Creator in the Heavenly Spiritual world, and we will be just like Jesus Himself.

Clearly the Samaritan woman could only think in terms of the earthly water without the Spiritual awakening given by Jesus. Just as Nicodemus could not conceive of being born again in a Spiritual body and was also stuck only in earthly realities of birth. Jesus helps us all to awaken from the body of flesh to realise we have another body of Spirit with us right now and then guides us to open our Spirit up by following His Teachings and Spiritual Way of Love and Non-violence. Then we are prepared to fully receive and live out of the Loving Spiritual Life-force from our Loving Creator in the Heavenly Spiritual World.

It is the Spirit Who Gives True Life the Flesh Profits Nothing

John 6:63

Jesus said, "It is the Spirit who gives True Life, the flesh profits nothing. My words that I speak to you, they are Spirit, and they are Life."

Jesus again says it is our Loving Spiritual Creator who gives us True Life and His words will awaken your Spiritual Life and save you and clearly states the fact that we all have two different bodies with us right now. Our Spiritual body and Soul are our ultimate identity and True Eternal Life given to us by our Loving Spiritual Creator while our temporary body of flesh is worth nothing once it dies. Our Earthly body needs earthly nourishment to have a limited life and is temporary while our Spiritual body only needs Spiritual nourishment to have True Life and is Eternal. The words of Jesus are nourishment indeed for our Spirits, but we must understand them correctly.

Understand My Words and Pass Through Death to Life

John 11:25

Jesus said, "I am the Living resurrected Spiritual Life that has arisen from the body of flesh. The one who believes in Me and My Teachings concerning this, even if his body of flesh is dying, he will still be Spiritually alive. And everyone who has awoken to their True Spiritual Life by believing I am a Living Spiritual child of our Loving Creator in Heaven and follows My Way will never die."

John 8:51

Jesus said, "Truly I say to you, anyone who hears My words and understands them and lives out of them will never see death."

Jesus makes this statement seventeen times throughout the five Gospels in different ways. That is how important it is to concentrate on His words above all else in the Jewish/Christian Bible and you do not need the Old Testament at all to understand His words. In fact, it can pervert His Teachings if you try to mix them together as He warned. Our Spiritual body is Eternal our body of flesh dies. Here Jesus says that anyone who hears and understands His words will become like Him. A fully awakened Spiritual child of our Loving Spiritual Creator on Earth with a Spiritual body that does not die. But it is concealed and covered in the body of flesh, so Jesus has to reveal its existence to us by teaching us that it is there and how to find it and become at one with it.

My Words Are Living Water

John 7:37-38

Jesus said, "If anyone is thirsty, let him come to Me and drink from Me. He who believes I am a Spiritual child of our Loving Spiritual Creator from within the innermost being of his Spirit will flow rivers of Living water." This is the Spiritual Life-force of our Loving Creator that gives Life to our Spiritual body or innermost being within the body of flesh out of which will flow endless streams of Loving Life-force if we awaken into our Spirit.

In the Thomas Gospel Jesus says this again, "Whoever drinks from My mouth will be like Me, and I shall be like that person and what is hidden within will be revealed to that one." Here Jesus again is clearly saying that if you listen to His Teachings and come to understand them you will be transformed by them, and you will find your Spiritual body and Soul will come to Life just as His did. But it is hidden within the body of flesh, the Treasure hidden in the field.

In the Thomas Gospel someone said to Jesus, "Lord, many are around the well, but no one is in the well." This saying describes how many children are only living out of their body of flesh that surrounds their Spiritual body at the center of their True being which holds the well of Living water or Loving Spiritual Life-force, that springs up to Eternal Life. They are not in their Spiritual bodies; they are not in the Spiritual water of the well. They are like children who are only being the vase but not the water held within the vase.

When we look around at the world today in 2025 with violent wars, poverty, the rise of the material cult of the filthy rich, a degenerating culture of self-serving, cold hearted individuals and climate change due to our greedy way of material living, we need a Spiritual revolution of Love.

I Have Spiritual Nourishment You do not Know About

John 4:31-34

While still at the well the disciples returned and were urging Him saying, "Teacher, eat something." But He said to them, "I have nourishment to consume that you do not know about." So, the disciples were saying to one another, "No one brought Him anything to eat, did he?" Jesus said to them, "My nourishment is to perform the Spiritual Way of Her who sent Me to you and to accomplish Her works."

Even His own close disciples were taking a long time to shift out of the Old Spiritual understanding of the Jews into the New Spiritual understanding Jesus was introducing them into. He is telling them He has another form of empowerment giving His Spiritual body Life that they do not yet know about, not realising they have two different bodies sustained by two different Life-forces. They were also still stuck in only thinking about the Earthly body of flesh and what it needs.

Earthly Food for Earthly Body Spiritual Food for Spiritual Body

John 6:27

Jesus taught, "Do not labor for the earthly food which perishes with your Earthly body but labor for the Spiritual nourishment from Heaven which endures within your Spiritual body to Eternal Life. I will give this to you for I am an awakened Spiritual child of our Loving Spiritual Creator in the Heavenly Spiritual World, and this is My joy to do so."

Again, we see Jesus trying to draw our attention away from concentrating only on maintaining our temporary bodies of flesh that always ends in death and leads us to search for and find our inner Spiritual bodies filled with the Spiritual empowerment of our Loving Creator's Life-force that provides real Eternal Life.

Our Spiritual Identity is Within

Gospel of Thomas

Jesus said, "Physical images are visible to men, but the Light and Spirit which is in them is hidden in the image of the Light of our Creator. Our Spiritual identity within, hidden in Her Light, will be revealed and come forth."

Here Jesus is once again clearly pointing out to us all that we have two very different bodies with us right now. Our bodies of flesh are easily visible to all of us by looking through the eyes of our biological bodies of flesh. Bodies formed of material elements can only perceive material objects.

But Jesus then says that our Spiritual body created by our Loving Spiritual Creator is hidden within us and is formed out of the Light and Life-force of our Spiritual Creator. It is a completely different form of body. It is hidden from our view because we have not yet fully awoken by becoming filled with Her Loving Life-force, to be at one with our True Spiritual body and Spiritual mind of Love.

Once we come to know that our Loving Spiritual Creator is only a Being of pure Love and kindness, and for us to be called Her Spiritual children on Earth we must also be filled with Her Love and kindness, then this will open up our Spirit and Soul to receive Her Loving Spiritual Life-force. Then our Spiritual body and Soul will truly come alive and will be revealed to us and come forth to be our primary body and identity on Earth and in the Heavenly Spiritual World.

When they asked Jesus where Heaven was located, He replied, "You will not find it by looking over here or over there upon the Earth because the Heavenly Kingdom is within you connected to your Spirit."

I Will Arise in Spirit as You Will Too

John 14:20

Jesus said, "On that day when I arise in Spirit you will understand that I am in our Loving Creator's Spiritual Life-force, and then you will also be as Me and I as you."

Jesus is referring to His body of flesh being killed and rising from it in His Spiritual body. Then Jesus is explaining that eventually they will catch on to the deeper meaning of His words. And when the Light goes on inside them and they awaken to their Spiritual body then they too will be empowered and enlivened by the Loving Spiritual Life-force from our Loving Creator. Then, having the same Spiritual Life-force in them as He does, they will all be brothers and sisters of Jesus in the Spiritual family of Heaven on Earth.

Healing Spiritual Body then Body of Flesh

Matthew 9:2-6 Luke 5:19-23

Jesus was Teaching inside a home when they brought a paralytic man lying on a bed to Jesus, and due to the large crowd, they had to lower him through the roof of the house so Jesus could see him. Seeing the man lowered on the stretcher and their great faith in Him to go to such lengths Jesus went up to him and said, "Friend, your sins are forgiven you."

When the scribes and Pharisees heard this, they were upset that Jesus was blaspheming against their God who they believed was the only one who could forgive sins. Jesus said, "Which is easier to say, 'Your sins are forgiven' or 'Get up and walk?" Then He said to the paralytic, "Get up and walk, and take your bed home with you." And he got up and went home.

Jesus is clearly showing us that His main concern for the man was the state of his Spiritual body and Soul as that is Eternal, so the very first thing He healed was that. He only moves to heal his body of temporary flesh after criticisms from the Jews and does so. The man's primary Eternal Spiritual identity was of much more concern to Jesus than healing his secondary body of temporary flesh that would die one day anyway.

Flesh is From Below Spirit is From Above

John 8:23

Jesus said, "You are still from below connected primarily only to the material Earth world and body of flesh therefore you are of this world. I am from above connected primarily to the Heavenly Spiritual World through My Spiritual body therefore I am not of this world anymore but just standing on the Earth for a while in My temporary body of flesh."

Jesus is simply telling them the body He now lives out of is His primary Heavenly Spiritual body and identity that has come fully to Life through the Loving Spiritual Life-force of Our Loving Creator flowing into Him. While they were still stuck in the Earthly life-forces and body of their flesh. Clearly Jesus is confirming that our Eternal Spiritual identity is superior to our temporary physical identity.

As He said to Nicodemus, "Spirit gives birth to Spirit. Marvel not that I tell you. You must be born again from above."

Heaven is the Home of Spiritual Children not Earth

Luke 9:57-58

As they were going along the road, someone said to Jesus, "I will follow You wherever You go." Jesus replied. "The foxes have holes, and the birds of the air have nests to call home, but the Spiritual child of humanity has nowhere here in the material

JESUS TEACHES WE HAVE TWO BODIES IN ONE

world to lay His head for My home is now in the Heavenly Spiritual World."

Here Jesus is telling the person that if he really wants to follow Him where He is eventually going, he must become an awakened Spiritual child of our Loving Creator in the Heavenly Spiritual World while here on Earth to get there. He then simply states that this world is not His True home anymore as He is now transformed and now living primarily out of His Spiritual body while still on Earth until He enters the Heavenly Spiritual World to live there Eternally. Heaven is the Eternal home beyond all suffering for all Spiritual children who awaken and become Spiritual.

Jesus consistently taught this two body Truth and wants us all to follow His Way of Love and Non-violence to awaken our Spiritual body and follow Him to the Heavenly Spiritual World before our temporary body of flesh dies and returns to the earth.

1 John 4:7 "Children let us Love one another for Love is from our Loving Spiritual Creator, and everyone who Loves is born into True Life from Her and knows Her. The children who do not Love do not know our Loving Spiritual Creator for She is Love."

GOD IS LOVE LOVE IS LIFE

Two bodies at One in purpose.

To bring Heaven's Love to Earth.

Chapter Five

Powerful Two Body Events Called Miracles

One of the most powerful demonstrations Jesus performed showing that we all have two different bodies was to bring the Spiritual body back into a dead body of flesh that was miraculously restored and revived through the Spiritual Life-force of our Loving Creator in Heaven that was now empowering His awoken Spiritual body and Soul mind of Love.

Jairus's Daughter Brought Back to Life

Mark 5:22-24

A large crowd had gathered around Jesus and one of the synagogue officials named Jairus came up to Jesus and fell at His feet. He earnestly implored Him saying. "My young daughter lies at the point of death. Please come and lay Your hands upon her that she may be healed and will live." And Jesus went off with him and a large crowd followed. Mark 5: 35-43 While He was still on the way to the house of Jairus a man from the ruler's house came and said, "Your daughter is dead, do not trouble the Teacher anymore." But Jesus heard what the man was saying, and He said to Jairus, "Do not be afraid, but only trust and believe." And when

He came to the house, He permitted no one to enter in with Him except Peter, John and James and the parents of the child.

At the house there was a great commotion with many people wailing loudly and weeping over the girl's death. But Jesus said to them, "Do not weep, for the girl is not dead but only sleeping." And they all ridiculed Him.

Jesus then put them all outside and went in to where the girl was laying. Taking her by the hand, He called to her saying "Talitha cumi," meaning, "Little girl I say to you awaken." And her Spirit returned into her dead body of flesh and immediately the girl arose filled again with Life and walked about, she was twelve years old. And those watching were completely astounded. But Jesus strictly commanded them that no one should be told about what He did. Then told them to give her something to eat.

The girl's body of flesh is dying so Jesus goes with Jairus to heal her. Then the news that her body of flesh has died comes to them while on the way. But Jesus has committed to heal the girl and now faced a more serious situation beyond using His Spiritual power to simply heal her illness for now her Spiritual body had completely left her physical body. Jesus reassures Jairus not to lose faith in Him and proceeds on despite the person giving the message believing it is hopeless now to save her.

Jesus only wants three disciples and the parents with Him when He brings her Spiritual body back into her body of flesh. He also plants a suggestion in the people that she is only sleeping and not really dead.

He did this for two reasons. Firstly, because they were not Spiritually ready to understand we all have two different bodies, and they did not know the True Spiritual Loving Creator and Her Loving Life-force now with Him which allowed Him to heal. Secondly, He often warned those He healed not to tell anyone else what He had done as His main work was not to be a doctor of the flesh but a doctor of the Spirit. No matter who He healed or brought back to life all their temporary bodies of flesh still died later. His main purpose was to bring those dead to their Spirit back to Eternal Spiritual Life in the Heavenly Spiritual World by helping them find and awaken to their Spiritual body and True identity as a Spiritual child on Earth of our Loving Spiritual Creator.

He speaks the words of healing to the Spiritual Soul of the girl, as her body of flesh had no life in it. Her Spirit and Soul were now possibly in the Heavenly Spiritual World with our Loving Creator. But as He is connected with our Loving Creator in Heaven and must perform His Spiritual works to help other children become Spiritual, His Loving Creator sent the girl's Spiritual body and Soul back into her body of flesh at His request. As always it is Her Loving Spiritual Life-force flowing through the Spiritual body of Jesus into the girl's dead body of flesh that performs the miraculous healing of her body.

The interesting Greek word Jesus uses when telling her to 'awaken' can also mean to 'arise.' In this case her Spiritual body and Soul are reentering into the body of flesh and then that body can arise together with her Spiritual body now back within her as one. With the death of Jesus, it was the opposite as His Spiritual body and Soul arose and left His body of flesh leaving it lifeless. This is what He kept telling the disciples would happen, that His Spiritual body would rise again from His dead lifeless body of flesh. His flesh did not need to come back to life as He was now finally living fully in His Spiritual body.

Widow of Nain Son Brought Back to Life

Luke 7:11-17

Jesus went to a city called Nain and many of His disciples and a crowd went with Him. And when He came near the gate of the city a dead man was being carried out the only son of his mother a widow. And a large crowd from the city was with her.

When Jesus saw her, He had compassion on her and said, "Do not weep." Then He came and touched the stretcher the body was on, and those who were carrying it stood still. And He said, "Young man I say to you, arise." The dead man sat up and began to speak. And Jesus gave him back to his mother.

Then everyone was filled with awe at what Jesus did and they glorified the Loving Creator saying, "A great prophet has awoken amongst our people." And this report about what Jesus did went throughout Judea and all surrounding regions.

Once again, the son's Spiritual body and Soul had left his body of flesh which was now lifeless. The True life had gone out of him. As a living Spiritual child on Earth of our Loving Spiritual Creator Jesus only had to speak the words, and She created exactly what He asked for as Her Life-force in Him flowed into the son's dead body. The son's Spiritual body and Soul were returned into a miraculously healed body of flesh. Our Loving Creator is a Spiritual Creator and Her power can alter any material thing on Earth motivated by Love.

Jesus deliberately chooses to restore the life of the widow's only son having compassion for her. In those times to have lost your husband and only son was a serious predicament for a woman. Jesus was also ready to perform the miracle in front of a crowd unlike the daughter of Jairus. He was clearly beginning to demonstrate and manifest the power of our Loving Creator's Life-force in Him more openly.

All the miracles were performed so children would see this Spiritual power in action and seek Him out. He was also gaining a reputation for someone to be listened to. Then He could teach them how to bring their Spiritual bodies and Souls alive by giving them His Spiritual words from Heaven to help awaken their True Spiritual identity. For He knew it was their Eternal Spiritual body and Soul that was the most important body that had to be brought back to Real Spiritual Life. Flesh is only temporary.

Lazarus Brought Back to Life

John 11-46

Now a certain man was ill named Lazarus of Bethany from the village of Mary and her sister Martha. It was Mary who anointed Jesus with ointment and wiped His feet with her hair whose brother Lazarus was ill. Therefore, the sisters sent a message to Him saying, "Master he whom You love is ill."

When Jesus received the message He said, "This illness will not end in death, but for the glory of our Loving Spiritual Creator, so that the Spiritual child of our Loving Creator may also be honoured through it." Now Jesus loved Martha and her sister and Lazarus but when He heard that he was ill He remained two more days in the place where He was.

Then after this He said to the disciples, "Let us go to Judea again." The disciples said, "Teacher the Jews are seeking you to stone you to death and are you going there again?" Jesus answered, "Are there not twelve hours in the day? If anyone walks in the day, he does not stumble for he sees the light of this world. But if one walks in the night he stumbles because the light is not with him."

He then said to them, "Our friend Lazarus sleeps but I go so that I may awaken him." Then the disciples said, "Master if he sleeps, he will get well." However, Jesus spoke of the death of his body of flesh, but they thought He was speaking about restful sleep. Then Jesus spoke plainly to them, "Lazarus's body of flesh is dead. And I am glad for your sakes that I was not there so that you may believe. But let us go to him." Then Thomas called the twin said to his fellow disciples, "Let us also go that we may die with him and also be awakened by Jesus."

Now Bethany was near Jerusalem about two miles away. When Jesus came, He found that Lazarus had been in the tomb four days. And many of the Jews had come to be with those comforting Mary and Martha concerning their brother's death. Now Martha as soon as she heard Jesus was coming went and met Him, but Mary stayed in the house. Martha said to Jesus, "Teacher, if you had been here my brother would not have died. But even now I know whatever you ask of our Loving Creator She will give it to you."

Jesus said, "Your brother is raised up." Martha said to Him, "I know that he is raised in the resurrection of the Spirit on the last day." (Possibly a reference to the book of Daniel 12:2 where it wrongly refers to many dead people rising from the dust at the end of the world. The apocalyptic belief of some Jews and Jewish/Christians but not of Jesus.)

Jesus said to her, "I am the resurrection and the Spiritual Life. He who believes in Me, though he may die to the flesh he shall Live in the Spirit. And whoever believes in Me and Lives out of the Spirit shall never die. Do you believe this?" She said to Him, "Yes Master I believe you are the anointed one a Spiritual child of our Loving Spiritual Creator who has arisen in this world."

And then she went and called her sister Mary privately saying to her, "The Teacher has come and is calling for you." As soon as she heard that she rose quickly and came to Him. Now Jesus had not yet entered the town but was still in the place where Martha met Him. Then the Jews who were with Mary in the house comforting her saw Mary get up and quickly go out and followed her saying, "She must be going to the tomb to weep there."

Then when Mary came where Jesus was and saw Him, she fell down at His feet saying to Him, "Master if you had been here my brother would not have died." And when Jesus saw her weeping and the Jews that came with her also weeping His Spirit was deeply moved and distressed. And He said, "Where have you laid him?" They said to Him, "Master come and see." And Jesus wept. Then the Jews said, "See how He loved him." And some said, "Could not this man who opened the eyes of the blind also have kept this man from dying?"

Then Jesus deeply moved again in His Spirit came to the tomb. It was a cave, and a stone lay against it. Jesus said, "Take away the stone." But Martha said to Him, "Master by now there will be a stench for he has been dead four days." Jesus said to her, "Did I not say to you that if you believed you will see the glory of the Loving Spiritual Creator."

Then they took away the stone from the entrance to where Lazarus had been laid. And Jesus lifted up His eyes to Heaven and said, "Loving Spiritual Creator I thank You that You listen to Me. And I know that You always listen to Me but for the sake of the people standing by I spoke this allowed that they may believe that You sent Me to them." When He had said these things, He cried out in a loud voice, "Lazarus come out!" And the dead man came out with his hands and feet bound with bandages and his face wrapped in a cloth. Jesus said, "Unbind him and let him go."

Therefore, many of the Jews who came to Mary and saw what Jesus had done, believed in Him. But some of them went to the Pharisees and reported what Jesus had done to them which upset them because Jesus was becoming so powerful in Spirit that many Jews were now following His new Spiritual Way of Love and ignoring them.

We can see a clear escalation again by Jesus demonstrating the awesome Spiritual power of our Loving Creator in the Heavenly Spiritual World. At first, He raised the girl's dead body of flesh back to life within a very short time of dying with only five witnesses and told them to keep His Spiritual power a secret. Then He unexpectedly came upon the Son of the widow whose body of flesh had been dead for a longer time. Probably hours as the Jews usually buried their dead within eight hours. But He had shifted into performing this miracle in public. Finally, He pushes the limits of bringing a dead decaying body of flesh back to life after being dead for four days in Lazarus. And He deliberately delays going to heal Lazarus knowing his body of flesh would be dead before He arrives to perform the miracle for His disciples and those present, to increase their faith in Him and our Loving Spiritual Creator.

Jesus again uses the term that Lazarus has fallen to 'sleep' instead of 'has died' and Jesus is going to awaken him when first talking to His disciples about Lazarus. Jesus knew it was the simplest way to talk to them about the miracle of his Spiritual body and Soul returning into his healed body of flesh. They take His words literally and He has to speak more plainly to them that the body of flesh of Lazarus is dead. Even the disciples still did not understand His Teachings until after His body of flesh died and He appeared to them in His Spiritual body.

Jesus tells Martha Lazarus has already risen in Spirit. She says that she understands the resurrection of the Spirit takes place on the last day. Jesus then reveals to her that He is already resurrected into His Spirit and Spiritual Life and anyone who believes in His Teachings and follows them will also come alive to their Spiritual body and Life which does not die like the body of flesh. And all those who awaken to this have Eternal Life. This dialogue of Jesus is profound as He is saying we can all be exactly like Him and should strive to be born again into our Spiritual body and Soul right now just as He did before our body of flesh dies.

At the tomb Jesus talks allowed to His Loving Spiritual Creator in Heaven so all those present know where the real power to raise Lazarus is coming from. And that He is a True awakened Spiritual child of Hers and is fully at one with Her Loving Spiritual Life-force in His Spiritual body now fully alive. He only has to think and speak the words of what He wishes His Loving Creator to do for Him and She does it in a most spectacular way due to Her Loving Spiritual Power. She can only Love and give Life and never take it from any of Her children. We may seriously damage the gift of Spiritual Life She has given us, but we can always come back to Her and ask Her to restore it for us.

The Spiritual body and Soul of Lazarus had left his body of flesh, and it was lifeless. But our Loving Creator returned his Spiritual body and Soul from a Spiritual place back into his body of flesh that She had miraculously restored, removing all signs of decay or disease creating a new healthy, living body of flesh for him. She did this simply because a Spiritual child of Hers on Earth, Jesus, asked Her to do it for Him so it may be a powerful demonstration of everything He had been teaching about Her and True Spirituality to help those present understand and bring their Spirits back to Life.

GOD IS LOVE LOVE IS LIFE

If our Spirit is asleep, we need to awaken it.

If we have covered it in filth, we need to clean it.

If we want to bring it fully alive, we must fill it with Love.

Chapter Six

Disciples Don't Understand Jesus

The following are examples of the disciple's inability to easily grasp the deeper Spiritual meaning of the Teachings of Jesus. Especially that our Loving Spiritual Creator is only Love not a two headed God of Limited Love and War as the Jews believed. It was a massive task to undo the years of distortions of the Jewish beliefs and teach the followers a new Spiritual Way and Truth that went against their old dualistic religion in just three years. Despite their failure to easily grasp the deeper Truths while with Him they did pass on His Life saving Spiritual words and Spiritual Way of Love for everyone in the world to be awoken to Spirit.

Matthew 19:23-26

And Jesus said to His disciples, "Truly I say to you, it is hard for a man rich in material wealth to enter the Heavenly Spiritual World. Again, I say to you it is easier for a camel to pass through the eye of a needle than for a man rich in material wealth to enter the Heavenly Spiritual World."

When the disciples heard this, they were very astonished as the Jews thought that those rich in material wealth were especially blessed by our Loving Creator. So, they asked Jesus, "Who then can be saved if the rich cannot?" And looking at them, Jesus said, "With people who rely only on the flesh this is impossible but with those who rely on our Loving Spiritual Creator all things are possible for them."

The disciples still haven't even grasped the difference between the Teachings of Jesus concerning Spiritual treasures such as Love, Compassion, Forgiveness and selflessness that we need in order to awaken into our Spiritual body and Soul and material Earthly treasures which in the end are as useless helping us enter Heaven as our dead bodies of flesh.

Matthew 15:11 and 19

Jesus taught, "It is not what enters into the mouth that defiles a man but what proceeds out of the mouth this defiles a man. For out of the heart come evil thoughts, murders, adulteries, fornications, thefts, lying, and slanders." Peter said to Him, "Explain this parable to us." Jesus replied, "Are you still lacking in understanding also?"

The disciples understandably have a very difficult time grasping that Jesus is teaching that we have two very different bodies in one with us right now formed from two very different sources. One is formed from the earth elements, and one is formed from our Loving Spiritual Creator's Life-force. The Jews had many laws about what type of foods you could eat and foods that were not allowed or you would be defiled by them. The disciples were still stuck in the Old Testament understanding of Spirituality. Jesus states that putting any earthly foods in your temporary earthly body of flesh does not defile you because you are not really that body of flesh anyway. It is our Spiritual body we must not defile as that is our ultimate Eternal identity and body we can be at one with in the Heavenly Spiritual World of Love.

We have a beautiful, perfect Spiritual body and Spiritual mind of Love within our dualistic body of flesh, created for us to become at one with right now to enter the Heavenly Spiritual world after our last earthly experience called death. But it is empowered only be a clean Loving Spiritual Life-force from our Spiritual Creator. And it can only be damaged or defiled if we choose to do evil things by our own free will. If our minds are full of evil, greedy thoughts they will poison the purity of our Spiritual Life-force and Spiritual minds of Love. So, that is the most important thing to avoid to remain Spiritually alive and well. Personally, I believe it is also very good to be a vegetarian if you can, to reduce the suffering of other sentient beings.

Mark 4:10-13

After Jesus gave the Sower of the Seed parable His disciples began asking Him to explain it to them. And He said to them, "To you has been given the mystery of the Heavenly Spiritual World but those not ready to receive it openly it must be given to them in parables. Do you not understand this parable of the Sower? How then will you understand all the other parables and the Spiritual Teachings they contain?"

Again, Jesus is frustrated at the slow progress they are making in understanding His New Spiritual Way and the deeper Spiritual meanings in His Teachings.

Matthew 16:6-9 Mark 8:15-21

Jesus said to the disciples, "Be warned! Beware of the leaven of the Pharisees, Herod and the Sadducees." They began to discuss this among themselves saying, "He must be talking about how we did not bring any bread with us." But Jesus heard them and said, "You men of little Spiritual faith why do you discuss among yourselves that you have no bread? Do you not yet see or understand? Do you have hardened hearts?

Do you not remember the five loaves of the five thousand and how many full baskets you picked up? Or the seven loaves of the four thousand and how many large baskets you picked up? How is it that you do not understand that I was not speaking about edible bread but the dangerous misleading Teachings of the Pharisees." Then they understood.

Again, Jesus has to explain for them what He was really talking about as they were still Spiritually asleep and unaware they had a Spiritual body within the body of flesh. They were still only thinking about food for the flesh, not aware of the Spiritual food and Way of Love He was giving them with His words to nourish and strengthen their Spirits and bring them alive. His words are True Spiritual nourishment. The Pharisee's words are not.

Mark 9:31-32

Jesus was teaching His disciples and telling them, "The Spiritual child of our Loving Creator will be delivered into the hands of men, and they will kill Him and when He has been killed, He will rise again from the dead." But they did not understand what He was saying and were afraid to ask Him what it means.

The disciples had been with Him for some time but because they still had no experience of their own Spiritual body and Loving mind, they had no idea we all have one as well as a temporary body of flesh. They could only think that Jesus was talking about His body of flesh coming back to life which makes no sense as it returns to the earth. They did not realise He was actually talking about arising from His dead body of flesh in His Spiritual body. They couldn't grasp at that stage the profound Spiritual Truth that He was teaching them and all of us.

Matthew 16: 21-23

From that time on Jesus began to show the disciples that He must go to Jerusalem and suffer many things from the elders and chief priests and scribes and be killed and be raised up from the dead. But Peter took Him aside and began to rebuke Him saying, "May our Loving Creator forbid this Lord. This should never happen to you." Jesus turned to Peter and said, "Get behind Me satan! You are a stumbling block to Me, for you are not setting your mind on Spiritual things but on things of the flesh."

Jesus makes a clear demarcation between our Spiritual body and Life and our material life of the flesh. In this case Peter, one of His closest disciples, still had no understanding that we have two different bodies with us in one. He thought Jesus only had a body of flesh so didn't want Jesus to die not realising He would arise again in His full Spiritual body to appear to them. Jesus is upset with Peter still not understanding this.

Jesus strongly rebukes Peter by saying that he is aligning himself with satan, the ruler of this dualistic, material world instead of with the Spirit. We see this also in the temptation by satan of Jesus while fasting to turn stones into bread for the body of flesh. Jesus responds that we do not live by earthly bread and flesh alone but by every Spiritual word that nourishes our Spiritual body and Soul that comes from our Loving Spiritual Creator."

Luke 9:38-41

A man from the crowd shouted saying, "Teacher, I beg You to look at my son for he is my only boy, and a spirit seizes him, and he suddenly screams, and it throws him into convulsion with foaming at the mouth and only with difficulty does it leave him mauling him as it leaves. I begged your disciples to cast it out and they could not." Jesus said, "Oh you generation who are distorted and cannot be trusted, how long shall I endure patiently with you? Bring your son to Me."

While he was still approaching the demon slammed him into the ground and threw him into a convulsion. But Jesus rebuked the unclean spirit and healed the boy and gave him back to his father. Matthew 17:19-21 Then the disciples came to Jesus privately and asked, "Why could we not drive it out?" And He said, "Because of the littleness of your own Spiritual belief for truly I say to you if you have Spiritual belief the size of a mustard seed you will say to this mountain 'Move from here to there,' and it will move, and nothing will be impossible to you. But this kind does not go out except through prayer and fasting."

Jesus is frustrated with the disciples still holding onto the distorted Jewish belief in a two headed God instead of believing only in our Loving Spiritual Creator so they can't be trusted to perform healings yet due to their own ignorance of the Spiritual Truth. The Jews have never worshipped only one Loving Spiritual Creator of Universal Love.

And because they did not fully understand the True Loving Creator is a beautiful Spiritual Being of only Love, they could not yet be filled with Her Loving Spiritual Life-force to strengthen their own Spiritual body and Soul to empower them to heal other children. Jesus taught that until their 'eye is single and their Spiritual body full of Light,' they will remain dualistic and divided within themselves and be in the dark.

If you worship a God of war and a God of limited Love at best, you can only be half full of Love. This is why He told them to fast from the material world and possibly eat less as well and concentrate on increasing their Spiritual connection or nexus with our Loving Spiritual Creator in the Heavenly Spiritual World. For they needed to awaken their Spirits and become Her children and feel Her Spiritual Loving Life-force in their own Spiritual bodies. Then they could ask Her for any Spiritual thing they need and She will grant it. Interestingly nearly all of the miracles Jesus performed were mainly about reducing the suffering of other children whose bodies of flesh were injured or ill. The Spiritual power of Love is all about caring for others and never hurts anyone.

John 14:2-11

Jesus said, "In My Loving Creator's Heavenly World there are many dwelling places. If it were not so I would have told you for I go to prepare a place for you. And if I go and prepare a place for you to come anew, I will receive you to be near Me so that where I am there you will be also. And you know the Way to the place where I am going."

Thomas said to Him, "Lord we do not know where you are going so how do we know the way?" Jesus said, "I am the Spiritual Way, the Truth and the Spiritual Life, no one comes to our Loving Spiritual Creator except by My Spiritual Way. If you had truly known Me as a Spiritual child, you would have known our Loving Creator also and from this moment on you do know Her and have seen Her Love clearly through Me."

Philip said, "Lord show us the Loving Spiritual Creator and it will be enough for us." Jesus said to him, "Have I been so long with you and yet you have not come to know who I am Philip? He who understands and knows Me, a Spiritual child of our Loving Spiritual Creator, knows Her so how can you say 'Show us the Loving Creator' when I am standing right in front of you?

Do you not believe that I am living in the Loving Spiritual Life-force of our Loving Creator and the Loving Spiritual Life-force of our Loving Creator is in Me? The Spiritual Teachings I give to you are not mine but are from our Loving Creator whose Spiritual Life-force lives in Me and does all the works I perform. Believe Me when I tell you I am living in the Life-force of our Loving Creator and Her Life-force is living in Me. Or if you do not believe Me then believe because you have seen the miracles and works I have done empowered by Her Love."

This is quite a revealing dialogue as it takes place at the last supper after being with Him for over three years listening to His Teachings and watching Him perform miracles and explain the nature of our Loving Spiritual Creator. But they were still unable to grasp the deeper meaning of all of His Spiritual Truths and Teachings. Thomas can still only think in Earthly terms of following Jesus to where He is going in their body of flesh. He has yet to realise there is a Spiritual Heavenly World just as real as this

Earthly world, but we go there through the inner awakening of our Spiritual body after our body of flesh dies.

He still has no idea that Jesus is talking about His Spiritual body going to Heaven after leaving His dead body of flesh as they still don't understand the concept that we have two very different bodies with us right now. But that is the Way we leave here to go to Heaven, not in our dead body of flesh, but in our Living Spiritual body brought fully alive through understanding the Spiritual Teachings and Way of Love of Jesus.

Philip's comment shows they still do not know who our Loving Spiritual Creator really is, unable to shake off the distorted dualistic God of the Jews. She is only Love and True Spiritual Life and Jesus is a Living example of Her Spiritual child on Earth who lived out of Her Loving Life-force to teach and guide children how to be with Her in Heaven. Helping them awaken to Her Loving Life-force within themselves by becoming at one with Her Love. He is amazed that after all this time Philip clearly still has little understanding concerning His core Teachings of the Spiritual Way of Love and our Loving Spiritual Creator that they lead us to.

So, Jesus being a Spiritual child is just like His Spiritual parent with the same characteristics and nature. This is what He called the 'New Covenant.' But they haven't fully understood this Spiritual relationship they all need to awaken into and then become connected to Her Loving Spiritual Life-force in their awoken Spiritual bodies. We must no longer be dualistic and divided within ourselves but full of the Light of Her Love to become Spiritual children like Jesus.

John 14:19

Jesus told the disciples, "After a little while the world will no longer see Me, but you will see Me because I will still be alive so that you will also come to Spiritual Life. On that day you will finally realise that I am in our Loving Creator's Spiritual Life-force, and you will be in the same Life-force in Me as mine will be in you. John 14:29 I have told you about this before it happens so that when it happens you may understand and believe all I taught you." Jesus is preparing them to see Him in His Spiritual body.

Jesus knows they still do not understand the deep Spiritual meaning held within His Teachings. So, He is opening up about their Spiritual bodies coming alive to their True Spiritual Life just like His has through the Loving Spiritual Life-force of our Loving Creator filling their Spirits. He is telling them they will only fully understand what He is saying once He rises in His Spiritual body from His dead body of flesh and appears to them again.

John 16:16-19

Jesus said, "In a little while you will no longer see Me and after a little while you will see Me again." Some of His disciples said to one another, "What is this thing He is telling us, 'In a little while you will not see Me and after a little while you will see Me' and 'because I go to Our Loving Creator?'" So, they asked each other, "What does this mean when He says, 'A little while?' We do not know what He is talking about."

This is easily the most startling revelation that the disciples had no idea whatsoever that the ultimate purpose of all the miracles He performed with our Loving Creator's Life-force in His Spiritual body and the Teachings He gave them, was to help them realise that they had two very different bodies with them right now. One of flesh will die and disintegrate back into the earth and one of Spirit empowered by the Loving Spiritual Life-force will live on returning to our Spiritual Creator reaping as it has sown.

Luke 9:51-56

Jesus was determined to go to Jerusalem, so He sent messengers on ahead of Him to a Samaritan village to make arrangements for them to stop and rest before continuing on. But the Samaritans wanted Him to stay with them and teach them like He did with the woman at the well and those Samaritans He stayed with for a few days. But because He was just passing through, they were upset with Him and refused accommodation.

His disciples James and John heard this, and said, "Master, do you want us to command fire to come down from Heaven and consume them?" Jesus turned and strongly rebuked them saying, "You do not know what kind of Spirit you are of, for the Spiritual child of humanity does not destroy men's lives but saves them." So, they went to another village.

This is another stunning example of the enormous difficulty Jesus faced trying to bring His disciples out of the distorted two headed God of the Jews into the singularity of the One True Loving Spiritual Creator. The two disciples were still under the heavy influence of the two headed God of the Jews with a violent, murdering, revengeful Godhead of war and a Godhead of Limited Love and saw no problem as followers of Jesus asking their God Yahweh in Heaven to send fire down to consume and destroy all the Samaritans in the town for insulting Him.

Being heavily indoctrinated and still trapped in the Jewish misunderstanding about who God really was, they were referring to an account in the Old Wine Testament in 2 Kings 10-12. In this account Elijah states he is a follower of their two headed God Yahweh and he calls down fire from the Heaven of this God Yahweh two times to consume two captains and their fifty men who had come to take him to their king. He did not want to go with them so murdered them all with help from the Godhead of war of the two headed Jewish God of Love and War Yahweh.

Clearly, the disciples had absolutely no idea who our Loving Spiritual Creator really is and even thought Jesus was still worshipping their two headed God like they were. He must have been extremely upset at what they were inferring about Him and our Loving Creator and amazed that they had made such little True Spiritual progress after being with Him for so long. His words say it all when He tells them they have no idea about what kind of Spirit their Spiritual Life comes from and so how would they ever find it by still following the distorted two headed God of the Jews. He then tries to bring them out of their delusional distorted belief about the two headed God of the Jews by telling them True Spiritual children of our Loving Spiritual Creator never destroy men's lives but only save them to Heaven.

Jesus never gave up offering or teaching the Spiritual Truth to children no matter how distorted their Spiritual beliefs were. That was His work. That was His Life. That was His purpose in giving words of enlightenment and Spiritual awakening to save all our lives to Heaven.

GOD IS LOVE LOVE IS LIFE

He who hears My words

and understands their meaning.

And becomes at One with them in their Spirit.

Will pass through death of the flesh to Eternal Spiritual Life.

Chapter Seven

Greatest Demonstration of Two Bodies in One

Jesus is about to provide the disciples with the greatest living demonstration of His Spiritual Teaching about the two bodies separating at death by appearing to them briefly only in His Living Spiritual body after His body of flesh dies and is buried. This is the culmination of all His Loving Spiritual Teachings and Way of living which He gave to us so we may also awaken to our own Spiritual body that is within us right now and enter the Heavenly Spiritual World of Love as He did when our bodies of flesh die and return to the earth as His did.

Jesus allowed His body of flesh to be killed on a cross by the Jews with Roman help. He did not have to do this but chose deliberately and extremely courageously to go ahead and let it happen. This extreme self-sacrifice of His temporary body of flesh had to take place in order to become a living demonstration on Earth to the disciples that we really do all have two very different bodies in one. The Spirit lives on after the flesh dies.

The disciples had already glimpsed His Spiritual body when He walked on the water and thought He was a Spirit. And again, at the transfiguration where they saw His face shine like the sun and His garments became as white as 'Light.' In both events He shifted more fully into His Spiritual body and the radiance of His Spiritual body shone through the outside of His physical body.

It is interesting that Jesus is described as being as white as 'Light.' In John 12:36 Jesus teaches, "While you have the source of Light with you, believe in the Light so that you may become children of the Light." Jesus is connected to the source of Spiritual Life or the Light of our Loving Creator. He is an awakened Spiritual child on Earth filled with the Loving Spiritual Life-force of our Heavenly Spiritual Creator and is telling them to become like Him and awaken to their own Spiritual body and identity also filled with Her Light and Loving Life-force.

Jesus Explains His Living Spiritual Body Will Rise from His Dead Body of Flesh

John 10:11 John 10:17

Jesus said, "I am the good shepherd; the good shepherd lays down His life for the sheep." John 10:17: Jesus said, "For this reason My Loving Spiritual Creator Loves and empowers Me because I lay down My body of flesh so I may take My Life up again in Spirit. No one takes it from Me, but I lay it down of My own free will. I have the authority to lay My flesh down and authority to take My Spiritual Life up. My Loving Creator has asked Me to perform this action for your benefit."

The voluntary crucifixion of His body of flesh on the cross by Jesus then arising from His body of flesh in His Eternal Spiritual body was His greatest demonstration of us all having two different bodies in one. He is emphasising this point by saying He is going to do this of His own free will because He knows He actually has two living bodies, and one will be laid down to die and the other will be raised up to Heaven. We saw this in His very direct Teaching when He said, "Two will be in a single bed. One will be received to be near our Loving Creator, and one will die and be food for the vultures." The first is the Eternal Spiritual body and the other is the temporary earthly body of flesh. And He could choose to do this because His Spiritual body was now fully awakened and empowered by the Loving Life-force of our Loving Spiritual Creator who is Eternal.

John 12:32

Jesus said, "If I am lifted up from My earthly body in My Spiritual body, I will draw all children to Me and our Loving Creator in the Heavenly Spiritual World." John 8:28 Jesus said, "When you lift up the Spiritual child of humanity then you will know that I am a Spiritual child of our Loving Creator."

Jesus knew His Spiritual body formed from the Spiritual Life-force of our Loving Creator was not going to die. He knew that once He was separated from His body of flesh by it being lifted up on a cross and crucified, He would then for the first time be able to appear before His disciples in His full Spiritual body only. And this is how He was going to draw all children to Him and His Spiritual Teachings and Way of Love that leads everyone to the Spiritual Heavenly World by also becoming awakened to our Spiritual body and Soul mind of Love. He simply demonstrated to the disciples that once our body of flesh dies, we will only be in our Spiritual body.

Many Jewish/Christians teach His body of flesh being physically lifted up on a wooden cross and crucified will cleanse us of our sins through His blood being spilled in this way. That belief is a Jewish overlay and misleading. They miss the main point of what He was really doing. Sacrificing His temporary body of flesh to show us we have another Eternal Spiritual body that lives on that we must become at one with before our body of flesh dies and returns to the earth.

They also wrongly teach His body of flesh rose up from the dead after three days. This is another Jewish overlay and is false and misleading. All flesh dies and is just food for the vultures.

John 8:23

Jesus said to them, "You have come out from below I have come out from above you are of this Earthly world I am no longer of this World but the Spiritual World above." Matthew 8:20 Jesus said, "The foxes of the Earth have holes, and the birds of the air have nests, but the Spiritual child of Heaven has nowhere here to lay His head and call His home."

Jesus tells them their primary identity is still based on their earthly dualistic body of flesh that they have and are living out of while His primary identity He is living out of is based on His Spiritual body and Soul mind of Love empowered by the Loving Life-force of our Loving Spiritual Creator in Heaven above. They still only know about their body of earthly flesh while He knows about His ultimate Heavenly Spiritual body.

And the real home of all Spiritual children who have awoken on Earth is the Heavenly Spiritual World. While all creatures and children who only know they have a body of earthly flesh are unaware they can also have a Heavenly Spiritual home.

John 8:21 John 13:33

Jesus said to the Pharisees, "I am going away from here and you will try to find Me but will die in your sin for where I am going you cannot come." John 13:33 Jesus said to His disciples, "Little children I am with you a little while longer. You will seek Me and as I said to the Jews, I also say to you, where I am going you cannot come." Peter said to Him, "Lord, where are you going?" Jesus answered him, "Where I go you cannot follow Me yet, but you will follow later."

Again, we see Peter not understanding anything about our Spiritual body that we all have with us now and its ultimate destination in the Heavenly Spiritual World, so he has no comprehension of what Jesus was really saying. Also, Peter had not yet realised that Jesus already had a fully awoken Spiritual body as well as a body of flesh. This is despite spending three years listening to His Teachings and watching Him perform miracles all empowered by the Loving Spiritual Life-force of our Loving Creator that was giving His Spiritual body True Life.

Jesus also explains that once His body of flesh dies and He leaves this material Earth world to enter the Heavenly Spiritual World in His Spiritual body they will be unable to find Him. He consoles Peter by telling him that he will eventually understand the deeper meaning of His Spiritual Teachings and also awaken to his Spiritual body and Soul and then be able to follow Him to where He is going. The Heavenly Spiritual Loving World.

He also warns the Pharisees that they are sinning and missing the chance of a lifetime to come out of their Earthly material ways of the flesh by following Him, otherwise they will never enter the Heavenly Spiritual World where He is shortly going.

John 14:19-20

Jesus said to the disciples, "In a little while the world will no longer see Me, but you will see Me in Spirit and because I live in Spirit, if you follow Me and My Spiritual Way, you will also live in Spirit. On that day you will understand that I am living in and out of our Loving Creators Life-force, and you will become like Me and I as you."

Again, Jesus is preparing them for the most extreme Spiritual thing He is going to show them knowing that they will have no idea about what is really happening and will think they are seeing a ghostly Spirit. When in fact they will be seeing Him for the first time in His actual living Spiritual body that has separated from His body of flesh. Understandably they will be completely confused. That is why He is forewarning them.

But He goes on to say to them that if they just follow His Spiritual Teachings and live by the Spiritual Way He taught them, they will eventually awaken to realise they also have the same type of Spiritual body like His. And on the day when that transformation of being born again into their Spiritual bodies and identities happens, they will understand everything He was teaching and become like Him. A living Spiritual child of our Loving Spiritual Creator in the Heavenly Spiritual World while still with the temporary body of flesh on Earth. And all who awaken to be Her Spiritual children of Love are sustained by Her Loving Spiritual Life-force in their Spiritual bodies.

John 16:26-27

Jesus said, "On that day of your awakening as a Spiritual child you may ask in My name to intervene for you with our Loving Creator, but I will have no need to do so for She loves you as much as Me and because you have loved Me as Her Spiritual child and believed that I am a Spiritual child of Hers She will hear you just as She hears Me."

Jesus was explaining to the disciples that He was about to leave in His Spiritual body and go to Heaven. But because He will appear to them in Spirit before He leaves this will be the final missing piece that He will reveal to them. Then once they awaken Spiritually as He has, they will have a direct connection with our Loving Creator in Heaven and have no longer any need to ask Him to intervene on their behalf.

Jesus is helping them realise that once they achieve being born again into their Spiritual bodies, they will be just like Him. For they will also be Her Spiritual children just as He is and can talk directly with their Loving Spiritual Creator any time they wish. This is the whole purpose of His Spiritual Teachings. To bring us all alive in the Spirit as independent Loving Children of our Loving Spiritual Creator while on Earth to then enter the Heavenly Spiritual World after we leave our dead bodies of flesh behind. Spirit gives birth only to Spirit. Our Creator is Spirit.

John 5:24-26

Jesus said, "Truly, truly I say to you he who hears My words and believes in our Loving Spiritual Creator who sent Me to teach you these words that come from Her in Heaven has Eternal Spiritual Life. And after death he shall pass out from the dead body of flesh into his Spiritual body and True Life."

Jesus simply states again the Truth about our temporary lives on Earth. We need to listen to His words and understand them and believe in our beautiful Loving Spiritual Creator and the Heavenly Spiritual World. Then we need to live out of His words and Spiritual Way and become transformed by them awakening to our True Spiritual identity and body. Then our Spiritual body and Soul will pass through the experience of the death of our body of flesh and if we are prepared, we will enter into Eternal Spiritual Life in the Heavenly Spiritual world.

John 16:28

Jesus said, "Once I awoke to My Spiritual Body and Soul which comes forth into us from our Loving Spiritual Creator in Heaven then I engaged with the world in a new Way as Her Spiritual child. And now I am leaving this Earthly world and body of flesh and am going to be with Her in Her Heavenly Spiritual World."

Jesus is saying He became a fully enlightened Spiritual child of our Loving Creator on Earth once He realised He had another identity and Spiritual body within Him. And He realised it was our Loving Spiritual Creator who placed it in Him just as She has placed it in all of us. He then merged with it fully becoming at one with Her Loving Life-force within Himself and this is what He came forth from into this world in His new Spiritual identity to teach other children they have it too. And He says He will soon be leaving this Earthly material world including His Earthly body of flesh and finally going home to the Spiritual Heavenly World.

The traditional Bible translations are, "I came forth from My Father and have come into the world, and I am leaving the world again (anew) and going to the Father."

The traditional Greek translations are taken by most Jewish/Christians to mean Jesus was in Heaven before Mary conceived Him and then came down directly from Heaven into Mary's body of flesh fully Spiritually enlightened from birth and now, He is going back. But that is a misunderstanding of these words. He had to seek and find His Spiritual body and Soul within His own body of flesh while being inspired and guided from Heaven by our Loving Creator to do so. And then He kindly teaches us all how to find it also within our own body of flesh just as He did. As He said, "I am the Way."

The words, "I am leaving the world 'again' and going to the Father," use 'again' instead of 'anew'. These translations should read, "I am leaving the world 'anew'. This would be closer to the Truth that He was leaving this world in His new Spiritual body that had come fully alive while here on Earth in the flesh.

John 16:20-22

Jesus said to the disciples, "Truly, truly I say to you, that you will soon weep and lament over Me, but the worldly ones will rejoice while you grieve but then your grief will be turned to joy. Whenever a woman is in labor, she has pain because her hour has come but when she gives birth to her child, she no longer remembers the anguish because of the joy that a child has been born into the world. Therefore, you too have grief now, but I will see you again and your heart will rejoice, and no one will take your joy away from you."

Jesus is saying the Jewish leaders, and their followers will be celebrating the death of His body of flesh while His disciples will be crushed with sadness until He reappears to them in His Spiritual body and then they will be filled with joy. He then uses an example that carries two meanings of a woman giving birth. Firstly, there is the reference to her pain being similar to their pain after He dies followed by rejoicing at seeing Him alive again just as the mother sees her living baby for the first time after a painful birth and rejoices.

The second meaning fits in perfectly with His earlier Teachings that, 'We must all be born again into our Spiritual bodies' which is what the disciples will fully see for the first time after He rises in Spirit from His dead body of flesh.

The Crucifixion Arising in His Spiritual Body

When Jesus voluntarily allowed His temporary body of flesh to be murdered and killed it was a supreme act of Love. He knew He had another Spiritual body that had come fully to Life empowered by the Loving Spiritual Life-force of our Loving Creator and could not die. But the disciples were still unaware they had one too as we all do, and they were still not understanding His Teachings enough to awaken it. This was like shock treatment to start a stilled heart when they saw Him after death in His Spiritual body only. Then they saw the full result of His Teachings that He was trying to awaken them with to help lift them up in Spirit out of their ignorance into enlightenment of who they really are. And who we all really are. Spiritual children of our Loving Creator.

Luke 23:46

At the moment when the body of flesh of Jesus died, He cried out, "My Loving Creator into your hands I commit My Spirit." His dead body of flesh hanging on the cross was now lifeless while His Spiritual body and Soul that was still fully alive left the dead body of flesh behind. As Jesus teaches, "One body is received to be near our Loving Creator and one body is redundant, of no use and dismissed." He had two fully functioning bodies. One died and was buried and one rose to live on.

John 20:14-17

After the dead body of Jesus was placed in the tomb Mary Magdelene came two days later to visit the tomb. But the stone was rolled back, and the body of Jesus was now missing for some reason. So, she sat and wept but then turned around and saw Jesus standing there but she did not recognise Him. Jesus then said to her, "Woman why are you weeping? Whom are you seeking?"

Supposing Him to be the gardener, she said to Him, "Sir if you have carried His dead body away tell me where you have laid Him and I will remove Him back to here?" Jesus spoke just one word to Her saying, "Mary." Upon hearing her name spoken by Jesus she turned and even though He appeared different now she knew it was Him. She said to Him, "Teacher!" And Jesus said to her, "Do not try and touch Me Mary for I have now risen up in My Spirit to our Loving Spiritual Creator, and you cannot hold on to Me anymore with your body of flesh."

Firstly, Mary was looking straight at Jesus but for some reason did not recognise Him. This is simply because He was now only in His Spiritual body and had no body of flesh for her to see, just a Spiritual body in the image of His body of flesh but not of the same substance. Spiritual bodies are formed from the Spiritual Life-force of our Loving Spiritual Creator while our bodies of flesh are only formed from Earthly material elements.

This account is the most obvious and most revealing of the Truth that He was now only in a Spiritual body with no flesh present in Him at all by telling Mary not to try to hold on to Him. Mary was still in a body of flesh and her physical arms and hands would not have been able to hold something now completely Spiritual. It is that simple.

The traditional words added in all translations as to why Jesus told her not to try and hold on to him are, "Do not try to hold on to Me, for I have not yet ascended to the Father." But this makes no sense. Firstly, as He was dying on the cross, He said, "Loving Creator into your hands I commit My spirit." He knew His Spiritual body and Soul were going straight to Our Loving Creator in Heaven right then. And this is backed up by the words of Jesus Himself when He said to the other person crucified beside Him, "Truly I say to you, this day you shall be with Me in Heaven."

That means Jesus is negating a final day of Apocalyptic judgement for this man and for all who have died as many Jewish/Christians believe and teach. Our day of judgement and reaping what we have sown occurs on the day we die. There is no doubt at all that Jesus is saying this here.

Road to Emmaus

Luke 24:14-16 and 28-31

Two followers of Jesus left Jerusalem for a village called Emmaus after Jesus was crucified. While they were walking and discussing what had happened to Jesus, Jesus Himself approached and walked along with them. But the two followers did not recognise Jesus at all and began talking with Him as they went along. And as they approached a village where they were going to Jesus acted as if He was continuing on. But they urged Him saying, "Stay with us, for it is getting towards evening and the day is nearly over." So, He went with them.

When He had reclined at the table with them to eat, He took the bread and blessed it and breaking it, He began giving it to them. Then they suddenly realised it was Jesus, and He then vanished from their sight.

Again, we can plainly see they did not recognise Him at all just like His very close friend and follower Mary. Mary had to only hear His voice call her name to know it was actually Him even though she thought He was the gardener. These two followers had a different catalyst to realise it was actually Him, when He broke the bread and offered it to them. This is the famous last supper tradition established by Jesus when He said, "Do this in memory of Me." Despite not recognising Him those words and action of Jesus jogged their memory and then they knew this man was Jesus. At that moment of their realisation Jesus just vanishes into thin air and disappears.

They did not easily recognise Jesus because He was in His full Spiritual body. He simply vanishes from their sight which a body of Earthly flesh cannot do. But the Spiritual body can.

Jesus Appears to the Eleven Disciples Including Thomas

Luke 24:33-38 John 20:21-22

After Jesus vanished out of sight the two followers got up that very hour and returned to Jerusalem to tell the disciples what had happened. When they arrived and entered the room where all eleven of the disciples were gathered, including Thomas, they began to relate their experience of meeting Jesus along the road. And how they did not recognise Him until He performed the breaking of the bread then He just vanished.

While they were telling these things to them, despite all the doors being shut, Jesus Himself suddenly appeared out of nowhere amongst them and said, "Peace be with you." But they were terrified and filled with fear and thought they were seeing a ghost or spirit not recognising it was Jesus.

Jesus said to them, "Why are you so troubled, and why do doubts arise in your hearts and mind? Jesus again said, "Peace be with you, as our Loving Spiritual Creator has sent Me to teach the Spiritual Way, I also send you." After saying this Jesus breathed on them and said to them, "Receive the Holy Spirit of our Loving Creator." Then He vanished out of sight.

The first accurate thing to note in Luke is that Thomas was there when Jesus first appeared to the eleven disciples. The account in John's Gospel of Thomas not being present and doubting his fellow disciples is false and John has added that in to distort and cover up the Truth.

The second thing to take note of is that His own disciples did not recognise Him and thought it was an apparition of a ghost or Spirit, and they were terrified and filled with fear. Exactly the same inability to recognise Him as Mary and the two followers on the road to Emmaus had and now themselves. None of them had ever seen a Living Spiritual child of our Loving Spiritual Creator before in the fullness of their Spiritual body with no body of flesh attached anymore. The scene of the transfiguration was the closest three of them came to seeing His Spiritual body shining through His body of flesh.

The third thing to note is that they actually received the blessing of the Holy Spirit of our Loving Creator right then and there directly from Jesus Himself. The way it is being described as Jesus breathing on them is a beautiful play on the Greek word for breath that can also mean Spirit.

The fourth thing to note again is that a body of material substance and flesh cannot appear out of nowhere in a locked room and then just disappear and vanish. Only someone in a Spiritual body like an Angel could do that. And that is the type of perfect Spiritual body all Spiritual children will have who enter the Heavenly World as Jesus Himself said.

Sea of Tiberias

John 21:3-13

The disciples were sitting by the sea of Tiberias and decided to go fishing. They fished all night but caught nothing. At daybreak Jesus appeared standing on the shore, but the disciples did not recognise Him. So, Jesus called out to them, "Children have you caught any fish?" They answered Him, "No." Jesus said, "Cast your net on the right side of the boat and you will find a catch." So, they cast their nets and caught so many fish they were unable to haul them onto the boat. Then one of the disciples said to Peter, "It is the Master." So, Peter dived into the water and swam ashore immediately. The others followed in the boat dragging the net filled with the fish they had caught.

When they came ashore Jesus said, "Bring some of the fish you caught and have some breakfast. So, they made a fire of coals and laid some fish and bread on it. None of the disciples had the courage to ask Him directly, "Who are you?" Knowing in their hearts it must be Jesus.

Once again, the disciples in the boat do not recognise Jesus until He also provides them with a catalyst of filling their nets with fish after following His instructions. Just like the time He did it after teaching by the shore from their boat giving similar instructions that were also fulfilled. We can read between the lines that Jesus up close must have still appeared different to them causing some serious doubts to arise about who He was. He was in His Spiritual body not body of flesh that is why. But intuitively following the catch of fish they knew it must be Him.

It is clearly obvious from all of these accounts that He had a different appearance after His Spiritual body rose out of His body of dead flesh making it hard for them to recognise Him. If He was still in His old body of flesh, as many Jewish/Christians still teach they would have immediately acknowledged that it was Him.

After the Earthly body of Jesus died and was buried and He arose out of it now fully in His Spiritual body He only appeared very briefly to the disciples on a few occasions and only gave brief instructions for them to follow. As well as blessing them Himself and giving them the Holy Spirit to receive from our Loving Spiritual Creator. The main purpose of Jesus sacrificing His body of temporary flesh by allowing the Jews to kill it was to provide an extraordinary actual living demonstration of what happens to us all at the time of our death.

If anyone listens closely to His words and understands them correctly, they will come to see that right throughout His Spiritual Teachings, He is preparing us for this very moment of departing from a dead useless body of flesh in our Eternal Spiritual body of Love. That was the whole purpose of His life, works and Teachings. To help us bring our Spiritual body and Soul fully alive to lead us out of a material world of danger, suffering and death through the Spiritual Way of Love. This must awaken within us to be able to enter a far more beautiful Spiritual Heavenly World where there is no more suffering or death but only Life and Love.

All the Spiritual practices that He taught and explained how to do are the very things that awaken our Spiritual body and Soul to real True Spiritual Life. And they are all empowered by only one motivation and one Life-force, Love. The flesh is prone to be dualistic but our Soul and Spiritual body can only be singular with Love.

Our earthly temporary bodies of flesh are only empowered by temporary earthly elements. Our Spiritual bodies and Souls and minds are only empowered by one thing. The Eternal Loving Spiritual Life-force of our Loving Spiritual Creator in the Heavenly Spiritual World so they never die. Our earth body disintegrates and returns to its source, the earth. Our Spiritual body remains intact and returns to its source, our Loving Spiritual Creator who formed it for us.

But we must all cross over the ever-flowing river of reaping what we sow to reach the shores of Heaven safely without sinking and being carried downstream to another destination for our Souls to be cleansed. Jesus gives us all the instructions we need on how to successfully cross over that river without sinking. Spiritual children of our Loving Creator just walk across the river in their Spiritual body just as Jesus walked on the water. Those weighed down by heavy evils they have committed in this world cannot do so and sink like a millstone and are carried away from Heaven downstream to be cleansed.

Added Words

In all Bibles there are words written that say Jesus rose in a body of flesh, that He ate some fish when He appeared to the disciples, He shows them the wounds on His perfect new Heavenly body and prompts them Himself to touch Him to see that He is not a Spirit but flesh and in Matthew's version there are a few women at the tomb who see Jesus and supposedly fall down and hold His feet. Unlike the Mary Magdelene account where Jesus says she cannot hold Him because He is obviously in His Spiritual body. And then there is the very powerful description in John of the Thomas event where Jesus supposedly says to Thomas, "Reach here with your finger and see the wounds in My hands and reach here with your hand and put it into My side at the wound." But this is only found in John's Gospel planted as a red herring while the Gospel of Luke correctly says Thomas was present when Jesus first appeared to the disciples together.

I will dedicate a chapter addressing this problem later in the book. The most important thing to remember is that He was still alive and well and appeared to the disciples in some type of different body that could just appear and disappear after they killed His body of flesh. The main thing as followers of Jesus is that we all believe that our life will continue after our body of flesh dies. There is little gain arguing over what type of body that will be but great gain in supporting each other to prepare ourselves Spiritually by following the Way of Jesus of Love and Non-violence to arise in our new Eternal body in the Heavenly Spiritual World.

GOD IS LOVE LOVE IS LIFE

I lay down My life of flesh

and I arise in My Life of Spirit

to have Life again Eternally in Heaven.

May we all follow His example and be ready to leave.

By bringing our Spirit alive through the Love that we all need.

Chapter Eight

Jesus Was a Pacifist Are You?

It is an undeniable, historical fact that Jesus was a pacifist and taught His followers that the only Way to pass safely through this temporary, material world of duality, dangers, dark evils and death of the flesh was by becoming at one with perfect Spiritual Love. And this only exists naturally in our Spiritual bodies as our bodies of flesh are prone to be dualistic in nature because they are formed from the earthly elements not from our Loving Spiritual Creator's Life-force in Heaven like our Spiritual bodies are.

Any Jewish/Christian who slanders Jesus and our Loving Spiritual Creator who gives us a Spiritual Life filled only with Her Loving Life-force by saying His followers can go to war and kill, is a Jew not a Chrisitan. And they are worshipping the two headed God Yahweh of the Jews not our Loving Spiritual Creator. That is the massive distortion that most Jewish/Christians hold on to which goes against Jesus and seriously damages His Spiritual Way of Love we must follow and our Loving Spiritual Creator. And without becoming at one with this perfect Spiritual Love while here on Earth by bringing our Spiritual body, Soul and mind alive through this perfect Heavenly Loving Life-force we will not enter into the Heavenly Spiritual World. Jesus Himself clearly said this in the sermon on the mount.

The reason I placed the preceding chapters dealing with the powerful Spiritual Truth that Jesus taught that we all have two very different bodies in one, is because without understanding and believing in that fundamental Spiritual Truth we may lack the Spiritual strength and courage to become a pacifist like Jesus. But once we awaken fully to our Spiritual body's existence being with us right now, and are living out of it as our primary identity on Earth and believe totally in Life after death then we can even face our body of flesh being killed by a demented child who has become a beast of the flesh but not retaliate against them in a similar way. Christians do not take part in wars.

Our responsibility as awakened Spiritual children of Heaven on Earth is to behave just as we will in Heaven and shine the Peace and Love of Heaven to those who are lost in the dark delusion of a false, violent, shadow identity devoid of Spiritual Life and Love. Jesus did exactly this by allowing the Jews to murder His body of flesh and not fight back physically because He knew He had another body with Him that was alive and well that was Spiritual which He was already at one with and living out of, that they could not kill.

Jesus was a pacifist, are you?

Peacemakers are the Spiritual Children of Our Loving Creator

Matthew 5:9

Jesus said, "Blessed are the peacemakers, for they shall be called the Spiritual children of our Loving Spiritual Creator in the Heavenly Spiritual World."

This short, simple Spiritual Teaching of Jesus describes the very nature of True children of our Loving Spiritual Creator. They only make peace for they are alive in Spirit and are filled with Her Spiritual Loving Life-force and in the face of violence and war they are the Spiritual Loving counterforce from Heaven to bring Peace on Earth. For only Love can overcome all hatred and violence and bring peace to this world of suffering.

Jesus was a pacifist, are you?

Love Your Enemies

Matthew 5:43-48 and Luke 6:27-28, 32-36

Jesus said, "You have heard it said of old, 'An eye for an eye and a tooth for a tooth,' but I say to you, you must resist retaliating evil with evil for revenge. But instead, whoever strikes you on your right cheek, turn the other to him also.

You have been taught of old, 'You shall love your neighbour and hate your enemy.' But I say to you, love your enemies, bless those who curse you, do good to those who hate you, pray for those who spitefully use you and persecute you. So that you may become the Spiritual children of your Loving Spiritual Creator in the Heavenly Spiritual World. For She makes Her sun to rise on the evil and on the good and sends rain on the just and the unjust and She is kind to the ungrateful and to the evil ones.

If you love only those who love you, what Spiritual reward do you have? Do not even sinners and corrupt children love those who love them. And if you joyously greet your fellow brethren only, what do you do more than others with only limited Spiritual Life in themselves. And if you will only do good to those who do good to you, your own Spiritual Life will remain incomplete and unfulfilled.

But I say, Love your enemies, do good and lend hoping for nothing in return and your Spiritual growth will increase greatly. Therefore, if you really want to become Spiritual children of your Loving Spiritual Creator and enter into Her Heavenly Spiritual World your Love right now must be as perfect as Her Love."

These Spiritual Teachings on Love and Non-violence which only a True pacifist follower of Jesus could do are the most powerful He ever gave to us to follow. All other Teachings and Spiritual practices He gave come forth from this one. For God is Love. But to reach this level of realisation and become a pacifist we need to understand that we are actually a Spiritual Child with an Eternal

Spiritual body with us right now that cannot die, empowered only by the Loving Spiritual Life-force of Our Loving Creator.

We need to begin understanding this by first learning His fundamental Spiritual Teachings like Love, Compassion, Forgiveness, Non-violence, Equanimity, Generosity, Honesty, Spiritual Truth and reaching out to help those who have fallen down. Then each fundamental building block slowly builds up your Spiritual strength and brings your Spiritual body and Soul to Life until they begin to form your Spiritual home to live out of on Earth based on the foundation of His Teachings that Jesus called the rock. "My words are like a man who built His home on a rock. And nothing could overcome it." Including demented children lost in darkness who may become our enemies and want to hurt us, but we only feel sorry for them and Love them in the best way we can as Jesus told us to do to bring them out of their darkness and guide them into the Light of Heaven.

Anyone can climb to this great Spiritual height and reach the summit of perfect Spiritual Love and non-violence by transforming into a Loving pacifist and then see the view of Heaven opening up and come into sight before them. For all children in the Heavenly Spiritual World of Love are pacifists. But only pacifists on Earth filled with perfect Love can reach the top of the mountain, and being Spiritually awakened by Jesus to understand that you have two different bodies in one is a powerful blessing to help you scale that summit.

Once you reach the summit there is only Heaven above you and all Earth below. At this point you realise the fullness of the Truth that Jesus did when He said in John 8:23, "You are from below, I am now from above. You are of this Earth world; I am not of this Earth world." And then your body of flesh can die and stay with the Earth it was made of, because you will leave in your perfect Spiritual body brought alive through His words of Love and non-violence that you took inside yourself and were nourished by. This is the Spiritual bread that came down from

Heaven that Jesus offers to all of us to partake in to have True Spiritual Life.

Jesus was a pacifist, are you?

Live by the Sword Die by the Sword

Matthew 26:50-52 and Luke 22:51

Then they came and laid hold of Jesus and seized Him. And one of those with Jesus reached and drew out his sword and struck the servant of the high priest and cut of his ear. Jesus then rebuked him saying, "Put your sword back into its place, for all who take up the sword shall perish by the sword." And He touched the servant's ear and healed him.

Jesus is clearly warning us that anyone who takes up the sword or gun or tank or drone or missile or any other weapon of death to kill another child of our Loving Spiritual Creator by becoming a beast of the flesh devoid of Spiritual Life and Love will face serious consequences. He cannot be more direct about this with the words He spoke right here.

Jesus wants us all to be pacifists for one extremely important reason. He wants us to be ready to enter the Heavenly Spiritual World after our body of flesh dies so we can come out of all the suffering and death in the Earth world into Eternal joy and Love in the Heavenly Spiritual World with our Spiritual Body and Soul intact. For a follower of Jesus to ignore this and kill other children of our Loving Creator is extremely dangerous for their own Spiritual body and Soul.

Jesus gave us a beautiful example when arrested of how we deal with a violent situation as a True pacifist follower of His should. Firstly, He immediately intervenes with the follower who drew the sword and rebuked him to stop any further bloodshed. He then demonstrated His perfect Spiritual Love by healing the enemy's injured ear.

Sadly, I have heard many Jewish/Christians pervert these words of Jesus and teach the opposite to children that we can kill our enemies. They quote examples of the distorted two headed War God of the Jews who helped them slaughter their enemies saying it is the same Loving Creator of Jesus, so we can do it too. Filthy slander. They are Jewish when they say this and are certainly not Christians or followers of Jesus when they teach this to children and poison their hearts and minds. The One Loving Spiritual Creator of Jesus is definitely not the same dualistic two headed distorted God Yahweh of the Jews.

Jesus was a pacifist, are you?

They Can Only Kill Your Flesh Not Your Soul

Matthew 10:28

Jesus taught, "Do not be afraid of those who can kill your body of flesh but cannot kill your Spiritual body and Soul. But rather fear sin, that can both destroy your body of flesh and damage and injure your Spirit and Soul."

Jesus is saying in this Earthly world we may face two different enemies but only one of them is fatal and that is the one we must always guard ourselves against no matter what. The external enemy who has become a beast of the flesh joining an army of children who are also beasts of the flesh to kill and steal from other children is not the one that is the most dangerous to your wellbeing. For we have two very different bodies to keep healthy so they both have life, and they can both be damaged but by two very different things. One only has a temporary short-term life that comes to an end at death while the other is Eternal beyond all suffering. Which do you think is the most valuable to protect?

Our body of flesh will die one day anyway and return to the Earth from which it was formed. It may just grow old and stop working, be killed in a sudden accident when young or killed by a disease at any time during our journey. Being killed by a demented child whose Soul is lost in darkness and evil is just another way our body of flesh stops working.

And although we will suffer a painful death of our body of flesh that the child lost in dark evil has caused us to experience with a bullet or evil weapon, our Spiritual body will not be impacted in any way whatsoever. A bullet is only made of earth and can only effect Earthly things. Our Spiritual body is made from a totally different substance that is vastly superior in every way. It is formed from the actual Living Loving Spiritual Life-force of our Loving Spiritual Creator in a Heavenly Spiritual World. It is Love, Light and Life itself and cannot die.

Only the internal enemies of wrong doings and evil that can arise from within our own minds by becoming a false, dark shadow figure can damage our Spiritual Life and Spiritual body and Soul by covering our True Spiritual identity of Love and Light with filth. Jesus said this is the One True Life to protect above all else. For if you lose this One True Spiritual Life you will lose everything. As Jesus said, "What does it profit a man if he should gain the whole material world but lose his own Spirit and Soul."

Only a pacifist follower of Jesus who believes in their Eternal Spiritual Life could accept such an horrific end to their physical life on Earth by being killed by a child who is demented by their own evil without killing the other child first to protect their body of flesh. For that would damage their own Spiritual body and Soul mind of Love and their entry into the Heavenly Spiritual World of Love. And that poor child of our Loving Creator is already lost in the darkness of their own evil and they are dead to their Spirit and devoid of True Spiritual Life anyway and cannot enter the Heavenly Spiritual World like that.

And if we do take their life in self-defense to protect our body of temporary flesh, we have robbed them of the chance to repent and turn away from evil and enter Heaven. A very serious thing to do to a lost child of our Loving Creator who still Loves them and only wants them to come out of evil and be saved to Heaven not killed. As Jesus said, "I did not come to condemn but to save the sinners who are lost in the darkness surrounding their Soul."

Jesus was a pacifist, are you?

It is the Spirit Who Gives Life the Flesh Profits Nothing

John 4:24 and John 6:63

Jesus said, "Our Loving Spiritual Creator is Spirit and those who Love Her must come to Her in Spirit and in Truth. It is the Spirit who gives Life, the flesh profits nothing."

This is another very powerful Teaching of Jesus to help us all become strong Spiritual children and pacifists in a dangerous material, dualistic world. Jesus very clearly states again that it is the Spiritual body and Soul created for you by our Loving Creator in the Heavenly Spiritual World that is the only Real Life you have. Real Life is ongoing as it is Life itself, and our Spiritual bodies and Souls are only empowered by one thing, our Loving Creator's Living Spiritual Eternal Loving Life-force, therefore we have Eternal Life if we are at one with our Spiritual body and Soul before we die. As Jesus said, "It is the Spirit who gives Life."

Our body of flesh is obviously not the True Eternal Life that Jesus often spoke of because it dies. It only has a brief life span based on Earthly elements that is cyclic. But it gives us time to find the Treasure within us of our True Spiritual body and Soul mind of Love to awaken and arise up into Eternal Life in a Heavenly Spiritual World before our body of flesh dies.

And Jesus says that if we want to come to where our Creator is in Her Heavenly Spiritual World of Love we must come to Her in our Spiritual body and in Truth not our body of flesh which once dead has no life in it anyway. And He very bluntly states that at the end of our life on Earth when the body of flesh dies it is absolutely of no use to you whatsoever anymore and is just food for the vultures.

To become a true pacifist follower of Jesus in this dangerous material world we must understand the power in this profound Spiritual Truth He is often Teaching. It can fill us with a Spiritual strength that other worldly children do not have. While they may take up the gun to kill and therefore worship death, we take up the Spirit to heal and so worship True Life. And as Jesus warned everyone, we will all reap as we have sown.

Who has the greatest courage in this material world? A demented child who has become a beast of the flesh full of hatred, greed and murder whose only strength is to pull the trigger of an evil satanic gun or the Loving Spiritual child of Heaven who is so strong in Spirit that they Love him even as he is pulling the trigger or nails them to a cross.

Jesus was a pacifist, are you?

Angry Words Can Hurt Other Children

Matthew 5:21-22 and 12:36-37

Jesus said, "You have heard that it was said to those of olden times, 'You shall not kill and whoever kills shall be in danger of damnation.' But I say to you, that whoever is angry with his brother or sister for no reason shall also be in danger of judgement coming down upon them. And whoever calls his brother or sister worthless, or a fool harming their Spirits will be in an even greater danger and fall into terrible suffering themselves as a consequence."

Jesus said, "I tell you that every careless word that people speak, they shall have to give an accounting of at their judgement day. For by your words, you will be justified and by your words you will be condemned."

Jesus says that while killing another child leads obviously to the destruction of your own Spiritual Life, anger can be just as dangerous for your Spirit and Soul as it can hurt other children's Spirit and damage your own Spirit of Love that is your True Life-force. And of course, any anger is like a smoldering coal that once the winds of hatred are blown upon it can set fire to a peaceful family home or whole country and plunge it into war. This is the level of Spiritual understanding we must reach to be True followers of Jesus to avoid using words as a weapon to deliberately hurt others instead of an instrument of Truth that helps bring those lost in darkness back to Spiritual Love and Life and supports reconciliation and peace.

Pacifists are full of Spiritual Love, Peace and Non-violence. But they have a strong Spiritual sense of what is right and wrong when engaging with other children and must speak the Truth calling out any Evil they encounter. Pacifists along with being Non-violent are usually also the ones who are sympathetic and use supportive words of healing and understanding to help resolve any difficult situation. This is the Spirit of their Love and our Loving Creator working through them for others.

In these modern times of social media unfortunately dominating young people's lives there are deeply disturbing events where some teenagers have taken their own lives after being attacked online by other callous children who drive them to kill themselves by just hurting them using evil words. Words can hurt our own Spirits if we are not in control and even kill other children when used as weapons of evil.

While Jesus was very forthright and critical at times when speaking the Truth with the corrupt Jewish leaders and people, the words that He used when dealing with those who were sick, outcasts or fallen down into sin were nothing but comforting, supportive, Loving and forgiving to lift them up into peace, hope and Spiritual Life. Pacifists are Loving but Truthful to reveal corruption and set children free from sin and lift up those who have fallen down with words of Love and Compassion.

Jesus was a pacifist, are you?

The Lost Sheep Parable

Matthew 18:12-14 and Luke 15:1-7

Then the tax collectors and sinners drew near to Jesus to hear Him teach. And the Pharisees and the Scribes complained saying, "This man receives and associates with sinners and He eats with them." Jesus overheard them and spoke this parable to them, "What man among you, having a hundred sheep and if he loses one of them does not leave the ninety-nine in the countryside and goes to find the one which is lost?

And when he finds the lost sheep, he lays it on his shoulders rejoicing at having found it. And when he comes home, he calls together his friends and neighbours saying to them, 'Rejoice with me for I have found my sheep that was lost!' I say to you there will be more rejoicing in the Heavenly Spiritual World over one sinner who repents than over ninety-nine virtuous children who need no repentance. For it is the will and intent of My Loving Spiritual Creator in Heaven that not even one of those lost and least in Spirit should ever be destroyed."

This beautiful image of a Loving non-judgmental shepherd going to great lengths to bring the wayward lost sheep back home to safety is a wonderful lesson to us all as followers of Jesus. He doesn't beat it or punish it for getting itself lost but only rejoices to have it back home safely. The lost sheep is any child on Earth who has turned away from our Loving Spiritual Creator and Her Light and Love to become a dark beast of the flesh to whatever degree. From being just selfish and uncaring to becoming a satanic warmonger slaughtering children through the evil of war.

Yet Jesus clearly states that not one of these gone into darkness will be destroyed due to the unending Love shining on them from Heaven of our Loving Spiritual Creator who gave them Spiritual Life to live out of even though they may have rejected it for now. Our Loving Spiritual Creator is a Being of pure Love and is the ultimate pacifist and we must all become Her Spiritual children now to enter Her Heavenly Spiritual World of Love and Peace after our body of flesh dies and returns to the earth. We shine the Light to bring other children out of the darkness they have gone into. We never become like the darkness that they have become at one with otherwise we would both be lost.

However, such lost children who do not repent and change their ways while alive on Earth will have to undergo burning realisations in accordance with the intensity of the wrongs they committed. This is the neutral Divine Spiritual Law of Reaping What We Sow acting like a mirror reflecting what they have done to others back to themselves to experience it and be Spiritually cleansed after their body of flesh dies. How long this takes and what the intensity may be will depend on the extent of the suffering caused by each individual child. Another reason to never have to kill a child of evil and remain a pacifist in the face of evil because they will all suffer after death anyway.

For the worst offenders, especially every child involved in killing other children in any war for any reason, will all suffer beyond any horror they could imagine. Neither our Loving Creator nor Jesus will cast them into a Hellish experience or cause their suffering for they create it themselves by killing other children of our Loving Creator. But Jesus and our Loving Spiritual Creator will still be there for them when their Spiritual cleansing is finished to embrace them once again with their Love. As Jesus Himself said while dying on the cross, "Loving Creator forgive them for they know not what they do."

Jesus was a pacifist and so is our Loving Creator.

Spiritual Children Save Lives We Do Not Destroy Them

Luke 9:52-56

When Jesus was travelling to Jerusalem, He wanted to stay the night in a Samaritan village, but the people refused Him accommodation being upset that He would not stay and teach them. When His disciples James and John heard that they were insulting Jesus in this way they said to Jesus, "Master, do you want us to order fire to come down from Heaven and consume them just as Elijah did?"

Jesus immediately turned around and strongly rebuked them saying, "You do not know what sort of Spirit you are of or from. For a Spiritual child of our Loving Creator only saves lives and never destroys them."

Jesus states very plainly that Spiritual children of our Loving Spiritual Creator in the Heavenly Spiritual World never destroy other children's lives because we are empowered only by Love for them. Only a True pacifist and follower of the Spiritual Way of Jesus can be insulted, persecuted or attacked by another child and remain peaceful towards that child. How else can we show them the Way to Heaven, Love and Peace if we do not live out of these Spiritual powers ourselves.

Jesus was a pacifist, are you?

The Good Shepherd Lays Down His Life for the Sheep

John 10:11

Jesus said, "I am the good shepherd. The good shepherd lays down His life for the sheep."

Jesus voluntarily allowed His body of flesh to be killed by the Jews without fighting back or killing them to defend His own body of flesh. He did not form a righteous army to kill them and save His physical life. In the face of being unjustly crucified to death by evil minded children He was nothing but peaceful and forgiving towards them because He was a Spiritual child of Light and True Life empowered only by Love. While they were still children of darkness in Earthly dualistic bodies of flesh empowered only by hatred, envy and death.

Jesus was a pacifist, are you?

Love is the Greatest Spiritual Practice of All

Matthew 22:37-40

Jesus said, "The greatest Spiritual commandment is to Love our Loving Spiritual Creator with all your heart, with all your Soul, with all your mind and with all your strength. And the second greatest is like it. You shall love your neighbour as yourself. All Spiritual practices come forth from these two."

A pacifist like Jesus is empowered only by a Spiritual Loving Life-force from the Heavenly Spiritual World and our Loving Spiritual Creator. A pacifist sees all other children as being potentially Spiritual children of our Loving Spiritual Creator just like themselves and does not dominate, take advantage or abuse anyone or be violent towards them but treats them all as close friends. Some may be lost in darkness and evil, so we help them find the way out by giving them the Truth about Spiritual Life and the distorted identity they have become. Some may be in great physical need or ill, so we give them the appropriate comfort they need. Without True Spiritual awakening and Love inside you it is not possible to follow in the Way of Jesus and be a pacifist like He was and become a Living Spiritual child of Heaven on Earth.

Jesus was a pacifist, are you?

GOD IS LOVE LOVE IS LIFE

Love your enemies.

Turn the other cheek.

Pray for those who hurt you.

Forgive and you will be forgiven.

Put your sword back into its place.

Die to the flesh and Live in your Spirit.

Chapter Nine

Pacifist Teaching of Jesus Destroyed

Pacifist Martyrs of the Original Christian Church

Jesus established beyond any doubt whatsoever that True followers of His Spiritual Way cannot kill other children even when they are about to kill your own body of flesh. The first original Spiritual Community of Divine Love or Christian Church that Jesus Himself founded were all pacifists for over three hundred years. They would rather be murdered in horrific ways by children lost in darkness than give up their Spiritual Life of Light and Love that lives on after the death of their temporary body of flesh just as Jesus did. This is an historical fact and anyone who disputes this does not know Jesus, our Loving Spiritual Creator or the Way to the Heavenly Spiritual World and slanders Jesus and our Loving Creator.

The first recorded follower of Jesus who was martyred was Stephen who was brutally stoned to death around 36 A.D by the Jews for not denouncing Jesus. He did not fight back or hurt those killing his body of flesh. The historical records show there were countless Christian martyrs put to death from as early as 64 A.D. by Roman Emperors as well such as Nero.

PACIFIST TEACHING OF JESUS DESTROYED

This still went on up until around 305 A.D. by Emperor Diocletian who wanted the Christian Spiritual Way of Love and Non-violence completely wiped out throughout the Roman Empire. A decree was issued by the Emperor forbidding Christians to gather and pray, all Christian writings were to be burnt, and any churches demolished. And any Christian who did not voluntarily surrender their scriptures or refused to renounce their Spiritual Way and faith were executed.

Ways True Christians Were Executed

Along with being stoned to death by Jewish zealots the Romans had a selection of brutal ways to kill followers of the Christian Way of Love and Non-violence of Jesus.

Burning Them Alive

Many Christians were brutally murdered by being burnt alive tied to a stake after being coated in tar.

Dismemberment

Some Christian's bodies of flesh were literally torn apart into four sections by tying each limb to a horse and driving the horses until each limb was physically ripped from the torso.

Eaten by Lions or Killed by Other Wild Animals

This was one of the more common ways to murder Christian martyrs by using them as public entertainment in the coliseums. The lions or other animals were deprived of food for some days then set upon the defenseless followers of the Spiritual Way of Jesus of Love and Non-violence to be literally eaten alive. Some even had animal skins tied to them stained with blood to provoke the Lions to attack them.

Crucifixion

This was another common way to murder Christian followers of Jesus by tying or nailing their bodies to a cross until exhausted by agony and thirst their hearts finally stopped beating. Just as the heart of Jesus stopped beating by being murdered in this same brutal and cruel way.

An Actual Account of the Christian Martyr Perpetua 203 A.D.

Perpetua was a young mother twenty-two years old with an infant son born into a well-off family. She was preparing to be baptised into the Spiritual Way of Love and non-violence of Jesus that leads us to the Heavenly Spiritual World, in the city of Carthage along with several other believers in the Spiritual Way. These included Saturninus, Secundulus, Revocatus and Felicitas who was pregnant.

Roman authorities found out about them and arrested them for refusing to worship the Roman deities. Perpetua and her infant along with the others were sent to prison to await trial. In loyalty to them another member of their Christian group, Saturus who was not arrested with them, voluntarily turned himself over to the Roman authorities to join them.

Perpetua's father visited her in prison and pleaded with her to leave her newfound Spiritual Way of Love and Non-violence taught by Jesus. But Perpetua pointed to a small clay pitcher in her cell and asked her father, "Is that a clay pitcher or something else?" He replied, "It is a pitcher." Perpetua asked again, "Can it be called by any other name than what it actually is?" "No," he replied. "Neither can I be called by any other name than a Christ-

PACIFIST TEACHING OF JESUS DESTROYED

ian of Love and Non-violence a follower of Jesus." Her father was furious at her refusal and left her.

Perpetua and her fellow Christians were secretly baptised into the faith while in prison. Perpetua continued to nurse her infant while in the prison dungeons. Perpetua's brother suggested that she ask our Loving Spiritual Creator for a vision to help her understand the Spiritual Way ahead.

That night Perpetua had a dream and saw a tall, narrow ladder made of gold stretching up to Heaven. Although the ladder was beautiful all types of evil weapons such as daggers, lances, hooks and swords were attached to the sides, placing climbers at serious risk. And at the base of the ladder, she saw a large crouching dragon waiting to consume those who could not make the climb to the top of the ladder.

In her vision, Saturus made the climb first and reaching the top encouraged Perpetua to follow him up. The dragon lifted its head as she approached the ladder but undeterred she stepped on its head as the first step upwards. She climbed to the top and she found herself in an immense garden. A white-haired shepherd sat there milking his sheep. Around him were gathered thousands of children in white robes. The shepherd looked at Perpetua and said, "You are welcome, daughter." He offered her some cheese he had made and as she ate it the surrounding children also said, "Welcome" to her. She realised from the vision that her life on Earth would end as a martyr.

Her father visited her again to plead with her to change her mind, but she refused. So, he took her infant son with him and left. Soon, they were brought to trial and the procurator ordered Perpetua to make offerings to the Emperors. Perpetua said, "I will not." He asked her, "Are you a Christian?" She replied, "Yes I am." The procurator ordered they all be thrown into the arena with wild beasts to kill them.

While waiting in prison for their execution a warden grew to like them impressed by their courage in the face of a certain terrible death. He allowed other Christians to visit them. Secundulus died in prison while waiting execution sparing him a violent death and Felicitas was hoping to give birth before the execution so she could die with them. A few days later she did give birth, and her baby was given to a Chistian woman to care for her.

While she was in painful labor one of the women who came to help asked her, "You are suffering now, but how will you cope when they throw you to the beasts?" Felicitas answered, "I suffer what I am suffering now, but then there will be another within me, who will suffer for me because I am about to suffer for Him."

Perpetua had a final vision before being murdered by the Romans. In it she was in an arena and was challenged by a large violent gladiator, but she overcame his attack upon her life and crushed him to the ground with her fists. Upon awakening she realised she was being shown that although she may lose her physical life to the beasts, she would successfully defeat the real enemy, the devil.

As they were led into the arena for execution they called out and reminded the procurator, "You have judged us, but God will judge you." A bear, a leopard and wild boar were released to attack the defenseless Christians. As Saturus was being killed by the leopard he called out to the kind warden who admired them, "Farewell, and take note of my Spiritual faith. Do not let these events disturb you but rather strengthen and confirm what you witness of the power of the faith."

Perpetua and Felicitas were stripped naked and thrown into the arena with a wild bull who trampled them repeatedly. Then those Christians left alive after the animals attacked them were put to death by the sword including Perpetua.

These first Christian followers of the Way of Spiritual Love and Non-violence of Jesus were the original Church community in accord with the Teachings of Jesus. There are many such historical accounts of the martyrs and True followers of the Spiritual Way of Love and Non-violence of Jesus before His powerful, pacifist Spiritual Teaching began being destroyed by Emperor Constantine in 312 A.D. and the complicit corrupt Church leaders that followed.

These early True Christian followers put nearly all modern-day Jewish/Christians to shame. Their total belief in Jesus, what He taught, and the Heavenly Spiritual World enabled them to face a painful physical death that was avoidable in order to arise up out of the flesh and be welcomed into the Spiritual Heavenly World. How many of us who claim to be followers of Jesus could do this today? As Jesus said, "Why do you call Me Lord, Lord but do not do the things I say? I do not know you and you do not know Me."

The Good Early Christian Leaders

As the Spiritual Way of Jesus slowly spread during the first three hundred years after the death of Jesus throughout the Roman empire some Roman soldiers were privately converting to being Christian while still serving as soldiers. This was starting to cause some dissention amongst the early church leaders and became a much more serious concern once Constantine stopped the persecution of Christians and eventually openly supported them. Constantine would not appreciate his soldiers of war being told by the Church leaders to leave his armies to become True Christian pacifist followers of Jesus.

At first most early Christian leaders were against anyone in the military involved in war becoming a Christian. These included Justin Martyr from around 160A.D. who wrote, "We ourselves were involved in war, murder and all things evil but all of us have traded in our weapons of war. We have exchanged our swords for ploughshares, our spears for farm tools and now we cultivate kindness towards our fellow man through the Way given to us to follow to Heaven by Jesus."

Tatian wrote around 185 A.D., "I do not wish to be a king, or be rich and I reject serving in the military."

Athenagoras (133-190 A.D.) wrote, "We now express the values of our Master's Teachings through our daily lives. When struck we do not strike back, when robbed we do not sue, to those who ask we give, we love our neighbours as ourselves and cannot endure to see any man being put to death even justly so."

Minucius Felix from the second or third century wrote, "It is not right for us to either see or hear a man being slain and so careful are we to abstain from human blood that we do not even partake in the blood of eatable animals in our food."

Irenaeus of Lyon (130-202 A.D.) wrote, "As the Teachings and Way of Jesus spread throughout the land it caused such a powerful change to take place that swords and war-lances were changed into ploughshares and reaping hooks for corn, instruments for peaceful purposes and instead of fighting when hit the followers of the Way now offer the other cheek."

(Pseudo) Hippolytos around (200 A.D.) wrote, "A soldier of the civil authority must be taught not to kill men and to refuse to do so if ordered by his commander. If he is unwilling to follow the Way of Jesus, he must be rejected from joining the faith for he has gone against our Loving Creator."

Clement of Alexandria (150-215 A.D.) wrote, "Shall not Jesus with a call of Peace issued to the ends of the Earth gather up his soldiers of Peace? Through His words He has assembled an army which sheds no blood in order to lead them to Heaven. Let us all then put on the amour of Peace as the Church is an army of Peace that sheds no blood."

Tertulian (160-220 A.D.) wrote, "Can warfare be justified for Christians and shall it be acceptable to take up the sword as an occupation, when Jesus proclaims that he who raises the sword shall perish by the sword? And will the son of Peace Himself take part in such battles with swords to kill. If a man in military service becomes a believer in the Way of Jesus, he must immediately abandon the way of war."

Origen (240 A. D.) wrote, "You cannot demand military service of Christians any more than you can of your own priests. We do not go forth as military soldiers. We by our prayers and Spiritual faith vanquish all demons who stir up wars and disturb the Peace and this is more helpful than those who go into the battlefield to fight and kill. We no longer take up the sword against nations or learn war anymore for the sake of Jesus and His Spiritual Way. And if all soldiers became Christians all wars would cease."

Cyprian (200-258 A.D.) wrote, "This world is soaked in mutual blood. When individuals commit homicide, it is called a crime, but the same thing is called a virtue when it is done in the name of the state or nation."

Didaskalia around (300 A.D.) wrote, "We forbid the acceptance of any money to help the Christian church from any of the magistrates of the Roman Empire who are polluted by war."

Gregory of Nyssa (335-395 A.D.) wrote, "This work our Divine Loving Creator gives to you, to cast out hatred and abolish war, to exterminate envy and banish strife, to take away hypocrisy and extinguish from within resentment of injuries smoldering in your heart."

John Chrysostom (347-407A.D.) wrote, "Understand this is a new kind of warfare we must engage in as followers of Jesus and His Way not like the old custom of killing each other. For we have a far greater and marvelous work to perform, to bring about a change of their Soul rather than to just kill their body. For as long as we are lambs, we will conquer, even though a thousand wolves stand around us. But if we act like wolves we are conquered, for then the Spiritual Aid of our Good Shepherd departs from us, for He does not foster wolves but sheep."

Maxamillion of Tébessa (295 A.D.) said, "I belong to the army of our Loving Spiritual Creator, and I cannot fight for this world.

You can cut off my head, but I refuse to be a soldier of this world, for I am a soldier and follower only of Jesus the Prince of Peace."

Arnobius around 300A.D. wrote, "We have learned from the Teachings of Jesus that evil should not be retaliated with evil, and it is better for our Soul and Spirit to suffer wrongs than to inflict them, even to shed our own blood rather than stain our hands and Souls with the blood of another."

Emperor Constantine Kills in the Name of Jesus and Our Loving Spiritual Creator

After Emperor Diocletian retired in 305 A.D. Constantine took hold of the title of Emperor of Rome after winning a battle against his final rival Maxentius, at the battle of the Milvian bridge in 312 A.D. The story is that prior to the battle Constantine had a vision or dream of a symbol of Jesus above the sun and heard the words, 'In this sign conquer.' So before going into battle Constantine reportedly got his soldiers of war to paint a symbol of Jesus, possibly in the form of a cross or letters representing His name on their shields.

He won the battle by taking the sword out of its sheath and raising the sword to kill other children with it in the name of Jesus. A complete perversion of the direct Spiritual instruction that Jesus gave concerning killing other children with weapons of war. Jesus said, "Put your sword back into its sheath. For all those who take up the sword, shall perish by the sword." This was the first reordered event of anyone killing other children in the name of Jesus and our Loving Spiritual Creator and became a catalyst for other followers of Jesus to do the same.

This was a total slander against Jesus and made a mockery of His own pacifist, self-sacrifice of His body of flesh to lead us all out of this material world to a Heavenly Spiritual World in our Spiritual body. This was the beginning of destroying and converting True Spiritual Christians of our Loving Spiritual Creator back into being Jewish/Christians who could kill other children in the name of the two headed God Yahweh of the Jews.

It perverted and destroyed the true identity of our Loving Spiritual Creator that Jesus was Teaching about and leading us towards being with in the Heavenly Spiritual World. Before too long all Jewish/Christians were no longer worshipping our Loving Spiritual Creator replacing Her with the two headed God of the Jewish religion again. One body called Yahweh with a revengeful, thieving, genocidal Godhead of War and a Godhead of Limited Love that Jesus tried to lead them away from and come to the One True Loving Spiritual Creator.

The Edict of Milan and Thessalonica

Constantine and Licinius, the Emperor of the Balkan region of the Roman Empire, joined together to produce the Edict of Milan in 313 A.D. This edict granted freedom for Christians and other faiths to be practiced without persecution in the Roman Empire. This was seen as a great help by Christians for the Way of Spiritual Love and Non-violence of Jesus to flourish but it was the beginning of slowly letting the Jewish religion and its two headed God Yahweh creep back in to poison the understanding of Our Loving Spiritual Creator and Jesus.

Jesus warned all of His followers saying, "New wine must never be put into old wineskins, for the old wine skins are not capable of holding the new wine and will burst and the new wine will be lost."

It took another sixty-seven years before the Edict of Thessalonica in 380 A.D. issued by Emperor Theodosius 1 made the Nicene Christian Church the official religion of the Roman Empire called Catholic. All other Christian branches of the Spiritual Way of Jesus including Arianism, which saw Jesus as a Spiritual child of our Loving Creator not part of the trinity of one God, were declared heretical and faced persecution.

This Roman Nicene Catholic Edict marked the beginning of Christian intolerance towards freedom of expression concerning the Spiritual Teachings and Way of Jesus. Anyone who did not tow the Nicene line were considered Spiritually condemned heretics and the Emperor could impose penalties against them. These included losing their legal rights and status within the Empire, their property could be confiscated by the Roman state, and they were forbidden from openly gathering for worship.

This was the influence of the Jewish religion old wine of punishment and dominance beginning to creep back in and overlay and distort the Spiritual Way of Love and Non-violence that Jesus taught and gave His life to establish for us all. And also, it began to further distort and mar the beautiful image and understanding of our Loving Spiritual Creator, therefore damaging children's Spiritual connection with Her.

Early Christian Leaders Became Jewish/Christians

Corrupt Christian leaders started appearing poisoning the Spiritual Teachings of Jesus after Constantine became Emperor following his initial slander of Jesus and our Loving Creator by killing in their names. They began to follow Constantine's way of the God of war instead of the Spiritual Way of Love and non-violence of Jesus and our Loving Creator. They betrayed Jesus by doing this destroying His Way of Love and Non-violence.

One of these was St. Athanasius (297-373 A.D.) when he wrote, "It is not right to kill, yet in war it is lawful and praiseworthy to destroy the enemy, accordingly, not only are they who have distinguished themselves in the field of war held in great honours, but monuments are put up proclaiming their achievements. So, the same act of killing is at one time and under some circumstances unlawful, while under others at the right time is lawful and permissible."

PACIFIST TEACHING OF JESUS DESTROYED

This is a complete destruction of the Peaceful Spiritual Way of Jesus who taught to Love your enemies and began converting all True pacifist Christians back into being Jewish to worship the two headed God of the Jews. A perverted God with one body called Yahweh and a Godhead of War and a Godhead of Limited Love. A distorted God where light and darkness are mixed together to form a dualistic, schizophrenic, volatile, dangerous God. Not the Loving Spiritual Creator that Jesus was at one with as Her child on Earth.

Lactantius (240-320 A.D.) wrote early as a Chrisitan leader before Constantine came to power that all Christians cannot kill even if the state commands it and cannot join the army in warfare to even defend the nation or support capital punishment and it is always unlawful to put a man to death.

But after Constantine became Emperor Lactantius was appointed by Constantine to be his adviser to guide his newly formed Christian policy and was also appointed to be his son's tutor. Constantine's corrupt influence over Lactantius saw a shift in his writings away from his hardline stance defending the pacifist Teachings of Jesus when he wrote, "Just as courage is good when fighting for your country but evil when rebelling against it, so too with the emotions. If you use them for good ends, they will be virtues; if for evil ends they will be called vices."

And in later writings he celebrates Constantine's military victories in war and omits any further condemnation of warfare and even defends capital punishment. He had become Jewish and abandoned the pure Spiritual Way of Jesus and poured the poison of the Jewish two headed God of the Jews into the One True Loving Spiritual Creator and mixed the two wines together.

Slowly the just war theory is creeping in to destroy the pacifist Spiritual Way and Teaching of Jesus until nearly all Christians are converted back into being Jewish with Jesus as an addon.

Ambrose of Milan (347-397 A.D) Early, before being corrupted by Constantine he wrote, "The Peace which removes the enticements of passions and calms the disturbances of the Spirit and Soul is far higher than that which puts down the invasion of enemies. For it is a greater thing to resist and conquer the enemy inside you than the one outside of you."

But as he came under the influence of Constantine, he changed allegiance and began preaching that Christians taking part in killing other children in a just war was acceptable as a follower of Jesus and our Loving Creator. He writes, "Indeed, a fair code of warfare has been drawn up in full accordance with religious scripture, from the religious laws of the Roman people for us to follow." And. "I must not detain you, Emperor Gratian, in this season of preparation for war, and the achievement of victory over the barbarians. Go forth, sheltered under the shield of faith and strengthened with the sword of the Spirit; go forth to victory in battle as promised in times of old."

He had capitulated and was now a Jewish/Christian with Jesus as an add on. He acknowledges the laws of the Roman people as being more important and superior to the Spiritual Way and Spiritual Laws that Jesus taught. He then blesses the Roman Emperor invoking the Spiritual Way of Jesus to shield him in battle and strengthen him with the sword of the Spirit. This is a total slander against Jesus and the Loving Creator to say they would have anything to do with supporting demented beasts of the flesh like the Emperor in killing other children of our Loving Creator.

Augustine (354-430 A.D.) One of the most corrupt and destructive Christians that ever-represented Jesus and His Spiritual Way of Love and Non-violence that Jesus taught us all to follow. He wrote the following guidelines for Christians to engage in war and kill other children of our Loving Creator but still be deluded into believing that you are a follower of Jesus and a Spiritual child of our Loving Creator.

His corrupt guidelines include, 'War must be declared by a proper authority, like a secular government, not by individuals or groups.' This neatly traps you into worshiping the laws of men not the Spiritual Way of Jesus of Love and Non-violence and Spiritual Way of our Loving Creator that leads us to Heaven.

Secondly, 'The war to kill other children should be waged for a just reason, such as self-defense or to punish those who have violated international laws of man.' Again, he wants us to leave Jesus and our Spiritual Life behind and worship and follow the judgement of men in power. He says Christians can now kill in self-defense when attacked; Jesus says to turn the other cheek when attacked. He says we can go to war to kill other children because they have done evil things. Jesus said, "I came not to condemn but to save." And "Our Loving Creator's Love is like the sun that rises and shines on the good and on the evil."

Thirdly, Augustine says, 'War is a way to restore peace and prevent further evil and should not be used to gain glory or plunder.' In all the years since Jesus the world has had war, after war, after war and it continues so this very day in 2025. Only an inner change in all children to become Spiritual will stop all wars as obviously the hundreds of wars since the time of Jesus have not been able to restore peace or prevent evil.

Augustine is cunningly shifting your focus onto protecting your body of temporary flesh and leaving your Soul and Spiritual body open to be damaged or destroyed. Jesus said, "It is the Spirit who gives True Life. The flesh profits nothing."

Augustine says, 'War should be a last resort after all peaceful means to do so have failed.' Here Augustine cleverly draws you into appeasing your conscience by trying to seek a peaceful way first to prevent you going to war. But if the enemies who want to sin and commit evil against you do not relent and begin attacking, then you as a Christian follower of Jesus the Prince of Peace and Love can kill them.

Peter asked Jesus how many times he should forgive someone who has sinned against him and wondered if seven times was enough before he no longer had to forgive them. Jesus replied. "I tell you not seven times, but seventy times seven." We must become forgiveness; not measure the amount of forgiveness we are willing to give before retaliating in kind. Augustine neatly destroys this very high level of Spiritual practice that will lead you to the Heavenly Spiritual World.

These are the main destructive instructions born out of being converted back into being Jewish to worship the two headed God of the Jews that Augustine regrettably taught to destroy the purity of the Spiritual Teachings of the Way of Love and Non-violence of Jesus. And this was rapidly infecting the entire Christian Churches as it still does to this day.

Once the Christian faith was lifted up out of persecution by Constantine and further supported by him the early church leaders became compromised and caved in to his Earthly power. They shifted their allegiance from Jesus and our Loving Spiritual Creator by replacing Her with the two headed perverted God of the Jews with Jesus as an add on. This then allowed them to return to the Jewish way of killing other children whenever they wanted to and appease Constantine by supporting his wars and all soldiers who could now become Christians.

The very heart and core message of Jesus about becoming a pacifist in this dangerous world to prepare for entering the Heavenly Spiritual World of Love became a new perverted Teaching attributed to Jesus and the Loving Creator of Jesus. Christians could now kill other children in the name of Jesus and our Loving Creator or for a secular Emperor and be hailed as heroes if they won. There are no heroes in war except those who refuse to take part in such horrific evil.

Satan had successfully infiltrated the Christian stronghold that Jesus built of Love and Non-violence through the corrupt Church leaders and is still amongst them to this day perverting the True understanding of our Loving Spiritual Creator and the Spiritual Way of Love that leads to Heaven.

This early corruption led to all the Christian wars that have ever occurred to this day. From the crusades in the eleventh and

PACIFIST TEACHING OF JESUS DESTROYED

twelfth centuries through to the Protestant and Catholic wars in the sixteenth century in Europe, and last century in Ireland and even the first and second world wars which were predominantly fought by Jewish/Christian countries.

Only Jewish/Christians take part in war who follow two different religions as being one. True Christians do not. And in today's Jewish/Christian armies you can still find Jewish/Christian ministers and priests blessing the troops in the name of Jesus and our Loving Creator before they go and kill other children of our Loving Spiritual Creator.

No true pacifist Christian who is a child of our Loving Spiritual Creator in the Heavenly Spiritual World, and follower of the Spiritual Way and Teachings of Jesus, took part in war. During the Vietnam war young people started waking up to the Spiritual Truth about how evil war is and demonstrated against it around the western world. Draught dodgers and some Christians like the Amish were True followers of the Way of Jesus and were persecuted and thrown into prison by their own governments just as the Romans did to early Christians.

Jesus, Mahatma Ghandi, Martin Luther King, all Christian martyrs and many others over the centuries, who practiced and taught the Spiritual Way of Love, Peace and Non-violence were often assassinated by beasts of the flesh living out of their false shadow identities worshipping the Godhead of war and death, all devoid of Spiritual Life.

Jesus warned us this would happen but stands beside us as we shine the Light of Love, Peace and Non-violence from the Heavenly Spiritual World to all children that gives True Life to our Spiritual Body and Soul. We must all try to help destroy the darkness and evil in this material world that can seriously damage the Spiritual Life of Earthly children. But the only weapons we have come from the Heavenly Spiritual World and are Spiritual Love, Non-violence, Compassion, Forgiveness and Equanimity. But these can overcome all personal evil in any child if they just take these words into themselves just as you would take physical medicine to heal a physical sickness. But these words would heal the Spiritual sickness in their Spirits if they only knew. As Jesus said, "My words, they are Spirit and they are Life."

GOD IS LOVE LOVE IS LIFE

He who lives by the sword

will perish Spiritually by the sword.

I came to save lost Souls not to condemn them.

Our Loving Creator's Love shines on the good and the evil.

If you wish to enter Heaven, your Love must shine like Her's.

Chapter Ten

Two Different Gods

Nearly all religions at the time of Jesus had different Gods to pray to for different aspects of their lives but they gave each one a distinct name and Temple to worship them. They rarely called their powerful Gods of War and murder by the same name as their Gods of Peace and Love. They understood they are opposite powers, and it would weaken their power and be illogical to say these very different natures are from one Divine being. But the Jews have always worshipped two opposing Gods of War and Love calling them by the same name Yahweh.

The Jewish God Yahweh is not a monotheistic God. It does have a monotheistic body called Yahweh but has two opposing Godheads on it making it a dualistic religion not a monotheistic religion. One brutal, murdering, thieving Godhead of War and revenge Yahweh 1 and a Godhead of Love and Peace Yahweh 2 on one body. This is not the Loving Creator of Jesus.

Jesus only acknowledges the Godhead of Love and Peace and cuts the Godhead of War off the body of Yahweh. The Loving Spiritual Creator that Jesus was an awakened Spiritual child of is Truly monotheistic as Her entire Being is only empowered by Her Loving Spiritual Life-force. True Christians only acknowledge Her as our source of Spiritual Life not Yahweh.

The Romans had twelve primary deities and two of those were the God of War called Mars, and a God of Peace called Pax.

They had their own separate dedicated Temples and ceremonies attached to their worship.

The Jews also worshipped two opposing Gods of War and Peace just like the Romans and Greeks and others but came up with a devious way of worshiping both opposing Gods at the same time by calling them by the same name Yahweh and placing them both in the same Temple.

The Yahweh 1 War God

The Roman War God Mars was worshipped and prayed to in his Temples and animal sacrifices of bulls, pigs and rams were made to Mars to gain the blessing of Mars for the military and bring success in wars. The animals were then eaten after offering some of the dead body of the murdered animal to Mars.

The Jewish priests and the one making the offering to their Yahweh 1 God of War, also sacrificed an innocent animal to their War God Yahweh 1 to help gain his blessing for their soldiers and bring success to kill in war and also ate some of the meat of the sacrificed animal.

Roman soldiers often gathered at the temple to receive a blessing from Mars and the priests of the War God Mars before going into battle to murder other children. Soldiers would swear an oath to the Godhead of War Mars. Emperor Augustus built a temple dedicated to him as Mars the Avenging God of the Romans.

Deuteronomy 20: 1-4 The Jews also had a Spiritual leader called the Meshuach Milchama especially anointed to bless the Jewish soldiers for war and killing other children. He would say, "When you go to battle against your enemies and see horses and chariots and people more numerous than yourselves, do not be afraid of them; for the Lord your God (Yahweh 1 of War and Death) is with you."

Yahweh 1, the Avenging Jewish Godhead of War, is the same brutal murdering God of War as the Roman Avenging God of War Mars, the Egyptian War God Sekhmet and the Greek God of War Ares. The Jews had the same type of rituals before going to War to kill other children as the Romans and others and worshipped the same War God under a different name. This Yahweh War God has nothing whatsoever to do with Jesus and our Loving Spiritual Creator. Revenge is a big part of the two headed Yahweh instead of forgiveness as Jesus explained concerning our True Spiritual source of Life.

The Yahweh 1 War God of Revenge

Yahweh 1 Godhead of War: 1 Samuel 15:1-3, 7-8 Then Samuel said to Saul, "The Lord (Yahweh 1) sent me to anoint you king over his people Israel; now listen to the words of the Lord (Yahweh 1 God of War and Death). This says the Lord (of War and Death) of hosts; I will punish the Amalekites for what they did in opposing the Israelites when they came up out of Egypt. Now go and attack Amalek and utterly destroy all that they have; do not spare them but kill both man and woman, child and infant, ox and sheep, camel and donkey. So, Saul obeyed the God of War Yahweh 1 and defeated the Amalekites. He captured Agag the king of the Amalekites alive and utterly destroyed all the people with the edge of the sword."

This describes the brutal, merciless, avenging God of War Yahweh 1 of the Jews who even murders infants like all War God followers are inspired to do. This is the exact same War God of other religions of the time. All War Gods are satanic.

Book of Nahum Yahweh 1 God of War

Here is another selection describing the brutal, avenging God of War Yahweh 1 worshipped and followed by the Jews in the book of Nahum in the Old Wine Testament of the Jewish religion. This refers to the Jews destroying the city of Nineveh and murdering the occupants and plundering the city.

A jealous and avenging God is the Lord. The Lord (God of War and Death) is avenging and wrathful. The Lord takes vengeance on His adversaries and reserves anger for His enemies. (Jesus said, "If someone strikes you on your right cheek, turn the other cheek to him also. Love your enemies for our Loving Creator is kind to the ungrateful and the evil so do likewise and be Spiritual children of your Loving Creator in Heaven.")

Who can endure the burning of His anger? His anger is poured out like fire. (Another common reference to fire being poured out from Yahweh 1) He will pursue His enemies into darkness. (Jesus and our Loving Creator bring you out of darkness.) "I am against you," declares the Lord Yahweh 1 War God (Jesus and our Loving Creator are always for you especially if you have fallen into sin.) "I will throw filth on you and make you vile and set you up as a spectacle to others who sin against me." (Jesus and our Loving Creator do not throw filth on us or make us vile for our wrong doings but help us wash ourselves clean through offering us their Spiritual Life-giving waters and unending support and Love that Jesus teaches about.) I will burn up your chariots, and a sword will devour your young and cut you down, many will be slain, a mass of corpses and countless dead bodies will be all that is left. I will restore the splendor of Jacob like the splendor of Israel." (Jesus said. "I have not come to condemn but to save. For I can only do what our Loving Creator Herself does and shows Me to do also.")

The above is an example of the Old Testament rantings of the Yahweh 1 Godhead of War and Death of Israel and all who follow it. Again, we see the violent, vicious, unforgiving anger of the murdering Jewish War God murdering even the innocent young ones. Only a God of War and Death does this. And it is only perpetrated by the children of darkness and death who worship such a perverse, violent God and become beasts of the flesh devoid of Spiritual Life and Love.

The Greeks also worshipped a God of War called Ares and a God of Peace Eirene. They had separate temples dedicated to them and sacrifices were made to them for success in War or Peace. Ares was praised as being a War God for his qualities of being violent, aggressive, insatiable in battle, filled with bloodlust and sheer brutality, enjoying manslaughter. Just like Yahweh 1 the War God.

War God Yahweh 1. Deuteronomy 20:10-17

"When you approach a city to fight against it, you shall offer it your terms of peace. If it agrees to your terms and opens to you then all the people who are found in it shall become your forced slaves to serve you. However, if it rejects your terms of slavery and defends itself against your attack you shall besiege it. And when the Lord your God (Yahweh 1 of War and Death) gives it into your hands you shall murder all the men in it with the edge of the sword.

Only the women and the children and the animals and all that is in the city, all its spoils, you shall take as booty for yourself; and you shall use the spoil of your enemies that you have stolen which the Lord your God (of War and Death) has given you. This you shall do to all the cities that are far from you, which are not the nearby nations.

Only in these cities that the Lord your God (of War and Death) is giving you as an inheritance you shall kill and murder everything that breathes and leave nothing alive. You shall utterly destroy them, the Hittite and the Amorite, the Canaanite and the Perizzite, the Hivite and Jebusite as the Lord your God (of War and Death) has commanded you." This is the total murdering, thieving, violent, genocidal War God Yahweh 1 of the Jews in full flight. Merciless, greedy and insatiable with bloodlust.

The Slaughter at Jericho

Joshua 5:12-6:27

Now when Joshua was near Jericho, he looked up and saw a man standing in front of him with a drawn sword in his hand. Joshua went up to him and asked, "Are you for us or for our enemies?" (Jesus said, " He who lives by the sword shall perish by the sword. Put your sword back into its place.")

"Neither" he replied, "but as commander of the army of the Lord (the War God) I have now come." Then Joshua fell face-down to the ground in reverence and asked him, "What message does my Lord have for his servant?" Now the gates of Jericho were securely barred because of the Israelites. No one went out and no one came in. (Understandably the people of Jericho were frightened of the marauding, murdering, thieving Jews.)

Then the messenger of (Yahweh 1 War God) said to Joshua, "See, I will deliver Jericho into your hands, along with its king and its fighting men. March around the city once with all the armed men. (Children of a War God) Do this for six days. Have seven priests carry trumpets of rams' horns in front of the ark. (Jewish priests and the ark lead the way to war, murder and death.) On the seventh day, march around the city seven times, with the priests blowing the trumpets. When you hear them sound a long blast on the trumpets, have the whole army give a loud shout; then the wall of the city will collapse and the army will go up, everyone straight in."

(The Divine Loving Creator and Jesus take no part in such evil acts and give no power to them. Only a War God of death would gladly give power to such evil actions of those who have become murdering, thieving beasts of the flesh.)

Joshua, called the priests and said to them, "Take up the ark of the covenant of the Lord (the War God) and have seven priests carry trumpets in front of it." And he ordered the army, "Advance!

TWO DIFFERENT GODS

March around the city with an armed guard going ahead of the ark of the Lord."

On the seventh day they got up at daybreak and marched around the city seven times in the same manner, except that on that day they circled the city seven times. The seventh time around, when the priests sounded the trumpet blast, Joshua commanded the army, "Shout! For the Lord has given you the city! (When someone gives you something as a gift you do not have to murder children to receive it.) The city and all that is in it are to be devoted to the Lord (our War God). Only Rahab the prostitute and all who are with her in her house shall be spared, because she hid the spies we sent.

But keep away from the devoted things, so that you will not bring about your own destruction by taking any of them. (Joshua tells his murdering Jewish army to not steal any of the treasures for themselves as they all belong to the War God Yahweh 1 and must be taken back and placed in their War God's Temple.) Otherwise, you will make the camp of Israel liable to destruction and bring trouble on it. (Their War God will punish them.) All the silver and gold and the articles of bronze and iron are sacred to the Lord (War God) and must go into his treasury."

(Jesus said, "You cannot serve mammon and God. My Temple, says the Divine Loving Creator, will be called a Spiritual house of prayer for all nations but you have made it a den of thieves." This is quite a stunning and deadly accurate statement by Jesus revealing the Temple was now dedicated to the false two headed God of the Jews because the gold, silver and mammon etc. they were taking back to honour their War God by placing them in his Temple, have all been stolen from the children of Jericho by the thieving Jews after murdering them.)

When the trumpets sounded the army shouted and at the sound of the trumpet, when the men gave a loud shout, the wall collapsed; so, everyone charged straight in, and they took the city. They devoted the city to the Lord and destroyed with the sword every living thing in it, men and women, young and old, cattle, sheep and donkeys. (They broke through the walls by force, not a magical power and mercilessly murdered every single person and even innocent little children of the Divine Loving Creator and all of their livestock. Just the sort of worship a War God of death desires.) Then they burned the whole city and everything in it, but they put the silver and gold and the articles of bronze and iron into the treasury of the Lord's (War God Yahweh's) house.

So, the Lord (The violent, murdering Yahweh 1 God of War) was with Joshua, and his fame spread throughout the land of men. (While in Heaven His infamy spread.)

Only a God of War would consider such stolen, material treasures as something to honour a War God's Temple with. The Divine Loving Creator only receives offerings of Spiritual Love that we must create with our own precious life She gives us by Loving other children. This is how we honour and thank Her for the gift of our Spiritual Life, our Spiritual body and Soul while here temporarily on Earth. Followers of Jesus are only children of Love and Life not death and War.

I challenged a number of Jewish/Christians from different denominations to explain to me how they can believe this violent God at Jericho and elsewhere is the exact same Divine Loving Spiritual Creator of Jesus. Here are a few of their answers.

1: "Maybe God had to destroy them all because they were going to interfere with Jesus being born." Obviously, this person feels it is fine to kill in the name of Jesus before He is even born.

2: "Maybe all those people were evil, so God had to kill them all." Even the innocent little children and animals?

3: "It has always puzzled me how the God of Jesus could do that, but He must have had a reason." Refusal to think for yourself by basing your understanding on blind acceptance of the lies you have been told while avoiding the obvious contradiction of the

Loving Teachings and Spiritual Way of Jesus is no real way to honour Jesus.

All of these children were indoctrinated into believing there is only One God in the whole Bible by faulty Teachings. Interestingly, all these Jewish/Christians loved studying the Old Testament Jewish religion, the two headed God of the Jews and the book of Revelation. They prefer the Old Wine to the New and so do not have a full and correct understanding of who our Loving Spiritual Creator really is as taught by Jesus or of Jesus Himself. They have mixed Jesus and the Loving Creator in with the two headed God of the Jews and lost the True understanding of what He was teaching as Jesus predicted they would if they did that. A very serious and damaging mistake.

Yahweh 1 War God of Fire

The Egyptians also worshipped a few different War Gods all violent killers. Sekhmet was one of their War Gods known for her fierce and destructive nature, a powerful warrior who wields divine retribution. She led them into warfare, was violent, viscous and bloodthirsty and could breathe fire against her enemies. They also made offerings of the blood of animals, food, drink, music and incense to her to gain her favour.

In the Old Wine Testament, we see in 2 Kings 1:10 where the Jewish prophet Elijah calls fire to come down from the Heaven of Yahweh 1 the God of War and Death to incinerate two captains and their fifty soldiers and the War God of death does it for Elijah.

In another example we see the Jewish War God mercilessly incinerate two children for offending him by offering the wrong incense to him in Leviticus 10. 'Now Nadab and Abihu, the sons of Aaron, took their respective firepans and after putting fire in them, placed incense on it and offered strange fire before the Lord, (Yahweh 1 War God) which he had not commanded them to do. And fire came out from the presence of the Lord (War God) and consumed them, and they died before the Lord.'

The Egyptian God of War Sekhmet who could breathe fire on her enemies and the Jewish God of War Yahweh 1 who does the same thing is the same God of War and Death under different names. When the disciples of Jesus wanted to invoke this fire of their Yahweh 1 War God to incinerate the Samaritans who had insulted Jesus, He rebuked them severely saying they had no idea who our Spiritual Creator really is.

There are many examples throughout the Jewish religion of this War God Yahweh 1. They are clearly not referring to the presence of Jesus or our Loving Spiritual Creator and their perfect Love and compassion being manifested in such a violent, murdering War God as these few examples show. Yet Jewish/Christian churches wrongly teach children this War God Yahweh 1 is the same Spiritual Loving Creator of Jesus the Prince of Peace and Love. Total slander and it must be stopped right now. Stop poisoning the Spiritual Way of Love for followers of Jesus by joining Him with the War God of the Jews Yahweh 1 and set Jesus free.

Jesus condemns this Jewish Godhead of War as being satan in disguise when He tells the Jews who worship this Godhead of War on the body of Yahweh in John 8:44, "You are children of your father the devil and you love to carry out your father's lustful desires. He was a murderer from the beginning, not standing in the Truth for there is no Truth in him. When he lies, he speaks from himself for he is a deceiver and the father of lies." Jesus knew the Jewish religion was dualistic worshiping a satanic War God and an opposing God of Love and Peace, a distortion of the One True Loving Creator and He tried to bring the Jews out of it. But they did not want to let go of their satanic War God Yahweh 1 and they still don't want to.

That way the Jews can oscillate between the two whenever they feel like it by calling them both by the same name Yahweh and cover their own evil in the name of their distorted two headed God Yahweh of War and Love. Murdering and stealing one day then Loving and caring the next all in the name of their two headed God Yahweh. A very contrived and convenient evil distortion to feed their own selfish agenda.

Jews stoned to death anyone who criticised their two headed God Yahweh. Is it any wonder they murdered Jesus who attacked their false, distorted two headed God so openly like no one else before Him by calling the God of War Yahweh 1 satan, to destroy the evil hold it had on the Jewish people.

Yahweh 2 the God of Love and Peace

The Roman God of Peace was called Pax. She was a God that was worshipped at her temples to bring an end to wars and provide successful pacts of Peace with adversaries. Emperor Augustus also popularised her to help bring peace to the Roman Empire. Around the fourth to fifth century as she declined in popularity the Christian faith based on Jesus took over her role as the symbol and power of peace and non-violence. Until it was corrupted by early church leaders misleading Christians to go back to worshiping the two headed Yahweh God of the Jews instead of the One True Loving Spiritual Creator of Jesus.

The Jews also had some Love and Peace instructions from the Yahweh 2 Godhead of Limited Love. Leviticus 19:18 "You shall not take vengeance, nor bear any grudge against the sons of your own people but you shall love your neighbour as yourself." This was an exclusive practice only for Jews between Jews.

But later in Leviticus 19:34 we see a glimpse of a universal Spiritual Way of Love that Jesus taught. The God of Love Yahweh 2 says, "The foreigner who resides amongst you shall be to you as a native among you and you shall love him as yourself." That would be the equivalent of saying today that all Jews should treat Palestinians as Jews and Love them as they Love other Jews.

Today only a very small group of Jews are capable of this higher Spiritual understanding and practice of Light and Love.

The Yahweh 2 God of Love and Peace is seen in Jeremiah 29:11. The God of Love said, "I know the plans I have for you. Thoughts of peace and not of evil. To give you a future and a hope."

Nehemiah 9:17. "You are a God of forgiveness, gracious and compassionate, slow to anger and abounding in Loving kindness; and you do not forsake us."

In Psalms 34:14 we see the God of Love again saying, "Depart from evil and do good, seek peace and pursue it."

In Isaiah 54:10, "For the mountains may depart and the hills be removed but my steadfast Love shall not depart from you, and my covenant of peace shall not be removed." Says the Lord Yahweh 2 of Love who has compassion on you.

In Nahum 1:7, The Lord Yahweh 2 of Love is good, a stronghold in the day of trouble and knows those who take refuge with Him.

These are some of the gold nuggets of Love Jesus found amongst the dualistic two headed God Yahweh of Love and War that reflect the presence of a God of Love. Jesus put all the gold nuggets together and formed a solid gold disc of Pure Love and Non-violence. This led Him out of the perverted and divided understanding of the two headed God of the Jews rejecting and condemning the evil Yahweh 1 God of War of the Jewish religion. As Jesus said, "If your eye or mind is single, your whole body will be full of Spiritual Light and Love. But if you are divided within, you will be full of darkness."

He tried to lead the Jews out also. But instead of following Him out of the God of War Yahweh 1 into the Loving Spiritual Creator of Universal Love they murdered Him, which is what all children who worship War Gods do. The Jews were always trying to trap Jesus into blaspheming their two headed God Yahweh to stone Jesus to death because He was constantly attacking their Godhead of War through His revolutionary Spiritual Way of Love and Non-violence and understanding of the One True Divine

Loving Spiritual Creator. That is why He often spoke in parables and not openly about the corrupt two headed God of the Jews. Anyone who offends a War God is killed by that War God and its followers. Even little egotistical human War Gods like Hitler or Putin will kill those who oppose them for they are shadow figures, beasts of the flesh, children of War and Death worshipers of the liar and murderer satan.

This is why Christians must never call Yahweh the Loving Spiritual Creator of Jesus because there are two different Yahweh's and only the Yahweh of Love and Peace has anything to do with Jesus. This is also why Jesus could never refer to our Loving Spiritual Creator as Yahweh in the Gospels as that would be misleading His followers. But the Jewish/Christian churches nearly all do it today misleading followers and slandering Jesus.

Jesus taught, "Our Loving Creator is Spirit, and we must come to Her in Spirit and in Truth." Our Loving Creator's entire being and consciousness is only Love and for us to be Her Spiritual children we must become at one only with Her Love. To describe Her as being anything else would be pure slander. Teaching children She is Yahweh is an insidious and disgraceful insult and leads children astray from our Loving Creator and Heaven.

Jesus gives a correct description of our Loving Creator He was a child of when He taught, "Love your enemies, pray for those who persecute you, bless those who curse you, do good to those who hate you, for our Loving Creator's Love is like the sun that rises on the evil and on the good. Her Love is like the rain that falls on the just and the unjust. She is kind to the ungrateful and the evil. If your Love is not as perfect as Her Love, you will not enter the Heavenly Spiritual World as Her child."

Does this description given by Jesus Himself match the Jewish Yahweh 1 God of War and Death? That God is not the Loving Spiritual Creator of Jesus who never hurts or kills any of Her children, even when they are evil. To deny this statement of Jesus and slander Him and our Loving Creator by saying this is the same

Yahweh 1 War God of the Jews is to deny the One True Loving Creator of Jesus and all that Jesus taught about Her.

True Christians know they are very different Gods because they are not Jewish. While all Jewish/Christians say they are the same God because they have mixed the New wine understanding of our Loving Spiritual Creator in with the Old wine two headed distorted God of the Jews which Jesus told them not to do. It is called 'The Bible'.

The Jewish religion is a seriously divided religion and should never be mixed in with the pure Spiritual Teachings of Jesus and our Loving Spiritual Creator. Darkness cannot exist where there is only Light and Truth. Jesus warned His followers, "No man tears a piece of cloth off a new garment and sews it onto an old garment. The new does not match the old and it will lift off and the schism between the two will be made worse." If anyone tries to mix the old into the new, they will make things more confusing for themselves creating a dualistic labyrinth they can never escape from and a distorted understanding of our Loving Spiritual Creator and who we must become as Her children of Love.

Children today are too smart and independent to swallow the lie that the two headed God of the Jews in the Old Testament is the One Loving Spiritual Creator of Jesus, so they stay away. It is for them that I wanted to write this book, so they do not throw Jesus and His beautiful life changing Spiritual Way and Teachings out with the two headed God of the Jews and the Judeo/Christian church organisations.

In general, the Jews were no different from the other waring nations at the time. They sacrificed animals to their two headed Yahweh God of War and Love and took symbols of their Godhead of War with them when they went to war to kill and murder other children. They prayed to their Yahweh War God that He will help them to slaughter their enemies so they can steal their lands and plunder them of their riches. The same as all War God worshippers do.

But when war and murdering was all over, they prayed to the Yahweh Godhead of Love, to help them love one another the same as all worshipers of a Loving Creator do. It is a two-faced God and not the One True Spiritual Loving Creator of True Spiritual Life that Jesus was at one with. He helps us to be at one with Her Love by following His Spiritual Way of Love and listening to His words becoming transformed by them to Spiritually awaken or be 'born again from above' as Jesus would say. Jesus instructed His disciples and us to, "Heal the sick and bring those dead to their Spirit back to Life." All True followers of Jesus should only believe in the One True Loving Spiritual Creator and come alive in Spirit as Her children of Love on Earth to bring Her Healing Love to all and bring Peace on Earth.

Despite this, many good hearted Jewish/Christian children have still found the Loving Creator through the Teachings of Jesus and understand that She and Jesus are Spiritual Love, Non-violence and forgiveness and have made their way to the Heavenly Spiritual World by just following the Way of Love of Jesus. That is because they generally completely ignore the Old Testament Jewish religion and the evil book of Revelation.

I however will gladly speak out about the distorted two headed God of the Jews to help all children come out of this deluded distortion and find the One True Divine Loving Creator of their Spiritual Life. I have had to write about this to defend Jesus and our Loving Spiritual Creator from the slander and misleading, poisonous words concerning them that are still being taught by many Jewish/Christian churches.

I hope my simple, clear understanding of Jesus and our Loving Spiritual Creator frees many of Her children from the distortion and confusion caused by mixing two different Gods and two different Spiritual Teachings together but calling them one and the same. A never-ending conundrum, labyrinth and maze that leaves you divided within yourself living in a dualistic state of existence. Instead of, "Your eye being single and your body full of Light and Love for everyone," as Jesus said we should all be as True Spiritual children of our Loving Creator.

It is extremely important that every Christian cut the Bible in two and separate yourself and Jesus out from the Jewish religion and rip out the book of Revelation and burn it. Put the Old Testament Jewish religion with a different two headed God that is poisoning the New Testament understanding that Jesus gave of our Loving Spiritual Creator up on the shelf with other religious books. There is usually some Love in all religions.

Our Loving Spiritual Creator is only Love. Jesus is only Love. She has always only been Love and always will only be Love. She only heals, saves and gives Eternal Spiritual Life to all children who wish to accept it, and She never gives Death for She is the True source of Real Spiritual Life. And to become Her Spiritual children in the Heavenly Spiritual World after our body of flesh dies we must be filled only with Her Love.

All War Gods are Gods of death, murder, thieving and destruction with a twofold effect. Firstly, those who worship their evil War God go and kill other children in battle destroying their lives and robbing them. But they can never kill a child's Spiritual body and Soul created by our Loving Spiritual Creator. Secondly, while doing this and deluding themselves into thinking they are as powerful as a War God by murdering other children without consequences, they are actually destroying their own Spiritual Life and Soul which are only empowered by the Loving Life-force of our Loving Creator. All soldiers of war do this to themselves. Jesus taught, "He who lives by the sword shall perish by the sword."

The Bible is one wine skin and contains the Old Jewish dualistic Wine and the New singularity of Love Wine of Jesus and they should never have been placed in the same wineskin as Jesus Himself warned. A two headed God can never be a single Loving Spiritual Creator; it is just that simple. Wake up, get over it and come Spiritually alive through the Way of Jesus of Universal Love, Non-violence and Forgiveness. I only have to refer to the Jewish two headed God and the Spiritual words of Jesus Himself to show this Truth, it is not just my opinion.

Please investigate this for yourself and draw your own conclusions. If you believe I am wrong then show me by having a sound, intelligent Spiritual reason based on Jesus and His words, not the Jewish Old Wine religion. Blind faith is dangerous without a logical, and intelligent Spiritual base.

It has been very important to me to spend time explaining this tragic seventeen hundred years lie and distortion. I do not like Jewish/Christians slandering my lifelong friend Jesus and Spiritual Teacher of the Way of Love and Non-violence that will hopefully lead me and everyone who follows His Way to the Heavenly Spiritual World beyond death. And I do not like anyone who calls my Spiritual Loving Creator a murdering, thieving War God leading children astray to worship the distorted two headed God of the Jews in the name of Jesus.

Love, Forgiveness, Compassion Non-violence and Equanimity are the cornerstones of the Spiritual Way of Love that Jesus taught that will lead us to the Heavenly Spiritual World. And although we cannot see it with our eyes of the flesh it is as real as this material world but Spiritual. We have to feel it within ourselves first before we can see it come into clear focus.

GOD IS LOVE LOVE IS LIFE

God is Love. Love is True Life. Become at one with Love.

Chapter Eleven

Two Identities

Body of Spirit and Body of Flesh

Jesus taught we have two bodies with us right now. One is based on a biological body of flesh, and one is based on a body of Spirit. By their very nature they are different. One is formed from the material elements of the Earth world and can be dualistic, and one is formed from the Spiritual Life-force of our Loving Spiritual Creator in the Heavenly Spiritual World and can only be whole and single empowered only by Her Loving Spiritual Life-force.

Jesus taught that the body of temporary flesh does not rise again from the grave when it dies at some last day of Apocalyptic judgement or three days later as the Gospel authors write concerning the dead body of Jesus. The only day of judgment for all of us is the day we die. He also taught this when He said, "Two will be in a single bed. One body will die, and one will be taken to be near to our Loving Creator. The dead body of flesh can be food for the vultures. The Living body of Spirit will be where the eagles fly." Jesus said, "It is the Spiritual Creator who gives True Spiritual Life, the flesh profits nothing."

He is saying, "Your Spiritual body leaves your body of flesh at the time of death, and you are taken in your Spiritual body to be near the Loving Spiritual Creator who gave it to you to reap as you have sown." He also said this fact to the thief on the cross saying to him, "This day you will be with Me in the Heavenly Spiritual World." He did not say, "You will be with Me in three days' time when I come back to life in My dead body of flesh."

He is telling us we all have two very different bodies, and all of His Spiritual Teachings are aimed at helping us awaken fully into our Spiritual Life and Eternal body of Love and live out of it before our body of flesh dies. He taught this when He said, "He who hears and understands my words will never taste death but will have Eternal Spiritual Life. He who hangs onto his physical life will lose it. But he who loosens himself from his physical life and finds his Spiritual Life will have it forever." And "Do not worry about those who can kill your temporary body of flesh but rather be concerned about damaging your Eternal Spiritual body and Soul by performing evil or wrong doings."

This is the simple Truth of what is really going on with our life after being born into this dangerous material Earth world. This Spiritual awakening and transformation that He went through Himself is the most important thing of all to achieve during our short life on Earth according to Jesus. That is why He became a Spiritual Teacher and gave us the ultimate medicine of His Teachings, to overcome all evil and be filled only with the Spiritual Loving Life-force and be ready to pass through the death experience of our bodies of flesh but still be well and alive in our Spiritual body of Love on the other side.

We see this in the important instruction that He gave to the disciples when He sent them out to awaken children who were lost in evil or ignorance. He said, "Heal the sick and bring those dead to the Spirit back to True Life." He acknowledges that our physical bodies can cause our Spirits great suffering and distress so explains how they can heal them with the Loving Spiritual Life-force of our Loving Creator. So, the immediate suffering of their bodies of flesh is healed for a while but all their bodies of flesh still die later anyway. He then says that as long as they are still dead to the Spirit, they have no real Life so awaken them and bring them to True Eternal Spiritual Life as I have awakened you. This is the ultimate Spiritual medicine, but He was very practical as well. This is the great and profound Way He taught to help children both physically and Spiritually but only the Spiritual healing brings Eternal Life.

The most direct statement of Jesus concerning this dynamic we are all involved in is found in His Teaching to Nicodemus. Jesus said, "Flesh only gives birth to flesh. Spirit only gives birth to Spirit. Marvel not that I tell you, you must be born again from above. " The word 'above' refers to our Loving Spiritual Creator in the Heavenly Spiritual World for it is Her Loving Spiritual Life-force we all need in our Spiritual bodies for them to have True Life. We have two bodies here but only one in Heaven.

Body of Flesh Identities Can Change

Firstly, we must be aware of the biological system of our earthly body. I know I am a Spiritual child of our Loving Spiritual Creator with a Spiritual body I cannot see on Earth that cannot change. And I accept that I have a material temporary body of flesh consisting of interdependent varied parts, chemicals and living organisms that will grow old and die. I know it can produce sensations and experiences of great pleasure and great agony from the various combinations of chemical reactions within its body for me to experience. Yet all the chemicals and elements are not who I really am. I am primarily a Spiritual child of Love but have another body of temporary flesh which can cause my Earthly identity and personality to dramatically change depending on the biological elements in my body of flesh and the chemicals affecting the brain organ. Or simply pain can shift my identity.

We are all unique due to the complex structure of our DNA and our natural personality is hard wired into our DNA. Some children are extroverted others are introverted. Some are naturally gentle and quiet while others are more boisterous and louder. We all have different gifts and aptitudes which is why some children can easily play musical instruments with a natural love for doing so, while others can easily repair car engines with a natural love for doing so. But our human biological identity and who we are as an Earthly person and our behavior can be altered by simply changing the chemistry of the brain.

At forty-two years of age, I stopped work to care for my beautiful Spiritual mother Lorraine who was eighty-two years old. Little did I know she would live on until she was one hundred and one years old and I was sixty when her Spiritual body finally left her body of flesh. That time of caring for her was the gold in my life. Anyone who has been a carer for the elderly will know that a slow physical degeneration usually takes place over time progressing from walking, to using a walker, to needing a wheelchair and being fed and showered. And some mental decline usually slowly appears also with some memory loss or general confusion but hopefully their personality remains stable. Some suffer the serious illness Alzheimer's disease which can totally destroy their personality and earthly identity.

My mother Lorraine was always selfless, caring, loving, extroverted and positive and never complained about her own troubles remembering that many others were worse off than her. The biggest swear word I ever heard her use when something went wrong was 'bum'. One week when my mother was ninety-six, she started to withdraw and go quiet. I knew something was unusual and she was even a little abrupt with me at times which she never was. Then at about 2 a.m. one morning she got out of bed and called to me saying I let someone take our car and she was going to call the police and tell them what I did.

I immediately realised something was seriously wrong and tried to calm her down and get her back into bed. But she started abusing me telling me to get out of her house or she will get the police. Then she said if I did not get out, she would go and get the police herself and made for the back glass door with her walker and tried to break through the glass door. For the first time in my life, I saw my mother being abusive, making angry threats and trying to be violent. I of course stopped her and got her back into the lounge safely where I just had to sit there with her. I was really shaken by this sudden demented, violent and aggressive shift in her personality and finally got her back into bed late in the morning but had to stay awake until I could call her doctor.

As soon as his surgery opened, I called and explained the situation and asked if he could make a house call as soon as he could. They said he would come later in the morning. When he arrived my mother was still unapproachable and angry, and I told him all the details of what had happened and asked him if he thought she may have had a stroke or something.

He calmly said to me, "It sounds like a urinary tract infection." I said to him that her entire personality changed, she was angry, abusive and trying to be violent and I had never seen her like that in my whole life. How could that be caused just by a simple urinary tract infection? He replied, "That is what these infections can do." He gave me a script for antibiotics, and I managed to get them into my mother with her food as there was no way she would take the tablet but just spit it out. Three days later she was the beautiful mother I had always known.

This provided me with a great insight into the complex and unstable identity of our body of flesh personality driven simply by chemicals. The infection may have been bacterial or yeast or fungal as all of these can alter your personality if they infect the body as they can produce neurotoxins that affect the brain. My mother's body of flesh had been cleared of the infection neurotoxins by taking an Earthly medicine, and her brain chemistry was balanced and healthy again, so she returned to being her natural lovely self. Spiritual Teachings are also a medicine if taken when Spiritually sick that restores our natural Spiritual Life to being good, well balanced and healthy again.

The chemical toxins had changed my mother's Earthly identity but her Spiritual identity is not made of chemicals so I knew she would still be fine Spiritually. But sometimes our dualistic biological body of flesh prevents us from behaving in a Spiritual way and it is no fault of our own. Another very good reminder for me not to judge someone who appears to be unstable and behaving in a bad manner. For all I know they may have a similar infection as my mother had. Jesus taught, "Judge not and you will not be judged. Condemn not and you will not be condemned. Forgive and you will be forgiven."

Many people commit suicide due to deep depression which is caused not by their inability to cope with life but a chemical imbalance in the brain caused by these infections. Modern psychiatrists almost never look for an infection in the body as the cause or an imbalance in the body's Biome of the intestines. Our Biome, which lives in our digested food passing through the bowel, is made up of trillions of various bacteria, yeasts and sometimes fungi. If the combination of good living organisms is in the correct balance, then they will produce feel-good chemicals that pass to the brain helping us feel uplifted.

If the Biome is full of the bad guys, then their toxins will take over and they will impact your brain and change your moods, behaviours and ultimately your personality. Over ninety percent of serotonin, the feel-good chemical, is produced in our intestines by EC cells but some specialists say it does not reach our brain. But an unhealthy Biome chemistry or infection certainly does. And no matter how beautiful you are in Spirit like my mother was, the chemicals of the body of flesh can take control over you. We must all be aware of this potential problem in our physical and Spiritual lives while here on Earth.

A case in Sydney Australia involved one of the first fecal transplant doctors helping a patient with decades of irritable bowel syndrome that made his life a misery. This involves taking healthy poo from a healthy gut Biome from one person and placing it in the intestine of another patient with a seriously compromised Biome imbalance. The patient was completely cured of the intestinal illness. At the last check up with his doctor he thanked the doctor for healing years of debilitating bowel trouble for him, and he never felt physically better. Then he added, "And I do not need to take antidepressants anymore as my depression has completely gone."

It wasn't because he was no longer in physical discomfort and always feeling very sad about it that he didn't need the antidepressants anymore. The bad Biome in his bowel had been poisoning his brain with neurotoxins causing chemical depression. The good fecal transplant introduced all the good bacteria he was missing, and they rebalanced the Biome to be healthy, and that altered the chemicals being produced in the bowel that were travelling to his brain. This was not a healing through Spirit, but his Spirit was freed from the toxic chemicals.

Our body of flesh Biome can be seriously damaged by eating too much junk food, sugars and alcohol and our brain chemistry can shift altering our personality without us ever understanding why we are so depressed, angry, impatient or abusive. Just as neurotoxic yeast, fungal and bacterial infections we are unaware of in our biological body of flesh can also change our Earthly identity and personality.

And we are all familiar with the effects that alcohol can have on a person's personality who gets drunk, as alcohol is essentially a poison to the body and brain and if you have too much it will even kill your liver. Not to mention all the modern, chemical, recreational drugs that are sold that damage children's bodies, minds and Spirits.

Although the Teachings of Jesus lead us to become Spiritual by taking care of our Spiritual body, Soul and Life through following the Way of Love we must also take care of our Earthly body and physical life. If our body of flesh is sick, as in my mother's case, we may not be able to connect to the Heavenly Spiritual

World through our Spiritual Bodies and Souls to express or bring the Love from Heaven to Earth. The body of the flesh chemistry can be very overwhelming. We see this in Jesus on the cross when He called out, "Loving Creator, why have you forsaken Me?" Even Jesus had to pass through the agonising biological death experience of His body of flesh which temporarily overwhelmed His Spirit to be fully born again in His Eternal Spiritual body.

I think of how most of our Earthly mothers had to pass through a very painful experience giving birth to our bodies of flesh so we would have Earthly life. And many women still die in childbirth around the world. They carried the pain for us to enter this material Earth world and although they can recall the agony the vast majority of us remember nothing about it.

When my Spiritual body is born out of my body of flesh, this time I am the one who carries the pain of being born again into the Heavenly Spiritual World, not my mother. But it can be just as agonising until the piece of meat called the heart stops moving. Then the birth will be over, and with a sigh of relief I will have left my body of flesh. Just like relief came after our birth was over for our mothers when our body of flesh finally left their body after hours of painful labour.

As Spiritual children we have an obligation to care for our temporary Earthly biological body and choose what we put in its body with care and thoughtfulness. I prefer being a vegetarian so as not to cause suffering to any animals. The extra benefit is that it seems to be healthier for our bodies of flesh. I like to think of myself as a Spiritual rider on my Earthly horse and I need to take good care of him so he is strong and healthy so we can ride together into Spiritual battle at one in purpose with the Spiritual weapons of Love, Non-violence, Compassion, Generosity and Forgiveness. Without my Earthly horse, body of flesh, I cannot manifest Heavenly Love in this dualistic, dangerous material world for other children of our Loving Creator and help bring Peace on Earth. Keeping his natural Earthly biological identity stable and well is very important for me to be able to express my natural Spiritual identity of Love through him.

Spiritual Body Identity Never Changes

Our Spiritual bodies, minds and Souls of Love all come from our Divine Loving Spiritual Creator who is perfect Love. She has always existed and always will exist as She is the True Spiritual Creator and is True Life itself. Everything Spiritual She creates is perfect and filled with Her Loving Spiritual Life-force which gives it Life. This is all that we need to empower our Spiritual Life which is also Eternal. Because it is formed from the one Spiritual Life-force of Love, it has no other complex elements or chemicals like our bodies of flesh have that can affect it.

We will find perfect stability when we leave our bodies of flesh and awaken fully into our Spiritual body and Soul mind of Love as children of our Loving Spiritual Creator in the Heavenly Spiritual World. No disturbances can arise or unsettle our Spiritual mind of Love including pain, suffering or death. Our Spiritual identity is singular, and we can only be Loving and kind as our Creator who created this Spiritual body for us is only Loving and kind. But we can each express Her Love in a unique way.

As Jesus said, "Our Loving Spiritual Creator is kind to the ungrateful and to the evil." Jesus, who upset the Jews with the Truth but was only Loving and kind told us this again when He said, "I can only do what My Loving Creator shows Me to do." And again, with Phillip He says, "Anyone who has seen Me and knows Me has seen and knows our Loving Creator."

Jesus had a full Spiritual awakening into enlightenment in the same way Buddha did. They were both pacifists and treated everyone as equals with compassion and Love. But Jesus took it to a higher level by actively going out into the streets to bring this Heavenly Love to those who were sick, outcasts or fallen into dark and evil ways. Both taught how to be selfless. Buddha mainly through detailed examination of your body and mind and Jesus by serving others in need. Both ways can free us up from selfish, false ego identities, and establish us in our True Spiritual identity of Love but the Way of Jesus had a wider impact through the power of Loving others in need.

When I was attending a Teaching in Melbourne given by the Dalai Lama some years ago, He said the following. "I am a Buddhist monk from Tibet, and you have come to hear the Buddha's Teachings. Australia was occupied for thousands of years by the native Aboriginals who had their own Spiritual Teachings. Then for the last few hundred years the Christian Spiritual Teachings of Jesus that came from Europe became the main Spiritual Teaching throughout Australia. We Buddhists should learn from our Christian brothers and sisters because they put the Loving Teachings of Jesus into action and build hospitals, schools and run many charities to help those in need. We should learn from them." The Dalai Lama acknowledged the powerful Spiritual Teachings of Jesus that have brought Love and real comfort to millions in need through His Spiritual awakening as a child of our Loving Spiritual Creator.

Buddha realised and experienced the state of mind called the, 'Clear Light Mind,' with no evil disturbances of any kind at all being present but only filled with Love and Light. Jesus underwent the same experience but used different terms to describe it when He taught, "If your eye or mind is single, your whole body will be filled with Light." Jesus had experienced the same singular mind Buddha found that was undisturbed by any evil, but Jesus called it a Spiritual Mind of Love and Light with a Spiritual body and Soul. Buddha simply called it; mind or consciousness cleansed of all negative adventitious interferences.

Buddha taught in great detail how we must clean out all the dark adventitious things within our minds that are blocking the Clear Light Mind experience of our True nature of Love from arising. Jesus said, "It is not the dirt on the outside of the cup that is the problem. It is the dirt inside the cup that needs to be cleaned out." He is saying the same thing, do not worry too much about your body of flesh being clean, it is your Spiritual body or mind within you that is the most important thing to keep clean and is the real problem if it is covered in evil.

It is the same understanding they both had and taught to other children using their own local cultural Spiritual terminology. And it is this singular Eternal Spiritual body and mind of Love that lives on and is found within our temporary body of Earthly flesh that Jesus is talking about when He says, "The Kingdom of Heaven is like a man who found a treasure hidden in a field and in great joy sold everything to buy that field and make the treasure his own."

Heaven is only a World of Love, and we must awaken now while we are in the body or field of the flesh, to become this beautiful Spiritual identity filled only with Love to be able to enter the Heavenly Spiritual world. When asked where the Kingdom of our Loving Creator was and when was it coming into existence He replied, "The kingdom of Heaven does not come through observation, nor will they say, 'Look it is over here!' or 'Look it is over there!' Realise this, the kingdom of Heaven is within you." By being born again into this Spiritual awakening while here on Earth, we have prepared ourselves to enter the Heavenly Spiritual World when we separate out from our body of flesh at the time of the death experience.

Our True Spiritual identity of Love never changes. Love is Love and is whole and complete. Nothing can overcome it. It is like a solid disc of pure gold and just like gold nothing can taint it. Sin or evil cannot take place when we are in our Spiritual Body and Soul identity simply because the one who created them for us never sins or commits evil. "Spirit can only give birth to Spirit." That is why Jesus was Her Spiritual child of Love. He found the treasure within, which opened the connection or nexus with our Loving Creator in the Heavenly Spiritual World and then taught us how to find it too through His Spiritual Way and Teachings of Love and Non-violence.

Jesus taught, "Everyone who comes to Me and hears My words and understands them; and practices them and lives by them, will be like a wise man who while building his home dug deep and laid the foundation upon a rock. And the rain fell, and the floods came, and the winds blew and beat violently upon that home but could not shift it and it did not fall because it had been founded on the rock." The words of Jesus are Truth and are very stable and unchanging just like our Spiritual body of Light and Love.

The floods and storms are the evil things that can undermine and overthrow our Spiritual Life of Love in this dualistic, dangerous material world. But deep inside us is the rock of our Spiritual body and Soul mind of Love which is Heavenly and unchangeable. If we awaken to be at one with our True Eternal Spiritual identity and live out of that, making it our home while here on Earth built from the words of Jesus, nothing material can overcome it. Even death cannot stop us entering Heaven.

This is what Jesus meant when He said, "In this world you will have troubles, but take heart for I have overcome the world, and you can too." Once we awaken into our True Eternal Spiritual identity while here on Earth, we will always see everything through the Eye or mind of Love be it good or evil. Our body of flesh is constantly changing from the time of conception to its death. Our Spiritual body does not grow old. Our dualistic body of flesh identity is changeable and short lived. But once our Spiritual body becomes filled with the Loving Life-force of our Loving Spiritual Creator we never change again because She never changes and is Eternal as we will be.

GOD IS LOVE LOVE IS LIFE
Two bodies working as one to bring Heaven's Love to Earth.

Chapter Twelve

Identity of Light or Identity of Shadow

In the last chapter we saw how we all have two fundamentally different types of bodies with us here on Earth. One Spiritual and one of flesh. Our Spiritual identity is only Love and is singular as Jesus said when He referred to our eye or mind must be single or whole to be filled with Light. Our body of flesh is dualistic by its very nature and its identity can shift due simply to chemical changes in the organ called the brain. These shifting identities are not through free will but are forced on to us by the chemicals in the brain. They do not represent a Spiritual wrongdoing and are not subject to reaping what we sow.

We now have to look at the identities that are free will identities of choice when our biological body of flesh is healthy and in perfect chemical balance. This is the separation between the sheep of Peace and Love and the goats of War and Evil that Jesus spoke about. It is this personal battle that has to be won against all odds and temptations to become a True Spiritual child filled with the Light and Love of our Loving Spiritual Creator to enter the Heavenly Spiritual World after death.

And what other way is there to transform this Earthly world into a Peaceful Loving world except by each one of us becoming Peaceful and Loving.

Identity of Light

John 12:35 Jesus said, "The Spiritual Light is with you a little longer, make progress now while you have the Light, otherwise darkness may overtake you. He who walks in darkness does not know where he is going. While you have the Light believe in the Light, so you may become children of Light."

John 8:12 "I am the Light of the world. He who follows Me shall not walk in darkness but have the Light of Spiritual Life."

John 12:45-46 "He who sees Me sees the One who sent Me. I have come as a Light into the material world, so that everyone who believes in My Way will not remain in darkness."

John 11:9-10 "If anyone walks in the daytime he does not stumble because he sees the Light of this world. But if one walks in the darkness of the night, he will stumble for the Light is no longer shining upon him."

Mathew 6:22 "The Light of the body is the eye of the mind, therefore when your vision is only of Love your whole being is full of Light and Love. But when the vision you have is evil your whole being is full of darkness. Be warned therefore that the Light you should have in you is not really darkness."

Thomas Gospel: His disciples said, "Show us the place where you are, for we must seek it?" He said to them, "Whoever has ears ought to listen. There is Light within an enlightened person, and it shines on the whole world. If the Light does not shine, it is dark." The Light of Love verses the darkness of no Love.

Thomas Gospel: Jesus said, "One who is whole will be filled with Light, but one who is fragmented will be filled with darkness. If they ask you, 'Where have you come from?' Say, 'We have come from the Light, from the place where the Light came into being from Her own self.' If they ask you, 'Are you Her?' Say, 'We are Her children, the chosen of the Living One.' Images of men are visible to men, but the Light and Spirit which is in them is hidden in the image of the Light of the Creator. The Spiritual identity within, hidden in Her Light, will be revealed and come forth."

These important Teachings of Jesus direct us to become Spiritual children of Light and Love in this dualistic material world of Good and Evil as soon as we can while we still have the opportunity to do so. As long as our body of flesh is still alive and healthy we can choose to awaken into our True, ultimate Spiritual identity through free will. Jesus was a fully awakened Spiritual child of Light and Love and at one with the Spiritual Loving Life-force of our Loving Spiritual Creator that was empowering His Spiritual body, mind and Soul.

His instructions and Spiritual Teachings along with His own life example enable us to all follow Him and undergo the same transformational experience of Spiritual awakening as He did. As He said, we must be born again into our new primary identity of our Spiritual body and Soul mind of Love and Light leaving our body of flesh with its dualistic mind to be our secondary identity to bring Heaven's Love to Earth.

We still need the body of flesh but only to manifest this Heavenly Love that empowers our Spiritual Life while we remain on Earth to help bring Love and Peace to this world and all the children born here. Our caterpillar flesh identity transforms into a Spiritual butterfly identity, but it still has its caterpillar body for a while to put to good use before it flies away to be in the Heavenly Spiritual World.

Jesus knew He had a Living butterfly Spiritual body that would not die on the cross. He knew He could leave His caterpillar body behind to return to the Earth it was formed from. His Spiritual identity became His primary identity, and His caterpillar body of flesh was a secondary identity that He used to teach and manifest Heavenly Love to other children in this material world to awaken them and lead them to Heaven.

Empowered only by this Loving Spiritual Life-force He could never harm anyone in any way. He could only heal them, restore them and bring them out of suffering and darkness by bringing those dead to the Spirit back to True Eternal Spiritual Life as children of our Loving Spiritual Creator. Once we become as He, we also become Living Spiritual children in an often-violent material world and shine the Loving presence of the Heavenly World and our Loving Creator to everyone we meet, even our Earthly enemies. How else can we help them find the Way if we do not display it to them. If we merely succumb to be like them, we will only be a mirror image of who they already are. Souls lost in the darkness, beasts of the flesh devoid of Spiritual Light, Love and True Eternal Life.

Our Spiritual identity of Light has five main characteristics. The first is Love, for all good things and all other Spiritual characteristics come forth from and are born out of Love. The second is Compassion, for this is the way we connect to all children of our Loving Creator who are in need. Compassion is the power of the Loving Spiritual Life-force that sustains our Spiritual bodies and Souls flowing out of us to others manifesting whatever they may need. The third is Forgiveness for it is a very high level of expressing Pure Spiritual Love and is vital for Peace. The fourth is Non-violence for there is no violence in the Heavenly Spiritual World or children of Love of our Loving Creator and the only counterforce to violence is Non-violence. The fifth is equanimity, for all human children on Earth are equally loved by our Loving Spiritual Creator so we must love all children equally too.

Love

Love is at the heart of our Soul and Spiritual identity of Light. It is Eternal and pure gold and cannot be contaminated in any way as it comes forth from the source of Pure Love Herself. We see everyone and everything through our Soul mind of Love and interact with them through our Soul mind of Love. Love is the guiding force within us that helps us understand how to handle any situation as a Spiritual child of our Creator.

If the situation involves violence, war or other such evils we engage with it through Love. If we come across a situation where a child is attacking someone, we may use physical restraint to stop them out of Love for the victim and also the child caught in darkness, so they do not damage their Spiritual Life any further. But we do not kill the child causing the evil. When warmongers and their armies of brain-dead sheep start murdering other children we stand openly against them and the armaments industry of satan in any way we can and give them no support whatsoever. We certainly never join in with their filthy satanic, beast of the flesh evil. Jesus said, "Love your enemies, pray for those who persecute you."

If the situation involves poverty, we share whatever we can to help give them a better life and reduce their suffering out of Love for them. Greed damages our Spiritual Life and Soul. If we see other children suffering in physical pain, we do whatever we can to help comfort them and alleviate their suffering out of Love for them. Love guides us with wisdom from Heaven to help us understand what is best to do in each situation we may encounter where Love is needed. And whenever we share our Love with others in need the Eternal wellspring of Heavenly Love within us fills us up again and we never run out.

Jesus said, we can only do what our Creator would do, and She is only Love. This is the rock that we stand on to help lift children out of the quicksand and cesspools of suffering, poverty and evil they may have fallen into. Love is our True Eternal Spiritual Life-force, and it is very powerful because it is Pure and comes forth from the Heavenly Spiritual World of Love. Love is vital for Peace on Earth.

Any child on Earth who lives only out of Love and the following four powers regardless of religion or no religion will enter the Heavenly Spiritual World of Love. For these are the empowering Life-forces that constitute our New Covenant identity, as Jesus put it, of our Eternal Spiritual bodies and Souls.

Compassion

We can see the compassionate example and practice of Jesus through His interactions with other children in need. The same compassion we must all have to become like Him and follow the Spiritual Way of Love to Heaven.

Matthew 15:32 Jesus said, "I feel compassion for the people, because they have remained with Me for three days and have nothing to eat, and I do not want to send them away hungry, for they may faint on their way home." Jesus manifested the miracle of the multiplication of the loaves and fishes to feed the hungry children who had come to listen to Him teach, for he was concerned about their physical well-being. How many homeless children do we see but never bother to offer them something to eat or drink. Followers of Jesus do offer out of compassion and Love for them.

Matthew 20: 30-34 While Jesus was traveling along a road, two blind men sitting by the roadside called out to Him to have mercy on them. Jesus stopped and asked, "What do you want Me to do for you?" They said, "Lord we want our eyes to be opened." Moved with compassion, Jesus touched their eyes, and they regained their sight.

Mark 1:40-42 A leper came to Jesus and fell down on his knees imploring Him, "If You are willing You can make me clean." Moved with compassion Jesus stretched out His hand and touched him saying, "I am willing; be cleansed." If we have a family member or close friend in need of medical support and care, we should oblige in any way we can. If no one close to us is in need of such help, we can support a charitable organisation in need of money to carry on humanitarian medical works to help those in need.

Luke 7:11-15 Jesus came to a city called Nain and as He neared the gate a dead man was being carried out, the only son of a widow. When He saw this, He had compassion for her and said to her, "Do not weep." Then He came and touched the stretcher and those carrying it stood still. And He said, "Young man, I say to you arise." And the young man sat up and began to speak and Jesus gave him back to his mother. We may not be able to bring the dead body of flesh back to life, but through compassion we can support those who have lost loved ones, especially those who are left in a vulnerable position as this widow would have been.

Luke 10:25-37 The parable of the good Samaritan is all about compassion, Love and equanimity. The man beaten and robbed by thieves and left to die was passed by twice by two Jewish men who had no compassion for him. But Jesus then says, "But a certain Samaritan, as he journeyed, came upon the dying man and when he saw him, he had compassion. So, he went to him and bandaged his wounds, pouring on oil and wine and placed him on his donkey and brought him to an inn and took care of him and left money with the innkeeper to also care for him."

Jesus teaches about having compassion for all children including strangers in this parable who are in need of help. If we see someone injure themselves near us, we must go over and assist them as Spiritual children of our Loving Creator and followers of Jesus. Compassion keeps our hearts and Souls warm, and we must thank those in need for providing us with the opportunity to be compassionate towards them keeping our Spirit alive.

Luke 15:11-24 In the parable of the prodigal son we see Jesus tell us that our Loving Spiritual Creator is compassionate towards us especially when we do wrong and return to be good. "The son arose and went to his father to ask forgiveness for his wrongdoings. But when he was still a great way off, his father saw him and had compassion and ran and fell upon his neck and kissed him and welcomed him back with a great feast and celebration." Our Loving Spiritual Creator is Love, Compassion, Forgiveness, Nonviolence and Equanimity. We as her children and followers of Jesus must be the same to enter Heaven.

Forgiveness

I will discuss forgiveness more fully in another chapter. In general forgiveness is our Spiritual shield protecting us from harming ourselves and others by falling out of our Spiritual Loving Life-force and hating other children who hurt us wanting to retaliate in kind. It is like the living water that Jesus spoke of preventing any fire of anger to take hold of you and burn your Spiritual home to the ground. Forgiveness is compassion. Forgiveness is a generous gift of Love we offer to others who hurt us in the hope they will change their ways of hurting and find Spiritual Love through our kindness towards them. Only a child who is separated from their True Spiritual identity and the Loving Life-force of our Loving Creator and therefore the Heavenly Spiritual World could deliberately hurt us.

So, we must feel sorry for them for they are living in darkness and do not even know who they really are and by doing evil they are cutting themselves off from the Heavenly Spiritual World. This can lead them into a hellish experience after their body of flesh dies. If we are to be children of Light, we must never condemn children who have fallen into darkness but try our best to save them, bring them out of their darkness and Love them to the Heavenly Spiritual World beyond all suffering.

If we do not forgive others who hurt us and we withhold our Spiritual Love from them, our Loving Creator cannot allow Her Spiritual Love to flow into us. The Loving Spiritual Life-force must always be flowing into and through us freely to others for us to have True Spiritual Life. And forgiving others prevents that flow from being blocked by our own refusal to forgive and Love those who hurt us. The Buddhists teach that the enemy is the jewel in our life because they help reveal to us the True depth of inner strength of our Spiritual Life-force of Love. Shallow Love will fail under the assault, but deep Spiritual Love for all will never fail. Forgiveness is vital for Peace on Earth.

Non-violence

Non-violence is the total commitment to being a Spiritual child of our Loving Spiritual Creator in the Heavenly Spiritual World above and beyond the death of the body of flesh. For the first three hundred and twelve years after Jesus established this Spiritual Way of Love to Heaven, all followers of His were pacifists. They were murdered, raped and thrown to the lions but never retaliated in kind to become beasts of the flesh like those who were persecuting them. As Jesus taught, "Do not fear those who can kill your body of flesh but only fear sin. For that will damage your Spiritual body and Soul mind of Love and prevent you from entering Heaven."

For they knew all flesh dies, rots and stinks and is nothing more than food for vultures, as Jesus taught. And only those who live out of their Spiritual identity and Soul mind of Love will enter the Heavenly Spiritual World after passing through their death experience. They were committing no evil, and they did not kill their persecutors to protect their bodies of flesh, so they were ultimately safe. They were True followers of Jesus who believed in Spiritual Life after the death of their body of flesh and the existence of the Eternal Heavenly Spiritual World for all Spiritual children of our Loving Creator to enter.

This powerful Spiritual instruction that Jesus gave of being Non-violent towards others saved them all to Heaven in the face of horrific persecution and violence impacting their temporary physical life and body of flesh. But those who had become beasts of the flesh devoid of Spiritual Life who murdered them, reaped the suffering that they themselves had caused after their bodies of flesh died, unable to enter the Heavenly Spiritual World.

Constantine and corrupt early Christian leaders destroyed this very high level of Spiritual practice that Jesus instigated for us all to follow in this material earthly world. Our Spiritual identity should even be willing to let go of our body of flesh in the face of violence without retaliating in kind to demonstrate this Truth to other children lost in darkness. Violent children need non-violent children to be able to see other possibilities and a better Way of Love for themselves. Just like Jesus we all have another body of Spirit that we know will rise from our dead body of flesh reaping as it has sown. We must keep it alive in Love.

So, we remain standing in this Spiritual Truth even in the face of death on the Spiritual rock that Jesus Himself established by giving us His Spiritual Teachings that awaken our Eternal Spiritual body and Soul of Love that brings us safely home to the Heavenly Spiritual World. Non-violence is one of the highest demonstrations of our belief in Spiritual Life after the death of our body of temporary flesh. Jesus on the cross of violence shows us the Spiritual Way of Non-violence, forgiveness and Love that will lead us all to the Heavenly Spiritual World if we just follow His Way. A commitment to Non-violence by all of us now is vital for Peace on Earth and essential for children in the future.

Our Spiritual identity is the ultimate True Life we can have. Our Spiritual identity can only support Life. Our Spiritual identity cannot take the life of another. Our Spiritual identity is Loving. Our Spiritual identity is caring and kind. Our Spiritual identity is generous towards others. Our Spiritual identity is understanding and patient. Our Spiritual identity is compassionate. Our Spiritual identity helps to heal all wounds and sufferings but never causes them. Our Spiritual identity always forgives others. Our Spiritual identity is not attached to Earthly material things but only the Loving Spiritual Way of the Heavenly Spiritual World. Our Spiritual identity stands strong and fearless in the face of all evil yet challenges all violence with Non-violence, understanding, wisdom and Love.

Our Spiritual identity and body of Light and Love will always be filled with the Loving Life-force of our Loving Spiritual Creator as long as we are always facing Her in Spirit and in Truth, as Jesus said to do. If we do not cover our Spiritual body and Soul in filth or evil that block us from receiving Her Light and Love or turn our back to Her that creates a false shadow identity, Her Loving Light will always be able to reach and warm our hearts and Souls. And we will always be connected through Her Love and Joy in our True Spiritual identity and enter the Eternal Heavenly Spiritual World and Life beyond all suffering after we pass through our final death experience.

All we do will be done out of Her Love that She freely gives to us to share with others as Her Spiritual children and we ask for nothing in return to do so. For our joy is to be Her Spiritual children filled with Her Loving Life-force which wells up inside our Soul and Spirit like a never-ending wellspring leading to Eternal Life. When we are fully centered and come alive to our Spiritual body and Soul mind of Love we can never hurt anyone. And once we have uncovered this buried Spiritual treasure within the field of our body of flesh, we will never want to be apart from it or lose it and will live out of it forever. Her Light and Loving Spiritual Life-force is indeed like the sun shining forever upon us to give us True Eternal Spiritual Life in the Heavenly Spiritual World of Love. All we have to do is accept it and be at one with it.

Equanimity

The following chapter will discuss equanimity, but we can clearly see that Jesus loved all children equally, whether young or old, rich or poor, sick or well, friend or stranger. It was irrelevant to Jesus who the child was or what condition they were in either Spiritually or physically. He simply addressed their personal need to help them come out of their Spiritual or physical suffering. As His Spiritual followers and children of our Loving Spiritual

Creator in the Heavenly Spiritual World we must do the same and see all children as our Loving Creator's children regardless of their present condition or situation.

Identity of Shadow

The only way to see your shadow is to turn away from the sun and turn your back to the Light. And right there before you spread on the earth will be a silhouette shadow figure of your living body of flesh. The shadow figure is in the shape of your body but has no life in it. Only your body of flesh has life in it. Yet when you raise an arm the shadow figure raises its arm. If you hold a gun the shadow figure holds a gun too. If you form a fist to hit someone the shadow figure does too. The shadow figure is animated by your will but there is no light or Spiritual Life in it. It is a figure filled only with darkness yet will do anything you wish it to do. All evil comes forth from the dark shadow identities children create from their own deluded imaginations to live out of a lie.

When we are facing our Loving Spiritual Creator, we have nothing to hide for we are fully exposed to Her Light and Love shining on us continuously, and there can be no shadow figure between us. We can think of Her warm Love holding onto us as Her willing child of Love which is how our relationship with Her should always be. But whenever we do anything wrong against Her Spirit of Love and goodness, we always have to turn away from Her sight and Light to do it. For our conscience alerts us when we are moving out of Her Loving Life-force into something darker and we do not want Her to see it. A useless endeavor as She is always aware of everything we do because She Loves us.

Our Loving Creator's Spiritual Life-force can never be involved in empowering anything evil such as lying, killing, war or theft. So, if we wish to go against Her and our True Spiritual identity of Love we must step out of our Spiritual body and Soul mind of Love and use another life-force to do it and another false identity. These are made up of the Earthly life force of the body of the flesh and a shadow identity with no Spiritual Loving Life-force in it that we create ourselves from the thoughts of our own imagination and is usually called Ego.

It is a shadow figure, literally a figment of our imagination and devoid of all True Spiritual Life-force but is capable of causing great suffering or hardship in this material world by using the body and brain mind of the flesh. Adolf Hitler was a false shadow figure of darkness as are all the current war mongers in the world today in 2025. They are all children of satan born out of their own dark thoughts, worshippers of death, beasts of the flesh not Spiritual children of our Loving Spiritual Creator who are worshippers of Life.

We create the dark, false shadow identity to serve and obtain our selfish desires that are born out of the dualistic mind of the body of flesh while ignoring our Spiritual body and Soul mind of selfless Love. The more we live out of our false shadow identity of darkness the stronger it becomes, and the weaker our True Spiritual identity becomes and Her Light within us begins to dim. This egotistical, self-serving shadow identity based solely on the body of flesh and its dualistic changeable mind is shaped by us to suit our selfish goals and utilises our body of flesh and its talents and abilities to achieve them. We create this monster layer by layer, thought by thought, action by action, word by word until it takes over and controls our Earthly life destroying our Spiritual Life of Love and Truth.

It is a calculating, manipulating perversion of who we should really be and all those who bring this dark shadow identity to life are living a lie unto themselves. This is the false satanic identity, the dark force that rises against Love to destroy the child's own Spiritual Life and bring suffering to other children. This false shadow identity destroys that child's chances of entering the Heavenly Spiritual World of Eternal Love and propels them into a place of burning realisations after their body of temporary flesh dies. This is the real enemy we all need to defeat. This is the evil one in the Lord's prayer that we pray to be delivered from and all the temptations that can lead us into becoming false shadow identities of darkness.

Jesus was threatened by these same temptations but overcame them by becoming a fully awakened Spiritual Child of our Loving Spiritual Creator filled only with Her Loving Life-force. He was born again into His Spiritual identity of Love and Light and He had to seek and fight to become at one with it as we all do. And He helps us to achieve this through following His words and example. As He said, "My words they are Spirit, and they are Life. You will have troubles in this Earthly world, but I have overcome this material world and so can you."

Our dark shadow, false identity devoid of Loving Spiritual Life-force has three main characteristics. Firstly, it is totally based only on the body of the flesh, worshiping only material things. Secondly, it is selfish, narcissistic, manipulating and self-serving and does not care about any other children and loves to dominate everyone and punish anyone who disobeys them. Thirdly, it's mind darkened by evil intent has no real belief in anything Spiritual or a Loving Spiritual Creator who gives them a Spiritual Life to come to the Heavenly Spiritual World in after death.

Many children have no belief in Spiritual Life but live a life full of Love, Non-violence and Forgiveness and are children of our Loving Spiritual Creator without even knowing it. As Jesus said, "You will know the children of our Loving Spiritual Creator by their fruits." And so will She. I often say to these children who have lived a life of Love but do not believe in Life after the death of the body of flesh, "I hope you get a lovely surprise when you die." Which I am sure they will, for no matter what religion or secular way of life they have lived they have lived it all out of Love. The Spiritual Way to Heaven is only through the power of Love.

Our body of flesh can provide us with high levels of chemical pleasure and satisfaction based on what we do with our body and what we put into our body of flesh for it to be healthy. Natural, healthy and harmless physical pleasures are a part of our Earthly existence with a body of flesh. These are often enjoyed and in the company of other children can provide us with many happy memories during our life on Earth.

While all the biological chemical pleasures and experiences our body of flesh creates are temporary the Clear Light Mind experience of Spiritual Love is Eternal. However, physical pleasures can be a way for us to express and share the Spiritual Loving Life-force in our Spiritual body and Soul identity with other children. But the false shadow identity of darkness uses the body of flesh for very different purposes.

Wide is the Way to Destruction

Matthew 7:13-14

Jesus said, "Enter through the narrow gate. For wide is the gate and broad the way that leads to destruction and there are many who enter in that way. For the gate is small and the Way is narrow that leads to True Life and there are few who find it."

The combinations of false shadow identities that children can create comes forth from a very wide selection of characteristics that all destroy Spiritual Light and Love. And many have gone this way and fallen into this trap to varying degrees. From the greedy and petty shoplifters and con artists to brutal warmongers who slaughter thousands of innocent children of our Loving Creator. They are all living a lie out of a false identity and the more they commit these acts the more they become like beasts of the flesh devoid of Spiritual Life-force. All flesh dies, rots and stinks only our Spiritual Life lives on.

The false identity can only come into existence if we step out of our Spiritual identity of Love and perform actions that go against Love. Love is the narrow Way and small gate that leads to our Spiritual Life in Heaven. The Spiritual Way is a path of Light made up of the words of Jesus that are like beautiful cobblestones beneath our feet. Our Spiritual identity is safe if we stay on this path. The false shadow identity can only be empowered if we leave this path of Light and are enticed to follow darker paths that branch off and lead away from the path of Light and Heaven.

One such path of darkness is to use our body of flesh to indulge in sensual pleasures and gratification just to receive the chemical intoxication caused by the physical indulgence. Taking alcohol or drugs to get a heightened chemical spike of experience in our brain is a very common abuse of our body of flesh. It is dangerous, addictive and can seriously imbalance the chemistry of our brains and minds. Alcohol and drug indulgence can lead us into violent behaviour, turning to crime and general ill health and in too many cases the death of our body of flesh. To harm our own bodies of flesh in this way that contain the Spiritual Treasure of Eternal Life within them, is a dark shadow identity action devoid of all Spiritual Life.

Another destructive dark path to go down is the selfish act of greed by worshiping money over Love for others and the source of our Spiritual Life. Children can amass millions and billions of dollars and buy any little physical indulgence they want yet walk right past homeless children of our Loving Creator living on the street and give them nothing. No love flows out of these dark shadow figures to others in need so no Love from Heaven above can flow into them. Covered in the darkness of their own false shadow identity of greed and selfishness their Spiritual lamps of inner Light and Love have dimmed. As Jesus said, "What does it profit a man if he gains the whole world but loses His Spirt and Soul? You cannot serve mammon and our Loving Spiritual Creator. And a man cannot ride two horses at once."

Another branch of the destructive path of greed the shadow identity indulges in is gambling. Many lives have been ruined in this pursuit and many crimes committed in order to feed and satisfy these needs of the false shadow identity of darkness we create. Needs that enslave our Spirit and can never free us to find contentment and peace by just living a simple Life of Love and Joy with other children. Once we start chasing after material things and money, putting them above Spiritual Love, we will never be satisfied no matter how much we own, and we will always want more. Love is self-fulfilling by its very nature for it is the True source of joy in our Spiritual Life and who we really are.

All other forms of general self-indulgent addiction that prevent, interfere with or destroy our Spiritual Life all come forth from these egotistical, false shadow identities of darkness we create from our own imagination. They are based on and empowered only by our body of flesh. These dark shadow identities can be found just about anywhere in anyone with varying degrees of darkness. In family homes, businesses, organisations, schools, hospitals, governments any workplace and even churches.

When they are just destroying their own Spiritual Life the false shadow identity of darkness is contained. But in extreme examples they can rise to dark power in gangs, governing bodies, governments and dictators and these false shadow identities of darkness can create extreme suffering and death to come upon other children. These are the ones who worship the satanic identity they themselves have become and are the children of satan on Earth, the thieving god of murder, war and death. They have set themselves up as a brutal War God to be obeyed and worshipped or they will punish and kill you. They turn their back on the beautiful Loving Spiritual Creator who is the source of their Spiritual Life and cover themselves in filth. Ignorant, blind, deaf and empty of True Love they hurtle themselves towards Hell.

These false shadow identities care about no one but themselves and love to dominate other children. These children of darkness are extremely dangerous to us all as they deliberately cultivate evil and poison the minds of other children to join in to do their bidding. All wars are started by these children living out of their false shadow identity of darkness. They couldn't care less how many children they murder, rape, torture or enslave. They are devoid of Spiritual Life and Love. Their shadow figure is addicted to dominating, hurting and murdering other children. Vampire figures feeding on bloodlust.

They are lost in the dark shadow of the beast of the flesh they have created and become, as Jesus said, "He who walks in darkness does not know where he is going." If they knew where their evil actions were taking them after death, they would stop their evil ways immediately, get down on their knees and ask for forgiveness. But they do not believe in life after death or reaping what we sow. They have no belief in Heaven and no idea about how to reach Heaven as they have no belief in the Spiritual Way of Love that leads to Heaven. And they do not believe in a Spiritual Loving Creator of Life. How much more lost can anyone be?

All because they rejected their Eternal Spiritual identity of Love by turning their back on our Loving Creator and stepped into their own pathetic creation of a short-term lifeless shadow identity of darkness and death to become beasts of the flesh. Intoxicated by their own evil they are blind to the Truth of what they have become. An empty shadow.

As Spiritual children of our Loving Spiritual Creator in Heaven we are the Light, they are a shadow. We are the Truth, they are a lie. We are Eternal, they are all temporary. The darkness can only exist in us while the Spiritual awakening of the Way of Light and Love that Jesus taught has not yet arisen for us to become at one with. All darkness and false shadow identities vanish out of existence once this takes place, and we are born again from above into our Eternal Spiritual Life.

May we all help each other to become enlightened and wake up to who we really are as Spiritual children of our Loving Creator in the Heavenly Spiritual world. And expose and help eliminate all evil and false shadow identities that many children have become trapped in to set them free and stop the suffering they cause to other children.

Our time on Earth is short and if we fill it with Spiritual Love and understanding making this world a better place for all, then we have achieved the greatest thing possible in a body of flesh by bringing the Heavenly Spiritual Way of Love to Earth for all children to find and follow home to Heaven. To awaken into being Spiritual is the True resurrection then we can rise from the dead body of flesh and enter the Heavenly Spiritual World of Love when our Earthly journey comes to an end.

John 3:20-21, "For everyone who dose evil hates the Light and does not come to the Light for fear that their wrong doings will be exposed. But the one who practices the Truth comes to the Light so that their deeds may be manifested through the Loving Life-force of their Loving Spiritual Creator in them."

GOD IS LOVE LOVE IS LIFE

Light is Love.

Darkness is Evil.

Where the Light is no darkness can exist.

Chapter Thirteen

Equanimity

In order to become like Jesus and also be a Living Spiritual child of Love on Earth of our Loving Spiritual Creator in the Heavenly Spiritual World of Love, we must have two very important Spiritual characteristics as part of who we are. They are Forgiveness and Equanimity. As we must become a bridge of Love flowing from Heaven to Earth for every child of our Loving Creator, both good and evil, it is vital we do not allow any blockages from arising in us that may prevent that flow of Love from going out of us to any other child in need.

What is Equanimity

Definition: A state of mental balance and even mindedness towards all.

Jesus said, "Our Creator's Love is like the sun that rises on the evil and on the good. Like the rain that falls on the just and on the unjust. If you wish to be Her Spiritual children on Earth your Love must be as perfect as Her Love towards all."

Jesus had perfect equanimity towards all children. As all children have a Spiritual body and Soul of Love to become at one with before their body of flesh dies, Jesus wanted everyone of them to find it. Unlike the Jews He mingled and dined with sinners, outcasts and children of different faiths. He allowed lepers to come near Him and touched them to heal them. He mingled with the poor and the rich, the young and the old. He gave the Teachings of Love to anyone who wanted them, even a Samaritan woman whom the Jews detest and have nothing to do with. He would heal any sick child of our Loving Creator who asked Him, even a Roman nobleman's child or a Roman Centurion's servant. He could forgive anyone, even those who nailed His body of flesh to the cross. He had perfect equanimity empowered by the perfect Love of our Loving Spiritual Creator and taught us all how to have it too. His Loving Spiritual Life-force flowed out to anyone in need.

Even the Pharisees knew He had equanimity when they said to Him, "Teacher we know that you are True and teach the Way of our Creator truthfully and have no regard for the position of men and show no favouritism."

There are many ways the flow of Love from Heaven in us can be blocked if we fail to have equanimity within our Spiritual character. Many followers of Jesus judge and condemn everyone else who do not follow Jesus saying they cannot enter Heaven. Some Jewish/Christian churches even judge and condemn other Jewish/Christian organisations by saying that their church are the only true followers of Jesus in the world. And other Christian organisations are evil because they teach the Teachings of Jesus in a different way to them.

This Jewish overlay of thinking they are the only chosen ones of our Loving Spiritual Creator in the whole world is seriously flawed and comes from the dualistic Jewish religion. It is not Christian. It immediately blocks them from receiving the fullness of our Loving Creator's Loving Life-force to share with all other children. This also applies to all other Spiritual religions who believe this exclusion dialogue too. For our Loving Creator Loves all Her children in this world just as Jesus did and Her Spiritual Way is inclusion not exclusion. Equanimity in us as Her Spiritual children is the base for inclusion.

Equanimity helps us see beyond the bodies of flesh or lifestyles that are different to our own to see the Spiritual child of our Loving Creator within and still Love that child of our Loving Creator. Without equanimity the flow of Love can be blocked by such things as racism and prejudice towards other groups of children different from ourselves. Arrogance and looking down on others judging them as being inferior to ourselves in the workplace, on the street or any given situation blocks the flow of Heavenly Love. This arrogance cannot arise in us if equanimity is present in our Spiritual character. Equanimity is the base for respecting others. As Jesus said, " Judge not and you will not be judged. Condemn not and you will not be condemned."

Withholding money from those you see in need when you have plenty to share blocks Heavenly Love flowing into you and through you. Equanimity helps us establish and manifest our primary Spiritual identity of Love by sharing extra money freely with those who have little or none. For we see them as being our siblings and equal as children of our Loving Creator. And money has no value anyway in the Heavenly Spiritual World to come, only Love does. Equanimity is a base for generosity and sharing by seeing others as ourselves.

Jesus said, "Give to him who asks you and from him who wants to borrow from you turn not away from him. It is easier for a camel to go through the eye of a needle than for a rich man to enter the Heavenly Spiritual World of Love."

Being unfair towards anyone blocks Heavenly Love from flowing into us and through us. Equanimity in our Spiritual character will always guide us to be decent, honest and fair when interacting and dealing with all other children treating them all like close friends or family. Seeing other children as strangers and not connected with you can block the flow of Heavenly Love flowing into you and through you to them.

I have a beautiful example of this from a great Teacher I had called Sandy 7. When caring for my elderly mother Lorriane, I would often take her in her wheelchair with our Labrador dog Sandy 7 to a beautiful 300-acre park called Westerfolds by the Yarra river in Melbourne. We would sit at the far end away from all the traffic noise and just rest in the natural surroundings of the park enjoying a chat, a drink and a bite to eat. Including a bone I always took for Sandy 7.

There was a bitumen one lane road that wound around the circumference of the park for bike riders and walkers. As we sat, I noticed some people walking down the road towards us some way off with a couple of dogs. I looked at Sandy 7 and could see her eyes asking me if she could go and say hello to them. I said to her, "Go on." She joyfully got up and started running up the hill towards the people with their two dogs with her tail wagging and her face smiling. The people stopped as she ran closer to them, and she greeted those strangers like they were long lost friends she hadn't seen for thirty years and completely ignored the dogs. She demonstrated perfect equanimity and Love towards those people and was more Spiritually advanced with perfect equanimity than many human children. She was a beautiful Spiritual being of Love and I miss her Loving companionship.

Another beautiful Teacher I had of living out of the Spirit, forgiveness and equanimity was my sister Joan. She was born in 1949 with cerebral palsy which rendered her left arm and both legs useless, her twin sister Anne died soon after birth. She spent her whole life of seventy-three years in a wheelchair. She sadly left her body of flesh in her perfect Spiritual body in 2023 from cancer. Our beautiful Spiritual mother Lorraine cared for her at home until she was too old to continue and Joan went into a care home for the last twenty years of her life. But by then she had an electric wheelchair and could be more independent.

She was a member and ardent supporter of the Australian Rules football team Collingwood. She would go to all the games she could in Melbourne. In 2018 her team made it to the grand finale against a rival team called West Coast Eagles. We got tickets and I took her there in the van we had with a hoist to take her out in. There was a crowd of 100,000 people at the M.C.G. stadium to watch the game.

Before the big game there were various entertainments and stalls outside the stadium for people to enjoy before the game. As we wandered through the grounds a family of West Coast Eagles supporters came towards us dressed up in their team's colours of gold and blue, while Joan was regaled in her black and white colours. As they came near, Joan called out to them, "Enjoy the game and good luck."

I do not know of many fans of any sporting club anywhere in the world that would wish the opposing team good luck. Only a Spiritual child of our Loving Spiritual Creator could do that. For Joan it was all about being alive and full of the Spirit. Not about who wins or loses a game of football. She was also able to forgive anyone who ever hurt her. She was a natural at it unlike most of us. From the start of her life on Earth she knew more than her four siblings that we are not our body of flesh. For although her body was damaged, she didn't need it fully working to be Spiritual and flow her Love out to others. Even the 'enemy' rival football team supporters.

Unfortunately, there are other children who also wear different coloured uniforms and are deadly rivals. But they are not like my powerful sister Joan. They are weak minded, evil and have become beasts of the flesh and worship the God of death, theft and destruction and are devoid of Spiritual Life. These are the warmongers whose teams of heartless soldiers wear different uniforms but are actually all on the same team of satan. He leads them into battle to kill and slaughter children of our Loving Spiritual Creator just like the War God of the Jews and other distorted Old world War Gods now replaced by satanic human leaders who are egotistical, psychotic killers like Hitler, Putin, Netanyahu, Hammas and others.

They love to dominate other children, seek revenge and to steal and force them to their will through punishment, death and war and are totally lacking in Spiritual Equanimity and Love. Without Spiritual equanimity any child could end up being filled with hatred and revenge towards other children becoming a dark, shadow figure devoid of Spiritual Life-force like all who take up the sword, gun or drone to kill other children.

Having the Spiritual characteristic of Equanimity within you is an important vital quality that acts as a base for Peace and prevents Wars and the slaughter of children. Equanimity allows you to see everyone as a child of our Loving Spiritual Creator even though they may be currently caught in the darkness of their own evil. We must see them through the eyes of Love and try to bring them out of that dark evil not become like them.

Jesus said, "I did not come to be served but to serve others. If anyone desires to be first, he shall be lowest of all and servant of all. Whoever humbles himself like a little child, is the greatest in the Spiritual Heavenly World. For he who is least among you all is the one who is great." My physically handicapped sister Joan and dog Sandy 7 were greater and more powerful in Spirit than all the deluded, evil warmongers of this world.

GOD IS LOVE LOVE IS LIFE

We are all children of our Loving Spiritual Creator

The only difference is some know it and some don't.

Chapter Fourteen

Forgiveness

Forgiveness is one of the highest Spiritual practices of Love we can perform in this dangerous, often unjust material world. Forgiveness is essential if we are to have the Spiritual wellspring of Eternal Loving Life-force bubbling up endlessly inside our Spiritual bodies and Souls. To not forgive another child who has hurt us would block the flow of Heavenly Love and Life-force from flowing into our Spiritual bodies and Souls which gives us Eternal Life in the Heavenly Spiritual World. And without it we would no longer be the Spiritual children of our Loving Spiritual Creator but just bodies of flesh.

Luke 6:37 Jesus said, "Forgive and you will be forgiven."

Luke 17:3-4 Jesus said, "If your brother sins against you rebuke him and if he repents forgive him. And if he sins against you seven times in a day and repents seven times forgive him."

Mark 11:25 Jesus said, "Whenever you stand praying if you have anything against someone who has wronged you forgive them, so that your Loving Spiritual Creator in the Heavenly Spiritual World can also forgive you for your wrong doings against Her Love for you." For as we sow, so shall we reap.

Luke 11:2-4 Matthew 6:9-13 Jesus said, "Pray with these words: Our Loving Creator who art in Heaven hallowed be your name. Your kingdom come, your will be done on Earth as it is in Heaven. Give us each day our daily bread and forgive us our sins, as we forgive everyone who is indebted to us. And lead us away from temptation and deliver us from evil."

Matthew 6:14-15 Jesus said, "If you forgive others their transgressions against you, your Loving Spiritual Creator will forgive your transgressions against Her and Her Love for you. But if you do not forgive others, then She cannot forgive you." For as we sow, so shall we reap.

Luke 23:24 Jesus said as He was dying on the cross, "Loving Creator forgive them for they know not what they are doing."

Matthew 18:21 Peter came and asked Jesus, "Master, how often shall my brother sin against me and I forgive him? As much as seven times?" Jesus said to him, "I will not say seven times to you but seventy times seven. For the Heavenly Spiritual World is like a Lord who wished to settle accounts with his workers. When he had begun to settle them, one who was indebted to him owing ten thousand talents came before him. But he had no means to repay the Lord his debt, so the Lord commanded him to be sold along with his wife and children and all that he owned to repay the debt.

So, the worker fell to the ground and prostrated himself before him saying, 'Have patience with me Lord and I will repay you everything.' And the Lord of that worker felt compassion and released him and forgave him all of his debt. But that worker went out and found another worker of his Lord who owed him a hundred denarii; and he seized him by the throat and began to choke him demanding, 'Pay back what you owe me.'

So, his fellow worker fell to the ground and began to plead with him saying, 'Have patience with me and I will repay you.' But he refused to do so and threw him into prison until he should pay back what he owed. When his fellow workers saw what had happened, they were deeply upset and went to their Lord and reported all that had happened to their fellow worker.

The Lord called back the worker whose debt he had forgiven and said to him, 'You wicked worker, I forgave you all your debt because you asked me to. Shouldn't you have shown mercy also to your fellow worker in the same way I showed mercy to you?' And his Lord was angry with him and handed him over to the torturers until he should repay all that was owed to him.

Our Loving Creator will also give to you what you give to others. So always forgive from your heart and Soul all those who are indebted to you or have wronged you, no matter what it is or in what way they have wronged you. Then our Loving Creator can forgive all the wrongs you have committed against Her and Her Love for you." For as we sow, so shall we reap.

The Impacts of Forgiveness

When we are hurt by someone in any way, especially if it is deliberate, we normally feel wronged, saddened, hurt, upset and even angry. We all know how anger can lead to violent action and retaliation in kind against the child who caused it. And this can even escalate to murder or even war. Jesus said, "Do not retaliate against an evil child but if anyone strikes you on your right cheek, turn the other to him also."

Forgiveness can de-escalate potential violent situations from arising. And the emphasis is not on the wrong doer saying sorry to us, as many will never be Spiritually strong enough to do so, but on us to forgive them regardless. We must be the Light of Love in this world even to our enemies who hurt us by always forgiving them. We do not wait for them to say sorry to us but instead feel sorry for them. For only a child not living out of their Spiritual body and Soul mind of Love filled with our Loving Creator's Life-force could hurt someone. They are lost in the darkness and ignorance of not knowing who they really are and become shadow figures devoid of Spiritual Life. It is our Spiritual responsibility to be strong and fearless as a living example to them of how a Spiritual child filled with our Loving Creator's Spiritual Life-force behaves. We must be the Light in their darkness.

To hurt someone is easy but to take the blow of that hurt and absorb it without hitting back takes great Spiritual courage and inner strength. That strength is only found in our Spiritual bodies and Soul minds of Love, not in our bodies of flesh. I remember listening to a radio program talking about a Jewish family in Nazi Germany. The false dark shadow Nazis pulled the Jewish man, his wife and children out of their home onto the street. They took the man aside and then shot his family to death right in front of him. They let him live because they wanted him to be an interpreter at a concentration camp as they knew he was multilingual.

He said in that split moment of time he knew he had two roads that he could take. Hate those evil satanic Nazis for the rest of his life and never be free of the prison of hatred he made for himself or forgive them and be free of any hatred within his own Soul. He chose to keep his Spirit free of the poison of hatred and forgave them. He had chosen the high road to be a Spiritual child of our Loving Spiritual Creator in that instant instead of a beast of the flesh. He was taken to a camp and helped many inmates to stay alive until they were freed.

The Nazis were all false shadows of darkness, beasts of the flesh, worshipers of death and satan and all flesh dies, rots and stinks. Only our Spiritual body and Soul live on after death and hopefully that man was reunited with his innocent family beyond this material world in the Heavenly Spiritual World. Like all warmongers, those Nazis would reap the Hell that they had sown, unless they fell down on their knees and asked for forgiveness from all the children they hurt and from our Loving Spiritual Creator for killing Her children.

There is a wonderful Buddhist saying, "Your enemy is the jewel in your life." This may seem ridiculous, but it has a sound Spiritual reasoning. None of your good friends or loving family will ever deliberately hurt you. And even if they did unintentionally hurt you in some way they would immediately say sorry to you. We may think we are strong Spiritually if these are the only children we associate with as we do not hurt them, and they do not hurt us.

But only the one who hurts you and never says sorry, behaving like an enemy helps you to see just how strong your Spiritual strengths of forgiveness and Love really are. They may expose a weakness in your Spiritual life that you were unaware of and need to strengthen. So, we must forgive them and thank them for giving us the opportunity to grow stronger as Spiritual children of our Loving Creator in the Heavenly Spiritual World. But we must also acknowledge their wrong doings and try our best to help them change their ways.

Always Forgive Pray and Forget

When Peter asked Jesus how many times in total, he should forgive someone before he no longer has to, Jesus said seventy times seven. Meaning there is no total number of times that you can reach when you no longer need to forgive someone because you become forgiveness itself as part of your growing Spiritual identity. My late sister Joan was a Spiritual natural at doing this but most of us must work at it.

When we forgive, we must let go of the incident that caused harm or hurt to us by the other child and not hang on to it by remembering it over and over. It happened, it was possibly unjust, it may have seriously impacted our Earthly life but it's over. And although we may still have to live with daily reminders of it due to injury or other real-life consequences, there will be no more pain or suffering for Spiritual children who reach the Heavenly Spiritual World in a healthy living Spiritual body of Love. That is why the more we live out of our Spiritual body and Soul mind of Love each day, we will have greater Spiritual strength to look beyond any present suffering caused to our life by others or just by encountering disease and old age on our Earthly journey.

Jesus clearly said our Spiritual body and Soul mind of Love are our real Eternal identity and this is the most important thing of all. He said, "Do not fear those who can kill your body of flesh (or any disease) but can do nothing more to you. Only fear sin which can destroy both your body of flesh and also damage your Spiritual body and Soul."

As part of our Spiritual practice of forgiving others we must add the next layer of praying for them to help them and further strengthen our own Spiritual identity. This is a very powerful and cleansing practice if done sincerely from our heart and Soul. It can wipe out any anger or hatred we are holding onto against them and prevent these from poisoning our Spirit and Soul.

We must first ask our Loving Creator to forgive them and help them to come out of any darkness they may have fallen into that led them to hurt us as they are Her children as much as we are. We ask our Loving Spiritual Creator to fill them with Her Loving Life-force and transform them into Heavenly children so they may be saved, and we send them our own personal Spiritual Loving Life-force from within our Spiritual body and Soul mind of Love as well to help them.

It is important we must pray deeply and sincerely for that child of our Loving Creator out of Love and concern for them. We must pray that they will recover their Spiritual Life and enter Heaven after passing through their death experience. And even look forward to hopefully seeing them there after overcoming all their sin as we must too.

I cannot stress enough how powerful this practice is to overcome any blockage to Love the one who hurt us, keeping the Love from Heaven flowing into us and through us to everyone, even the enemy in our life. That Heavenly Spiritual Love is our Spiritual Life-force for our Spiritual body and Soul, and we must not starve ourselves of it by hating anyone and not forgiving them blocking the flow of Love from Heaven into us.

We must learn to let go and forget of wrong doings against us. We all live day by day and we can only Love in the present moment no matter how the conditions or restrictions in our life may change or who or what caused them to change. That is why Spiritual children can forget the past and concentrate on each new day to bring what Love they can from Heaven into this dangerous material world. This is how we heal and feel comforted from still being open to Heaven's presence and Love flowing into us. We must always remember the Heavenly Spiritual World is as real as this world but Spiritual.

As this is our great joy and True Life to share our Loving Creator's Love in us with other children then to do that we must be in the present moment and not living in the past and regret. Jesus reminded us of this when He taught in Matthew 6:34, "Therefore do not worry about tomorrow, for tomorrow will have its own worries. Today has enough troubles of its own to deal with."

Forgiveness keeps the river of Heavenly Loving Life-force bubbling up inside our Spiritual body and Soul mind of Love that brings us into Eternal Life in the Heavenly Spiritual World. By forgiveness becoming a natural part of who you are, you will become a Living Spiritual child of our Loving Spiritual Creator in the Heavenly Spiritual World on Earth.

GOD IS LOVE LOVE IS LIFE

**Loving Spiritual Creator
forgive them for they know not what they do
or who they really are.**

Chapter Fifteen

Judge Not Condemn Not

John 12:47 Jesus said, "And if anyone hears My words and does not believe, I do not judge or condemn them for I did not come to judge the world but to save the world."

John 8:2-10 One of the most profound and beautiful dialogues of Jesus can be found concerning the woman caught in adultery. In the morning Jesus came into the temple and taught. And the scribes and the Pharisees brought to Him a woman caught in the act of adultery. And they placed her in the midst of them and said to Jesus, "Teacher, this woman was caught in the act of adultery. Moses in the law commanded us that such a woman should be stoned to death. But what do you say?"

They said this to try and trap Him and accuse Him with blasphemy so they could stone Him to death also along with the woman. But Jesus just stooped down and wrote words in the dirt in front of them with His finger for them all to see, ignoring them. But they insisted He answer their question. So, He stood up and said to them, "He who is without sin amongst you, let him be the first to throw a stone at her." Then He stooped down again and continued writing words on the ground.

When they heard Him speak these words, and saw what He was writing on the ground, they began to leave one by one beginning with the older ones first until they had all left. And Jesus was left alone with the woman in the center of the courtyard. When Jesus stood up and saw the woman alone, He said to her,

"Woman, where are those who accused you? Has no one condemned you?" She said, "No one Master." Then Jesus said to her, "Neither do I condemn you but go your way and sin no more."

The Jews worshiped a two headed God and the Yahweh Godhead of War and Death whom they loved to serve any chance they could get, was the source of this violent condemnation and potential murder. The Godhead of Love is ignored when they murder and steal. Jesus had a very difficult situation to contend with but dealt with it on a number of levels through the Loving Spiritual Life-force and understanding that empowered His Spiritual body and Soul mind of Love.

Firstly, He had to save the woman's life. Then He had to do it without committing blasphemy against the two headed God of the Jews that they worshiped to avoid being murdered by them Himself for contradicting their two headed God Yahweh and Moses. If He openly spoke that Moses followed and worshiped a false two headed God, they would have killed Him on the spot. He accomplished this in a very simple, effective and powerful way that the murderers could not easily get out of by writing down many of the rules and laws of the Jewish religion on the ground for them to see.

He knew they were all imperfect in some way and had undoubtedly broken these laws also. Once they saw these other laws He wrote on the ground each individual realised they were guilty of transgressing a law also like this woman. And since they did not want to be stoned to death if anyone found out it prompted their own conscience to walk away from committing murder as Moses instructed them to do. This sought of profound wisdom can only arise through being a fully awakened Spiritual child of our Loving Spiritual Creator as Jesus had become.

At the same time as saving His and the woman's life He was helping them question their own perverted religion to help them see how brutal their Yahweh 1 Godhead of War and Death really is. They were devoid of True Spiritual Love and Life so He was directing them to find the One True Loving Spiritual Creator who can never hurt any child. And in this instance, He was being a True living example to them of how a Spiritual child of our Loving Spiritual Creator in this world behaves.

Finally, He pours out His and our Loving Creator's Love over her shame to heal her of this wrongdoing and its consequences and lovingly advises her to continue on her way in this world towards Heaven by not sinning anymore. Unlike the two headed God of the Jews and its followers, He and our Loving Spiritual Creator cannot murder or kill anyone for their entire mind and being is empowered only by Her Loving Spiritual Life-force. They are single in their identity and are not divided within like the two headed God of the Jews and are full of Light and Love for all Her children and only save them to Heaven and never condemn them.

Here, Jesus gives us all a beautiful example of how to engage with any child who has committed a wrongdoing through seeing them through the eye of Love, compassion and forgiveness instead of hatred and brutal judgement.

Matthew 7:3-5 Jesus taught, "Why do you point out the speck in your brother's eye but do not consider the plank in your own eye?"

Luke 19:1 Jesus taught, "For the Spiritual child of our Loving Creator has come to find and save those who are lost."

John 3:17 Jesus taught, "The child of our Loving Spiritual Creator comes to save the world not to condemn it."

Luke 6:37-38 Jesus taught, "Judge not and you will not be judged. Condemn not and you will not be condemned. Forgive and you will be forgiven. For with what measure you give out it will be given back to you."

Matthew 9:13 Jesus taught, "I desire mercy not sacrifice."

Matthew 5:7 "Blessed are the merciful for they shall receive mercy."

Genuine critical opinions if given with Love to help someone can be very beneficial for anyone. But we often seek to justify and build ourselves up by running someone else down. We use them like a footstool to climb higher up into our ivory tower of arrogance built from the bricks of our own ego that eventually comes tumbling down. The only foundation to build our home on are the rocks of Love, Compassion and Non-violence.

We do not have the omniscient capacity of our Loving Spiritual Creator to know everything about everyone else's life to be able to condemn or judge anyone. Only our Loving Creator knows all the circumstances that may have led a child into darkness. And who knows how we would have turned out if we were in that child's place. We can and must only judge the action as being wrong or evil and try to help the child see this so they can change their ways and awaken to their True Spiritual identity of Love.

In Australia during an election, I delivered my own pamphlets to vote the Liberal government out of office after they denied a ship called Tampa, that had saved a boat load of refugees from drowning at sea, from putting them safely ashore in Australia. The Liberal leader and government deliberately ran a scare campaign to enflame hatred and racism against the refugees in order to win the election. To my shame as an Australian they won the election. But we must still try to bring in Love where there is none.

One morning around 6 a.m. while delivering my pamphlets into letterboxes I approached a house that was run down with a wrecked car in the front yard. A small boy around 4 years old with bare feet and dirty clothes suddenly appeared out on the pathway in front of me but facing away from me he did not see me coming. He suddenly saw me and shouted an expletive 'F_ _ K.'

His face was dirty, and I thought to myself, 'What hope have you got to grow up and lead a normal well-balanced life filled with Love.' I felt so sorry for him and wonder how he has turned out. As my mother used to advise us when we saw children down and out, we must always be compassionate towards them because 'there but for the grace of God go I.'

GOD IS LOVE LOVE IS LIFE

Judge not and you will not be judged.

Condemn not and you will not be condemned.

Forgive and you will be forgiven.

For with what measure you give out.

It will be given back to you.

Chapter Sixteen

Divine Spiritual Law of Reaping What We Sow

Jesus explained that the source of our perfect Spiritual body, mind and Soul empowered only by Love comes forth from a Spiritual being and Creator of perfect Love. And because Her Love shines forever on all Her children both good and evil equally, as Jesus Himself said, She can never harm any of them in any way whatsoever. Our Loving Spiritual Creator that Jesus was at one with does not commit infanticide killing Her own Spiritual children like the two headed God of the Jews does.

Matthew 10: 14
Jesus taught at the end of the lost sheep parable, "It is not the will or intention of your Loving Spiritual Creator in the Heavenly Spiritual World that even one of these littlest lost ones with the least Spiritual Life should be destroyed." Any Jewish/Christian who wrongly teaches that our Loving Spiritual Creator does murder Her own children who have fallen into darkness by throwing them into Hell is a Jewish believer in the Jewish two headed God. They are not a Christian believer in the One Divine Loving Spiritual Creator of Jesus.

However, there is perfect justice both for the evil and the good and everyone in between called, 'The Divine Spiritual Law of Reaping What We Sow.' Jesus warns us about reaping what we sow when He says to the man He healed, "You are physically well now. But do not sin less something worse happens to you." Jesus knew Spiritual sickness can lead us into the burning realisations of Hell experiences after death which are far worse than just having a lame leg for a while on Earth.

This Spiritual power of 'Reaping as We Sow' is completely neutral like a mirror that simply reflects back to us what we created with our life on Earth to experience ourselves. Those who created Love receive Love and awaken in the Heavenly Spiritual World of Love. Those who created suffering receive suffering and must undergo cleansing before they can enter Heaven. Jesus stated this very clearly when He taught, "With what measure you give to others that is the measure you shall receive." This is the same Teaching of Buddha regarding Karmic consequences of our actions, words and thoughts that also affect our next Life.

Our Loving Creator and Jesus are not our judges, as Jewish/Christians wrongly teach but only want to Love us to Heaven. As Jesus said, "If anyone hears my Teachings and does not do them; I do not judge him; for I did not come to judge the world but to save it." We can hurt ourselves, but they will never hurt us for they only Love us. We are all our own judges, and we also create our own suffering or Loving reward we shall receive after death, through our own free will actions while alive. This was the whole point of Jesus Teaching we must become Spiritual children of Love and Non-violence now while we have the chance if we wish to enter a Spiritual World of Love after our body of temporary flesh dies and returns to the Earth from which it is formed.

Many children do not believe this Spiritual Law exists or has any effect on us after we die because they have never seen it. That is like saying gravity does not exist because we cannot see it, yet all children come under its effect. A strong Spiritual belief in a Heavenly Spiritual World of Love that we can go to after death is a powerful shield against doing any wrong while here on Earth by knowing we shall all reap as we have sown. But the warmongering murderers hold no such belief and are therefore in great danger of falling into the evil trap that will send them into their own living Hell after death.

The Reaping What We Sow River

This Reaping as We Sow Spiritual Law is like a river that never stops flowing between the shore of the Heavenly Spiritual World and the shore of the material Earth world that we must all cross over to reach the Heavenly shore. Those who have been filled with our Loving Creator's Spiritual Life-force and lived out of it by Loving other children throughout their life while on Earth in a body of flesh, simply walk across the water in their Spiritual body after the death of their flesh to enter the Heavenly shore. Just as Jesus walked on the water through the Spiritual Loving Life-force empowering His fully awoken Spiritual body which carried His body of flesh. He overcame all temptations to do wrong and so had no adventitious filth waying Him down. And it is the same for all good Spiritual children of our Loving Creator who come alive and live out of their Loving Spirit.

    Each child crossing the river has a different Spiritual level of awakening of Light and Love mixed with some possible unresolved negativities produced from time to time by our shadow ego identity we may fall into. Most of us have a mixture of the goodness of white, maybe a few black spots with grey tones in between. Only the white areas of our life are Truly Spiritual, the black areas are any serious wrong doings, and the grey areas are the other less serious intensities of our wrong doings. For example, our white elements are all the selfless Loving we have given to others. The light grey elements may be just something like lying about being sick to get out of work. Stealing directly from others is a darker grey. Assaulting another child is very dark grey until killing another child of our Loving Creator is black.

All the grey and black areas we have accumulated that cover our Spiritual body and Soul mind of Love must be cleansed before we can enter Heaven. And they all cause us to suffer after death to varying degrees. Those of us who are mostly white but with some small grey areas and no black will enter the river in a shallow place with the water only up to our ankles or knees. The waters contain the Spiritual Truth of each of our lives on Earth.

We will undergo the cleansing of these grey areas covering our Spiritual bodies and Souls by experiencing any suffering we caused to others or our own Spiritual Life as the Spiritual waters wash over us. But because hopefully we were mostly white and lived out of Spiritual Love we should pass through the experiences saddened and remorseful for doing those wrongs but with no stronger levels of burning Hellish realisations. We will not be overwhelmed by our remorse, and I pray we will be allowed to reach the yonder shore of the Heavenly Spiritual World in short time ready to enter.

Those of us who have less white, a lot more shades of grey and some black will enter the river waste deep and have to struggle to reach yonder shore. For the experiences these children undergo will be of an increased intensity matching the increased suffering they caused to themselves or others. They will be deeply saddened and remorseful for the bad things they did and will experience longer and greater levels of burning realisation pains that equal those they caused to other children.

It will take longer for them to cross over as they struggle through these experiences of suffering, and they may be frightened they will be swept away downstream before they reach the shore. This is the arising of the burning realisations and fear they have created for themselves to undergo equal in intensity to what they caused to other children while in the body of flesh. They can form the torture and darkness of their own living Hell they have created for themselves, depending on the amount of evil they have covered their Spirit of Love in.

Those of us who have almost no white, numerous dark shades of grey and a massive amount of black covering our beautiful Spiritual bodies and Souls of Love in layers of stinking evil and filth through our own free will, sink like a millstone and are swept away downstream by the river to be cleansed of our evil and filth for as long as it takes. The flowing Spiritual waters washing over them will reveal every single evil act they committed and every single suffering experience they caused to others will now be their suffering. And they cannot escape it for they have no body of flesh anymore.

These children have entered at the deepest part of the river and the burning realisations they must undergo will be intense and can cause great suffering and agony as they experience the exact suffering, agony or deaths that they caused other children to experience. And the darkness they are in is caused by the evil filth of each evil act they have covered their Spirits in, preventing the Loving Light of their Loving Spiritual Creator reaching their Spirits.

These are the war mongers, armies of soldiers who murder, violent gangs and anyone who has deliberately created a false shadow identity of darkness and evil to live out of destroying the lives of other children in any way. These darkest ones who thought they were so powerful and strong on Earth will now be brought to their knees filled with extreme fear and frightened they will suffer for what may seem like an eternity for what they did cut off from Heaven and True Life. There will indeed be wailing and gnashing of teeth as they scream and cry out in the agony and Hell of their own making.

Suffering is Limited by Her Love for Us

Suffering is not Eternal and never ending as many Jewish/Christians teach. It is an indeterminate amount of time based on each individual's life. Jesus taught this in Matthew 18:33-34 when He said, "The wicked servant who was forgiven his debt by his master was thrown into prison and handed over to the torturers for not doing the same thing to a fellow servant who was indebted to him. And he would not be released until he repaid all of the debt, he himself had incurred to his master. Our Loving Creator cannot prevent this happening to you also if you do not forgive other children indebted to you." Jesus clearly states that once we undergo the suffering of our debt or sin and it is fully paid or fully experienced, we will be released from its effects of suffering. Reaping as we have sown each according to the severity of the evil we have done.

Our Loving Spiritual Creator knows everything that has happened to every single child of Hers and how it was caused. She knows the pain, agony and fear of every single child hurt, tortured or killed by another child and which child of Hers caused it as She is omniscient and the Creator of all of our Spiritual bodies in our bodies of flesh. She only has to re-create that child's experience we hurt for us to experience it in its fullness, and it is those actual experiences of the child we hurt, injured, or killed that we now have to experience ourselves that are called the 'torturers' in the words of Jesus.

She creates these experiences through shining Her Love, Light and Truth on us when our Spiritual body and Soul come into Her presence after we leave our body of flesh at the time of our death. Remember the words of Jesus, "Her sun rises equally on the evil and on the good." She is pure Love, Truth and True Spiritual Life exposing any false shadow identities of darkness we may have created which cover our Spirits in filth. She is the cornerstone that breaks our false identities to pieces to reveal our True Spiritual identity.

A clean child of Truth and Spiritual Love who dies and comes before Her feels Her warm Love shine right into their Soul as our Loving Creator welcomes Her child into Heaven after their long Earthly journey. Another child covered in filth and evil of their own making who dies and comes before Her cannot receive Her same warm Love shining into their Soul for, they have blocked it with their own filth.

And they are devastated knowing they have caused this to themselves and must remain in darkness and suffering until they are cleansed by Her Love shining on them. Her Love for them ignites the burning realisations of their own wrong doings they must now endure until they are all consumed through their own suffering in the Light of Her Truth and Love.

It is this outer covering of filth we created over what is left of our Spirit and Soul and are now imprisoned in that is revealed to us by being in Her beautiful, Loving presence. Too late to say sorry and ask for forgiveness and wash the filth away with the words of Jesus and Her Loving Spiritual waters. The filth has to be set alight or illuminated by Her Love, Truth and Light shining on us, so we realise the full extent of any evil or wrongdoing that we did. And Her Light and Love shines on the layers of filth and illuminates them to be cleansed through each painful, burning realisation experience we must undergo layer by layer, sin by sin, one by one for however long it takes until they are all removed.

But it is limited to the amount of filth needed to be removed. She never commits infanticide killing Her child's Spirit or Soul as some Jewish/Christians wrongly teach. Instead, She sets us free but not before we pay the price reaping as we have sown to be set free. All this could be avoided by not sinning in the first place or by saying sorry to Her and any children we have hurt and feeling sincere remorse for any wrongdoings we have committed and asking Her to forgive us. Then we are cleansed of all sin by Her Love for us as Her child of Truth, but we must try not to sin again.

Who is Destroyed by Our Loving Creator

Some Jewish/Christians still teach that our Loving Spiritual Creator and Jesus will destroy or kill all Her children who have fallen into becoming false shadow figures of darkness for all the evil they did to other children. But this is not the Teaching of Jesus. What is destroyed is the false shadow identity of darkness that they became which buried and covered their True Spiritual identity beneath.

In the 'Gospels of Jesus Unplugged,' in the wicked tenants parable, Jesus tells the Jewish leaders they are rejecting Him as the cornerstone of a new understanding of our Loving Creator. I translate the following saying of Jesus in this way when He says, "The very stone which the builders rejected has become the head and primary cornerstone and is our Loving Creator's doing. He who comes against this stone, his false identity will be broken to pieces, and on whomever this stone rests it will winnow him of his sins and reveal his True Spiritual identity." He does not break you or crush you as most Bibles say and many Jewish/Christians falsely teach but releases you from sin so you can become your true Spiritual identity of Love and enter Heaven.

Jesus talked about the false dark identities when He said in Matthew 22:13 "And the king said to the attendants, 'Bind him hand and foot and cast him into outer darkness, in that place there will be wailing and gnashing of teeth.'" Matthew 25:30 "And cast the worthless servant into outer darkness. In that place there will be wailing and gnashing of teeth." Matthew 8:12 While others will be thrown into the outer darkness. In that place there will be wailing and gnashing of teeth."

These children are being cast into the outer darkness of their own false shadow identity that they created from their own egotistical imagination to commit evil. It surrounds their True inner Spiritual identity of Light and Love with dark evil layers of filth made up from all the evil actions they created which now cuts them off from receiving the Love and Light into their Spirits and Souls from their Loving Creator that is still shining upon them.

It is this false shadow identity of darkness that is destroyed and dies as Her Love and Light reveals the truth about all the evil and dark things they committed that gave birth and life to this false shadow identity that they became. And as each evil suffering they caused is experienced now by themselves, they feel their shadow identity slowly being torn apart agonisingly dying and there is wailing and gnashing of teeth as they realise the full implication of what they did to themselves and others.

This is the Hellish experience of burning realisations that we cannot stop until they are all passed through. And there is no one else in your Hell and darkness, just you. For all those children are propelled into darkness by their own doing. The Hellish experiences are made all the worse by finally realising what life on Earth was all about. You threw away your Spiritual Eternal Life of Love in the Heavenly Spiritual World where many of the children you hurt or killed may now be, for a filthy dark shadow figure devoid of Spiritual life and are now paying the price for what you did to others.

But Jesus also points out that those torturous experiences you will undergo that you created by causing suffering to others will stop once you have experienced every single one of them. The Greek word often used for eternal or everlasting in the Gospels is 'aionios' which generally means lasting for a period of time which is indeterminant. As we all have different degrees of Spiritual cleansing that needs to be done after passing through our death experience the time is different for all of us so has to be called indeterminant. It is not eternal meaning never ending suffering caused by Jesus and our Loving Creator as some Jewish/Christians wrongly teach.

Jesus again refers to this limited Spiritual time that it takes for cleansing us of our debt of wrongdoing against the Way of Love in Matthew 5: 25.-26. Jesus said, "Make friends quickly with your opponent for your wrongdoings against him while you are still here with him, so that you may not be handed over to the judge, and the judge to the officer, and you be thrown into prison. Truly I say to you, you will not come out of there until you have paid up the last cent you owe." Say sorry before you die and make amends for your wrongdoings and you will not end up in a state of Hellish burning realisations after your body of flesh dies.

Jesus uses the term, 'every last cent,' to indicate every last wrongdoing not corrected and cleansed before our body of flesh dies will have to be accounted for and experienced by our Spirit and Soul identity until they are all cleansed. The judge is the mirror or river called 'Reaping What We Sow' of our Loving Creator that reveals our wrongdoings to us and the force and intensity of them propel us or throw us into any painful cleansing experience we must undergo. Our Loving Creator and Jesus never throw us into suffering of any kind as they are always trying to bring us out of suffering. We do that to ourselves while they wait patiently and Lovingly for us to pass through it.

Fate of the Warmongers

If we think of how many of our Loving Creator's children Hitler was responsible for killing in World War 2 it totals somewhere between twenty-nine and thirty-five million. Imagine if you had to experience every single one of those children's deaths exactly the way they died caused by you. Many died quickly while many lingered in agony before dying. If the average dying time was just one hour and one million hours equals one hundred and fourteen years, then thirty-two million children dying would total three thousand six hundred and forty-eight years. This would be the time Hitler has to endure constant dying over and over again until it is all experienced.

That would be perfect justice in exact accordance with what we cause. And as Hitler would have only been undergoing these deaths continuously for the last eighty years since he died, this being 2025, he still has another three thousand five hundred and sixty-eight years of continuous Hellish burning realisations of dying to undergo and experience that he caused before it is all over. Not to mention the millions left with bodies that were seriously damaged causing them years of suffering they had to endure before they finally died because of Hitler. And all those left with mental damage due to the war. We could probably add another three thousand years of continuous suffering for those children's pain. All his heartless Nazi soldiers devoid of Spiritual Love will of course reap what they caused personally as well.

What do you think will happen to the Hamas killers, Hezbollah killers, Putin and the Russian killers, Netanyahu and the Israeli killers and even the Ukraine killers and all warmongers when they all die after killing children of our Loving Spiritual Creator? Will they be welcomed into the Heavenly Spiritual World of Love and Peace carrying their satanic guns and drones and bombs? Or are they all heading the same way as Hitler? Jesus warned everyone, "He who lives by the sword shall destroy themselves by the sword."

They have no belief in Spiritual consequences after death, especially if they worship a War God so I give them this warning. Many children of our Loving Creator sadly commit suicide here on Earth. Some have suffered such horrific traumas that they have lost hope and the will to live and kill their body of flesh to release themselves from the mental torture they are experiencing. Others are suffering from a chemical imbalance in the brain chemistry often due to undiagnosed neurotoxic infections which cause a very deep mental experience of serious black depression which never stops.

Robbed of all joyful experiences the endless mental torture and depression drives them to kill their own body of flesh to be released from the agony of this endless mental torment. All of us who have suffered serious depression know about this. Never judge a child who takes their own life only our Loving Creator knows what they are going through.

They will all be released from that torture once the body of flesh dies and hopefully, they will enter the Heavenly Spiritual

World in their Spiritual body if they have lived a life of Love until this tragedy destroyed their lives. But when the evil-minded children of satan die, dark shadow figures, beasts of the flesh, the war mongers who propel themselves into the outer darkness and Hellish, burning realisations caused by what they did to other children, they can never kill their body of flesh to stop the mental torture because they have no body of flesh to kill anymore. Too late to say sorry.

Buddha would say it is their mind that is suffering their own Karma not their flesh, and it may possibly take place in another body they are born into in another lifetime on Earth. Jesus would say it is their Spirit suffering not their flesh. Both of these great Spiritual Teachers warned about this same Spiritual Truth of Reaping What We Sow.

If children have to take drastic action to kill their own bodies on Earth to stop the mental torture caused by illness or trauma which is not their fault. How horrific and agonising do you think it will be for those who are trapped in a similar living Hell of their own making but can never escape it until all the debt is paid and experienced down to the last bit of suffering, they caused to others. Be warned, just as Heaven exists so does Hell. Love your Way to Heaven or hate your Way to Hell it's your choice.

Although I am unsure how our Loving Creator deals with them once all their evil false identity is cleansed from their Spirit and Soul through their own suffering and they feel the warmth of Her Love and Light shining upon them again, I am reminded of something Jesus said regarding debts.

Jesus said that those who had the greatest debt but were forgiven loved the most. Although these children of evil will have to pay a very high price of suffering for their debt maybe the same principal applies when their living Hell is all over and they see and feel our Loving Creator still Loving them. Perhaps they will be the greatest devoted children of all in Heaven towards Her. A very hard way to have to come to Heaven but I would hope they get there at the end of their self-inflicted torture and suffering.

Dramatic Warning About Reaping as You Sow

Mark 9:43-47 Jesus gave this very dramatic warning to demonstrate the Divine Spiritual Law of reaping what we sow. Jesus taught, "Woe to this world because of temptations to sin. For circumstances in this world can cause them to come into existence. But woe to that one who brings the temptation to sin into this world.

If you commit a wrongdoing through using your hand or foot in an evil way and cannot stop doing so it would be better to cut them off to prevent yourself doing further wrongdoings. Then by maiming your temporary body of flesh to prevent your Soul and Spirit from performing wrongdoings any more in this evil way, you will rise after the death of your body of flesh into the fullness of your perfect Spiritual body in Heaven.

But if you continue performing wrongdoings using your hands and feet until your body of flesh dies you will propel your Spirit and Soul to enter the Hell of burning realisations from which there is no escape. Not until your Soul has experienced all the wrongdoings you have committed to others or yourself. Those who enter there will wail and cry aloud.

Think of the warmongers who use their hands and fingers to pull the trigger that kills or launches a missile or drone or fly's a plane to drop bombs on children or uses the foot to drive a tank only to kill other children. Better they were born lame so they could not commit such evil.

If you commit wrongdoings through using your eye in an evil way and cannot stop doing so it would be better for you to pluck it out to prevent yourself performing wrongdoings again. Then by maiming your temporary body of flesh to prevent your Spirit and Soul from performing wrongdoings in this evil way again, you will enter into the fullness of perfect Spiritual Life after the death of your body of flesh.

But if you continue to use your eye in an evil way it will propel your Spirit and Soul to enter the Hell of burning realisations after your body of flesh dies from which there is no escape. Not until your Soul has experienced all the wrongdoings you committed against yourself and others. There will be wailing and crying.

Think of the warmongers who use their eyes to get children in the sights of their gun to blow then away. Or the ones who fly drones to zero in on children to kill them using their eyes. Better they were all born blind.

While Jesus in no way wants us to actually cut off limbs or pluck out our eyes if we sin with them, He is just providing a very dramatic insight into how extreme the torturous experiences can be that we will have to undergo in the Hell of burning realisations caused by our own evil actions if we do not stop sinning.

This is a very serious warning He is giving us, and we would be foolish to ignore it as He only wants to save us from any Hellish suffering like this. All Hellish experiences are caused by cutting ourselves off from our Loving Spiritual Creator in the Heavenly Spiritual World and Her Loving Spiritual Life-force that gives Eternal Life to our Spiritual bodies and Souls. This is the greatest Hell of all.

We must remember one of the most important Spiritual instructions Jesus gave us to follow to reach the Heavenly Spiritual shore of Love and Peace in safety. "Do not fear those who can kill your body of flesh but can do no more to you. Rather fear sin, which can destroy both your body of flesh and seriously injure your Spiritual body and Soul of Love after you die. With what measure you give out to others it will be measured back to you."

Jesus was a pacifist, a Spiritual child of our Loving Spiritual Creator and is waiting for us all to commit fully to our Spiritual Life of Love and Non-violence and follow His Spiritual Way of Peace and Love to join Him in the Heavenly Spiritual World. All

DIVINE SPIRITUAL LAW OF REAPING WHAT WE SOW

bodies of flesh in the end are just food for the vultures they do not rise from the grave. Love your Way to Heaven in your Spiritual body and Soul mind of Love by becoming at one with them now as Jesus did. And I pray we will all meet there one day.

GOD IS LOVE LOVE IS LIFE

Be careful what seeds you sow

during your Lifetime here on Earth.

For the fruits of Love are very sweet.

But the fruits of evil are bitter indeed.

Chapter Seventeen

Spiritual Awakening

Two Become One

Jesus had to reveal to us that we have two very different forms of bodies in one human form. Without this understanding we could easily get disorientated and end up living just as a beast of the flesh. They perfectly overlap and we only see the body of flesh but not the Spiritual body. Our Spiritual body can only be empowered by the Loving Life-force of our Loving Spiritual Creator in the Heavenly Spiritual World while our body of flesh is empowered only by Earthly elements. He then directs us to make our Spiritual body and Soul mind of Love our primary identity as it is Eternal and manifest the Spiritual Love through our body of temporary flesh. To do this the two different bodies must become at one in purpose. His Teachings explain how to achieve this.

Thomas Gospel
Jesus said to them, "When you make the two into one, when you make the inner like the outer, and the outer like the inner, and the upper like the lower, and when you make male and female into a single one, so that the male will not be male and the female will not be female, when you make eyes replacing an eye, a hand replacing a hand, a foot replacing a foot and an image replacing an image, you will enter the Heavenly Spiritual World."

Here Jesus is simply saying our two bodies must be as if they are one body and the new identity formed from merging both in the image of our Spiritual identity is beyond the biological identities for both males and females and is Heavenly which He clearly states in the following.

Mark 12:25 Jesus said, "When they are resurrected in Spirit after the death of their body of flesh, they will neither marry nor be given in marriage for they will have bodies like Angels."

Spiritual awakening involves bringing our body of flesh into perfect alignment both mentally and physically with our Spiritual body and Soul mind of Love. This means all our thoughts, actions and words must come forth only from our primary Spiritual identity of Love and then expressed in the best way we know how through our secondary identity of flesh. In this way the two become as one in purpose directed by the Loving Life-force flowing into and through our Spiritual body from the Heavenly Spiritual World to be manifested through our body of flesh. When children see our body of flesh and the good way we live, they are really seeing our Heavenly Spiritual body and Soul mind of Love as well.

To achieve this, our physical life must be healthy in body and mind by caring for our body of flesh while following the normal, natural cycle of our Earthly human life. If we maintain a good balance of work, exercise and relaxation, eat well and avoid unhealthy foods or drinks, do not consume dangerous substances that can damage our bodies and minds and get adequate restful sleep, our body will be ready to share and manifest our Spiritual Love to our family and others. Like a car you maintain in good running order so your Spirit inside the car can take hold of the wheel and direct it to take you to anyone you wish to share your Spiritual Love from Heaven with.

Our Spiritual body and Soul mind of Love must also be healthy by caring for it in the same way we care for our body of flesh. We should only listen to and take in healthy words and advice that strengthen our Spirit and Soul and avoid all unhealthy temptations to do the opposite that could damage our Spiritual Life. We also need to maintain a good balance between performing Spiritual Works and time to be alone with our Loving Spiritual Creator and Spiritual Teacher Jesus and His words to recharge our Spiritual batteries.

We often see Jesus going away from towns into the countryside and nature to talk with our Loving Creator by Himself or with the disciples away from all the man-made distractions. I believe this is a vital Spiritual practice for all children in cities or large towns, so we do not burn out and get a break from the ever-increasing chaos, noise and stress of city life. We may also need a break from the collective consciousness of others who may not be Spiritually minded to strengthen our nexus with Heaven. And joining a Spiritual center can support our Spiritual journey.

So, with both our bodies on a good healthy path, one Earthly and one Spiritual we can study the words of Jesus, contemplate their meaning and begin applying them to our life to transform the way we think and live which will awaken us fully into our Spiritual butterfly identity before our caterpillar body dies.

Then if successful, we just fly away after we pass through the death experience of the body of the flesh and are born again fully into our Spiritual body and Soul mind of Love as Jesus was. We will then all be Spiritual children of our Loving Spiritual Creator in the Heavenly Spiritual World the same as Jesus. He brings those dead to their Spirit back to Life through understanding His words of Spiritual Love and Non-violence.

Basic Characteristics of a Spiritual Child

We cannot see our Spiritual bodies of Love with our eyes of flesh to see what they look like. So, we have to discover what it is like to experience being in a Spiritual body of Love instead and wait to see what they look like after we leave our body of flesh. We do this by listening to the Teachings of Jesus, contemplating them, understanding their meaning and implementing them in our daily life to come alive to our Spiritual body and Soul mind of Love. The Spiritual characteristics we adopt will bring us alive.

This is how we awaken to our True Spiritual identity. As well as seeing the living example of the Spiritual life of Jesus in action that shows us the eventual fullness of our own awakened Spiritual Life and character. It is more important to know who you are than what you will look like.

Once we awaken to our Spiritual Life we can easily relate to the general list of our Spiritual characteristics that Jesus describes amongst His Teachings that make us Spiritual children of our Loving Spiritual Creator. Then we can look into the deeper explanations found in His parables and other specific Spiritual dialogues to gain an even stronger understanding and belief in His Spiritual Way of Love.

The general list includes the following. Be merciful. Have a pure heart and Soul. Be peacemakers and pacifists. Always forgive everyone who hurts you. Be generous and share from your abundance with those who have none. Do not worship money, material wealth or Earthly power. Always be aware of all the various ways in this dangerous, material world that can cause your Spiritual downfall and avoid them. If you do fall down and stumble into wrongdoing, just acknowledge it honestly to yourself, feel remorseful for doing it and say sorry to our Loving Spiritual Creator and strive to not do it again. She always forgives Her children who are Truthful about their life and Her Love flows back into them as warm and beautiful as ever.

Always hold our Loving Spiritual Creator, the Heavenly Spiritual World and the Way that leads us there above all else in this material World. Be Heavenly while passing through this Earthly world. Do not be arrogant but humble like a little child and treat everyone as a friend. Love your neighbour as yourself and even show Love to your enemy. Do not be a hypocrite by pointing out the faults of others but avoiding looking at your own faults.

Condemn not and you will not be condemned. Judge not and you will not be judged. Become a Spiritual Light to those children lost in their own darkness. Become selfless and enjoy serving others in need with our Loving Creator's Loving Life-force in you.

Perform as many Spiritual good works for other children as you can. Help to bring those dead to their Spirit back to life by your example and sharing the Spiritual Way and Teachings of Love with them that lead us to the Heavenly Spiritual World. Remember the Divine Spiritual Law of Reaping as You Sow and only sow good seeds of Love. Never pick up a gun or join any military force in the world. Never kill your enemy and rob them of the chance to repent at a later stage in their life and also enter the Heavenly Spiritual World of our Loving Spiritual Creator. Never become a false shadow identity of darkness, a figment of your own imagination devoid of Spiritual Life by turning your back on Her Love and Light like all those who create evil.

Be compassionate and keep your Loving Spiritual Life-force flowing through you to everyone in need. Never let your Spiritual Love grow cold or be blocked by anything that happens to you in this dangerous, temporary, dualistic material world. Always remember the Heavenly Spiritual World is Eternal and your True Spiritual body and Soul mind of Love is also Eternal.

Awaken from the temporary life of the flesh and become a living Spiritual child on Earth of our Loving Spiritual Creator in the Heavenly Spiritual World today while you have the chance to do so. Our time on this Earthly world is limited so use it well.

Matthew 24:12 "Because of the increase of wickedness in this material world the Love of most will grow cold." So, let's all stay warm.

Luke 10:20, "Do not become arrogant because you have received the authority and Loving Life-force of our Loving Creator in Heaven to be able to heal children's sick bodies and drive out demons. But rather rejoice that such Love from our Loving Creator and Heaven can flow through you to others in need."

John 7:37, "If anyone thirsts for the Truth let him come to Me and drink from my words. And he who believes in Me and becomes like Me rivers of Living Water, the Loving Life-force of our Loving Spiritual Creator, will flow freely out of him from within his Spirit and Soul to all who are in need."

John 14:6, "I am the Way and the Truth and the True Spiritual Life. No one can come to our Loving Spiritual Creator in the Heavenly Spiritual World except through following My Spiritual Way of Love and Non-violence."

Spiritual awakening is a very personal endeavour and may take some time and constant effort for it to fully unfold inside us. But the fullness of its beauty and wonder remains unknown until you experience it for yourself. So do not be daunted by setbacks or slow progress but continue to grow in Spirit every day. The Eternal Spiritual Treasure is hidden in the field of our flesh, and we only have to seek it to uncover it as Jesus taught.

GOD IS LOVE LOVE IS LIFE

Heal the sick and bring those

dead to the Spirit back to Life.

Starting with yourself.

Chapter Eighteen

Manifesting Spiritual Love in a Material World

Matthew 5:42 Jesus taught, "Give to him who asks of you, and do not turn away from him who wants to borrow from you." Matthew 5:14-16 "You must become the Spiritual Light of the world, and no one lights a candle and puts it under a basket but on a lampstand, so it gives light to all who come near it. Let your Spiritual Light shine before other children so they may see your good works that are empowered by the Spiritual Life-force of our Loving Creator in you and give Her praise and thanks."

The Good Samaritan

Luke 10:25-37

A certain lawyer tested Jesus asking, "Teacher what shall I do to inherit Eternal Life?" Jesus answered him, "What is described in the law? What is your understanding of it?" He answered and said, "You shall love the Lord your God with all your heart, with all your Soul and Spirit, with all your strength, with all your mind and love your neighbour as yourself."

Jesus replied, "You answered rightly, do this and you will live." But wanting to be perfectly just the lawyer asked Jesus,

"Who is my neighbour?" Jesus then answered him with this parable. "A certain man came down from Jerusalem to Jericho and fell among robbers who stripped him and wounded him, then departed leaving him near death. By chance a certain priest came down that same road and when he saw the man lying there, he passed by on the other side. A Levite also passed that way and came to the place where the man lay seeing him wounded and also passed by on the other side.

But a Samaritan on his journey also came to where the wounded man lay. And when he saw him, he was moved with compassion. So, he bandaged up his wounds pouring oil and wine on them then placed him on his donkey and brought him to an inn and took care of him until the next day.

Then on the next day when he departed, he took out two denarii gave them to the innkeeper and said to him, 'Please take care of him and whatever more you spend on his care I will repay you when I return.' Which of these three do you think was a neighbour to the man who was attacked by the robbers?" He answered, "He who treated him with kindness and mercy." Jesus said, "Go and do the same."

Jesus is speaking to a Jewish audience, and He knows how they despise and look down on Samaritans as being inferior to themselves not regarding them as true children of God like themselves. He deliberately chooses the despised Samaritan to be the one who shows Love and mercy to the wounded man and describes the arrogant Jews as being inferior, cold hearted and uncaring. This would have been a very strong afront to the Jews that were listening who saw themselves as being the greatest and the only special chosen ones of God. Jesus shows here that anyone can be a child of our Loving Spiritual Creator empowered by Her Love no matter what religion you follow.

Jesus knew the Jews had boxed themselves into a corner by believing only they were the chosen children of our Loving Creator which created a religion of exclusion instead of inclusion.

Later on, this Jewish overlay was taken on by the Jewish/Christians who also said they were the only chosen children of our Loving Creator and only Jesus can save you creating another religion of exclusion instead of inclusion. Jesus swings a wrecking ball into the delusion of the Jews or anyone believing only they are the chosen children of our Loving Creator by making the despised Samaritan the honourable hero in this story. Jesus is breaking apart their false identity of arrogance in this confronting way.

He is trying to bring us into the understanding that we are all the children of our Loving Spiritual Creator depending on how much Love you live out of. The two Jews in this story had no Love for the wounded man so were not children of our Loving Creator but the Samaritan freely gave his Love to the wounded man and so was a child of our Loving Spiritual Creator. He even paid for further care for the man even though he was a stranger and had no family or cultural ties with him. Anyone who lives out of Love for others and hurts no one can enter the Heavenly Spiritual World.

The Samaritan had equanimity of Love and he put aside his own personal activities to give his time to the injured man. Sometimes the most valuable thing we can give someone is our heartbeats, because all of us only have a limited amount to spend. This is self-sacrifice and the selfless Loving action of a typical Spiritual child of our Loving Spiritual Creator on Earth.

The two Jews were selfish and would give nothing to the wounded man in need, so no Heavenly Love could enter them or flow through them to the wounded man. When we are selfish towards others in need, we are starving our own Spirits of nourishment instead of receiving unending Love by just sharing what we have with others. For whenever Love flows out of us to others it immediately flows in from above and we are never empty of Love for it is Eternally flowing for anyone who wants it.

Mark 9:35 Jesus taught them, "If anyone wants to be first and the greatest, he will be the last of all and servant of all."

Matthew 7:16-21 Jesus said, "You will know them by their fruits. Grapes are not gathered from thorn bushes nor figs from thistles. Every good tree bears good fruit, but the bad tree bears bad fruit. So, you will know them by their fruits." And our Loving Spiritual Creator also knows all of Her children by our fruits of Love or lack of them. "Not everyone who calls Me Lord, Lord will enter the Heavenly Spiritual World of Love but only he who does the will of our Loving Spiritual Creator will enter."

The Samaritan will enter and so can a Jew, a Buddhist, a Christian, a Muslim, a Hindu, a Sikh, a Jain, a Taoist, a Bahai, a Confucian, a Zoroastrian, a New Age child, an Atheist and any other human child of Love and Non-violence. For the fruit of Love always tastes the same no matter who is producing it, and they are all Living Spiritual children of our Loving Spiritual Creator.

The ticket into Heaven has only one word on it, Love. Have you got your ticket with you? If you have don't lose it. If you haven't got yours yet sell all your hatred, condemnation, selfishness and greed and buy one. And become a Universal Spiritual child of Love of our Loving Spiritual Creator in the Heavenly Spiritual World just as Jesus became and teaches us to also become.

The Sheep and the Goats

Matthew 25:32-46

Jesus said, "Children of all nations will appear before our Loving Spiritual Creator when they die and they will be separated into two different groups, as a shepherd separates the sheep from the goats. The sheep will be on Her right while the goats will be on Her left.

Then She will say to those on Her right, 'Come, you who are blessed with Love and inherit the Heavenly Spiritual World of Love prepared for those like you since the beginning of time. For

I was hungry and you gave me to eat, I was thirsty and you gave me to drink, I was a stranger and you took me in, I was naked and you clothed me, I was sick and you cared for me, I was in prison and you visited me.'

Then the children of Love will answer our Loving Creator asking Her, 'Loving One, when did we see you hungry and feed you, or thirsty and give you a drink? When did we see you a stranger and invite you in, or naked and clothe you? When did we see you sick, or in prison and visit you?' And She will answer, 'Truly I say to you, whenever you did these things to one of the least of My children you did it to Me.'

Then She will say to those on Her left, 'When I was hungry you gave Me no food, when I was thirsty you gave Me no drink, I was a stranger and you did not take Me in, naked and you did not clothe Me, sick and in prison but you did not come to Me.' And they will answer, 'Loving Creator when did we see you hungry or thirsty or a stranger or naked, sick or in prison and did not help you?' And our Loving Creator will say to them, 'Whenever you did not do this to one of the least of my children you did it not to Me.'

Then our Loving Creator will say to these self-centered, cold-hearted children lacking in the Spirit of Love, 'Depart from Me for you are not yet ready to enter the Heavenly Spiritual World.' Then they will leave and experience burning realisations of their own making until they are fully cleansed. While the Spiritual children of Love will be welcomed into Eternal Life in the Heavenly Spiritual World."

This one extremely powerful Spiritual message from Jesus has been a major factor in manifesting all the Christian charities in the world that help all those in need. He clearly establishes and teaches that we are all children of our Loving Spiritual Creator regardless of race or religion and She Loves and cares about every single one of us. Therefore, if we are to be Her True Spiritual children on Earth of Love and Peace we must also Love and care for every other child of Hers on Earth as well.

To do so means we will be filled with Her Light and Loving Life-force as Jesus said and be Spiritually alive. But to not do so would mean we are divided within and will be in darkness as Jesus warned and will be dead to the Spirit. Being in our Spiritual identity is how we share and bring our Spiritual Creator's Loving Life-force in us to other children and serve those in need. Our own joy is knowing that by helping others we are growing ever stronger in our True Eternal identity as Spiritual children of our Loving Spiritual Creator. And we have those in need to thank for helping us to do so by providing us with an opportunity to give our Love to them in any way we can.

Just as we must exercise our body of flesh to keep it healthy, fit and strong we must also exercise our Spiritual body and Soul mind of Love to keep them healthy, fit and strong. But instead of lifting weights or going to a gym, this can only be done through sharing the Living Loving Life-force flowing through us with others in need. It is like a never-ending stream of pure water which sustains and reinvigorates us in Spirit the more that flows through us to others. We give it freely and completely holding nothing back from the flow, and our happiness comes through seeing others made happy.

The list Jesus gives is just a small sample representing the many ways of how we can all manifest Spiritual Love in this material world depending on each child's circumstances and needs. Throughout our life, our Loving Creator will bring us into contact with others in need, family, friends, neighbours or strangers offering us a further opportunity to grow and become Her Heavenly Spiritual child of Love on Earth before we pass through our death experience. We should never think this is a burdensome, restriction on our life but rather the Gold in our life thanks to another child being in need of Love.

Jesus said, "I have not come to be served but to serve others. And just as I washed your feet, may you also wash the feet of others. He that is greatest among you will be your servant."

The Great Manifestations

The greatest demonstrations of manifesting Spiritual Love in this material world were given by Jesus. There are twenty-one separate accounts of Jesus healing a child's body of flesh that was injured or diseased in some way. And many others were spoken of but not recorded. Two accounts of manifesting Earthly food to feed the hungry crowds who came to hear Him teach. Stilling a storm at sea so the disciples did not drown. And He brought three children's bodies of flesh back to life as well.

He was able to do this, unlike the Jews, because He was a fully awoken Spiritual child of our Loving Spiritual Creator who is only Love, unlike the two headed God of the Jews. He could then pass Her Loving Spiritual Life-force that empowered His Spiritual body and Soul mind of Love into the child's body of flesh and restore it by just wanting to relieve that child's suffering. Or manifest any material thing He wished for. Our Loving Creator provided the material manifestation as only a Divine Loving Spiritual Creator of Love and True Life can do.

Jesus taught the disciples how to perform these same miracles manifesting Spiritual Love in this material world and told us we can also do it but for some reason it has died out. Could it be since Constantine and the early corrupt church leaders converted Christians who only adored our Loving Creator, back into being Jewish/Christians to worship the Two headed God of the Jews that the power has gone out of His Judeo/Christian followers.

I myself have been attempting to learn how to heal with our Loving Creator's Life-force based on the accounts and words of Jesus Himself. As there are few who can do this and teach it these days. Despite my naive but sincere efforts, I have yet to be blessed with such a wonderful gift from above to help other children and myself. If you believe our Loving Creator is only Love and not the two-headed God of the Jews that all Jewish/Christians pray to, perhaps if you try, you will receive this blessing to heal as Jesus said we would.

Manifesting Sounds

The most numerous way Jesus manifested Spiritual Love in this material world was by making sounds. These sounds formed words, and those words formed meanings and those meanings when understood and followed transform us into becoming a Spiritual child of our Loving Spiritual Creator in the Heavenly Spiritual World and lead us all home. This was the most important endeavour Jesus undertook to bring us all out of our suffering by becoming Spiritual like Himself and be welcomed at the end of our Earthly journey into the Heavenly Spiritual World of Love. We should share His words and Spiritual Way of Love and Non-violence with other children any chance we get. But we only offer this Spiritual Teaching we never force it onto anyone.

The Greatest Manifestation

The greatest personal manifestation that Jesus performed of Spiritual Love in a material world was to allow His temporary body of flesh to be brutally killed by the Jewish leaders and buried in order to appear in His full Spiritual body to the disciples after His body of flesh died. Although His new Spiritual body was no longer material, and they were unsure who He was, He was able to appear to them in a similar form as His old body of flesh and talk with them, so they realised it really was Him. This was the manifestation of all He taught them.

This was the important message the disciples were literally shown by Jesus to share with us all. That our body of flesh dies and is nothing but food for the vultures, but we have another Spiritual body of Love that can live on in Heaven if we have become at one with it on Earth. Rarely are Spiritual children or

Angels from Heaven allowed to appear to us to see them. Jesus was given an exemption to appear briefly to the disciples due to His great personal sacrifice and Love for us all.

May we all manifest the Spiritual Loving Life-force sustaining our own Spiritual bodies and Souls in whatever way we can to help other children in need. It may just be loving your children and providing for them until they can fend for themselves. Caring for your elderly parents when they can no longer care for themselves. Helping close friends and neighbours who are in need of help. Stopping to sit with a homeless child on the street and offer them some food or drink or other essential things they may need.

You may become a volunteer at any of the charity organisations you wish to be a part of by serving in an op shop or any other Loving Way that charities help others. You may join a human rights cause, anti-war group, an environmental group to protect nature or simply donate money to a worthy cause. Never stop caring about other children and be on the lookout for an opportunity to be of service to anyone in need for they are sent from Heaven to you to keep your Spirit of Love alive.

GOD IS LOVE LOVE IS LIFE

We are Spiritual riders on an Earthly horse.

At one in purpose Heaven's Love flows through us to all.

Chapter Nineteen

Commit to Being Spiritual

Jesus was constantly teaching that our Spiritual body and Soul filled with our Loving Spiritual Creator's Life-force is Eternal and lives on to reap as we have sown after our body of flesh dies. He encourages us to make a full commitment to awakening and becoming a True Spiritual child of our Loving Creator while still here on Earth. He gave many sayings concerning this because it is very important to establish our Spiritual identity and be prepared to pass through the death experience of our body of flesh and leave in a healthy Spiritual body with a Soul mind of Love.

Give It All You've Got

Mark 12:41-44

Jesus sat down opposite the Temple treasury and began observing how the people were putting money into the treasury and many rich people were putting in large sums of money from their abundant wealth. A poor widow came and put in two small copper coins which amounts to one penny.

Calling His disciples to Him, He said to them, "Truly I say to you, this poor widow has cast in more than all the contributors to the treasury, for they all put in out of their wealthy abundance but she out of her poverty put in all she owned, all that she had to live on."

The temple was supposed to be a Spiritual center, and she chose to hold on to her Spirit and let go of money and place her whole physical life and Spiritual Life in the hands of our Loving Creator. The woman was not holding onto material possessions or her temporary body of flesh. She was showing her complete trust in our Loving Creator who gives True Spiritual Eternal Life and was prepared to even give up the little material wealth she needed to support her body of flesh. Jesus would say her eye was single and she will be filled with Spiritual Light and Life.

But those who were wealthy held onto much of their wealth to maintain their physical life of privilege and indulgence that money can buy to enjoy living out of their body of flesh. Their Spiritual commitment was relatively far less than the woman's and they remained divided within themselves between the body of flesh and their body of Spirit. Jesus said in the Thomas Gospel, "One who is whole and single will be filled with Light. But one who is divided will be filled with darkness."

Although we all need money to physically survive for the short time we have a body of flesh, we should never place it above our Spiritual Way of Life and the things we need to grow in Spirit such as Love, Generosity, Forgiveness, Compassion, Equanimity and Non-violence. These are the vital Life-giving Spiritual Ways we need to commit to in this material world to bring our Spirits alive, that will lead us into an Eternal Spiritual Life in the Heavenly Spiritual World.

All we do should be guided by the Loving Spiritual Life-force that empowers our Eternal Spiritual Life and Soul mind of Love and money is just a way to help manifest it on Earth for those in need. It naturally starts usually within our biological family. Parents help their children and children help their parents. Then it may include friends, neighbours and those we work with. Until we break through all barriers of division within ourselves and are filled with the Light of Love for all. Some may even commit their life to working for a Spiritual or charitable organisation.

Commit And Don't Look Back

Luke 9:57-62

As they were going along the road someone said to Jesus, "I will follow you wherever you go." And Jesus replied, "The foxes have holes, and the birds have nests but the child of our Loving Spiritual Creator in the Heavenly Spiritual World has nowhere on Earth to rest His head."

Gospel of Thomas Jesus said, "Whoever finds his True Spiritual identity, this material world is no longer worthy of him."

Jesus is saying that to fully commit to following His Spiritual Way of True Life that leads to the Heavenly Spiritual World you must no longer be attached to this material world anymore. Other than to Love and help other children reach Heaven before you go there. This means giving up the Earthly material way of living only out of the body of the flesh and transforming into a Spiritual child waiting to go home to Heaven. This is a massive shift in your own inner identity by awakening into your Spiritual Eternal Life through a full commitment to do so. Buddha also taught to not be attached to this material world as it will prevent you experiencing your ultimate Clear Light Mind identity.

Another follower said to Jesus, "Teacher, I will follow you but let me first say farewell to those at my home." Jesus replied, "No one who puts his hand to the plow and looks back is ready for the Heavenly Spiritual World of our Loving Spiritual Creator."

Jesus said to a follower, "Come and follow Me." But he replied, "Teacher, permit me first to go and bury my father." Jesus said, "Let the dead bury their own dead, but as for you, go and proclaim everywhere the Heavenly Spiritual World of our Loving Creator."

Although these follower's requests seem quite reasonable, Jesus uses their delay to make a strong Spiritual point about total commitment to becoming a Spiritual child of our Loving Creator. There is no time to waste as our bodies of flesh are just temporary. And we must leave behind our own biological family as our primary connection that establishes our Earthly identity and join the greater, Universal Spiritual family of our Loving Creator by transforming our life from being based on the body of flesh to being based on the body of our Spirit and Love.

When the mother of Jesus and His family came to see Him, the house He was in was too crowded for them to get close to Him so they sent a message in telling Him they were outside. Jesus replied, "Who is my mother, brother and sister. Anyone who does the will of our Loving Spiritual Creator in Heaven is My mother, brother and sister."

It is quite a powerful statement that Jesus is making when He says to let those dead to the Spirit bury their own who are also dead to the Spirit and leave them and come alive to True Life and be Spiritual. But this doesn't mean we abandon our family or loved ones in need but only that we must overcome biased biological love and loyalty and transcend into Spiritual Universal Love and loyalty to be able to serve every child in need out of Love for them equally. Just as our Loving Spiritual Creator does and wants us to do also.

Dedicating our life to our family members who need our Love can become a powerful Spiritual practice to become selfless and grow in Spirit. But we may need time away from our family to develop our own Spiritual awakening and once we attain this to a greater degree we can return to our family and Love them more and help them also connect to their Spiritual Life.

Above all we must continue to Love whoever we are with and wherever we currently find ourselves. As the sixties' song says, "If you can't be with the one you Love, Love the one you're with." We must commit to becoming a True Spiritual child of our Loving Spiritual Creator in the Heavenly Spiritual World by Loving all Her children on Earth equally. We must over-ride our own self-serving interest, not allow it to dominate our life and give some of our time to serve others in need. Spend your heartbeats wisely. By investing in Loving others, you will gain Loving interest that enriches your Spiritual Life.

The Talents Parable

Matthew 25:14-30

Jesus said, "You must grow in Spirit. It is like a householder going on a journey who called his servants and gave one five talents, one two talents and the last one talent each according to his ability. Then he left.

The one who received five talents went at once and worked with them and he made five talents more. Likewise, he who had two talents did the same and made two talents more. But the servant with one talent went and dug a hole and covered the gift in dirt so it remained hidden and unused.

When the householder returned, he praised both of the servants who had used his gifts fully increasing their amount by one hundred percent, from five to ten and two to four and promised them greater gifts to work with, joyfully embracing them happy to have them as his servants. But the one who hid and covered his gift in the dirt and made no use of it at all because he was afraid to use it gave it back to the householder with no increase. The householder was very upset and called that servant lazy and took the one talent from him and gave it to someone else and dismissed that lazy servant from his service."

In this edited account of the parable, we see the two servants who put everything they had been given to work with into use, increasing the gift by one hundred percent and were called successful. They both committed everything to achieve this outcome. But the last servant made no effort to use any of the gift at all because he was frightened to commit to using it, so left it buried in the earth.

The talents represent Spiritual opportunities and gifts we are all given to grow with from our Loving Spiritual Creator. Some are given many gifts to use and accomplish many Spiritual tasks while others have fewer to use to accomplish their tasks. Each according to their circumstances and abilities. But it is not about the number of gifts or tasks we have to perform. For as long as each of us gives one hundred percent with whatever we have been given to use Spiritually, we are all equally welcomed into the joy of the one who gave us the gifts. Our Loving Spiritual Creator in the Heavenly Spiritual World is not interested in numbers but only if you tried your best with what you were given to grow in Spirit. Whether our Spiritual cup is small or large as long as it is full of love we have succeeded.

And it is a revealing, subtle message that Jesus gives us through the servant who hid the unused talent buried in the earth. He represents all of us who only hang onto living a material life out of our earthly body of flesh that covers up or buries our Spiritual Life and we never become Spiritually awakened because we were too frightened to let go and try. But we must remember Heaven can always see us and they will do all they can to encourage and support us to spread our Spiritual wings and fly. We will not fall down with Heaven's Love holding onto us but only be lifted up to the Heavenly Spiritual World of Love.

None - Partial – Full Commitment

Matthew 13 Mark 4 The Sower of the Seed Parable

None: Jesus spoke this parable to them, "A farmer went out to sow seed and as he sowed some seeds fell along the pathway and were trampled and the birds came and devoured them.

Partial: Some fell on stony ground, and they immediately sprang up, but they had no depth of soil. And when the sun came up, they were burnt because they had no deep roots and lacked moisture, so they withered away. And some fell among thorny brambles and the brambles grew up and choked them and they bore no fruit.

Full: But other seed fell on good ground and sprang up growing to fullness bearing fruit, some thirty-fold some sixty and some one hundred. He who is listening and considers this saying, let him understand it."

The disciples asked Him to explain the parable to them. Jesus said, "The sower sows the words of our Loving Spiritual Creator in the Heavenly Spiritual World. When anyone hears the Spiritual words but does not understand them the evil one comes and snatches them away from within their heart and Soul before they can sprout. Preventing them from believing and coming alive to their Spirit. These are the seeds that fell along the pathway.

The seeds on rocky ground are those who hear the words and initially receive them with great joy. But they have no deep belief within themselves, so endure for a while until tribulation arises in this world and comes against them, then they abandon the words and no longer believe.

The seeds sown among thorny brambles are those who hear the Spiritual words of Heaven but the cares of this world and the delight in material riches, smothers their Spirit and they do not mature Spiritually and are unfruitful.

The seeds sown on good soil are those who hear the Spiritual words and believe in them, hold onto them, understand them and with an honest and good heart they bring forth Spiritual fruits, some thirty, some sixty and some one hundred."

Jesus gives four different reactions of children who receive the Spiritual words of transformation. Some reject them outright and do not believe in Spiritual Life at all so do not awaken to their True Spiritual identity. Some are happy to believe in the Spiritual Way of Life while all is well, but when the harsh reality of this material world comes against them and challenges the strength of their Spiritual belief, they give up and their Spiritual Life withers. Some are happy to receive the Spiritual words but are distracted and spend their life enjoying the indulgences of the body of flesh. Ignoring the words which would have helped them grow into their Spiritual body of Love and produce many Spiritual works instead of none.

But some who hear the Spiritual words, believe and understand them, live out of them their whole life and everything they do is empowered by the Spiritual Loving Life-force of our Loving Creator that gives Life to their Spirit and brings Love to others. This last group is transformed and are fully committed to being Spiritual children of our Loving Creator through receiving the Spiritual words and Way of Love and becoming at one with them. Again, Jesus states it is not about the quantity but the fullness of our Spirits that counts.

Martha and Mary One Too Busy One Sits and Listens

Luke 10:38-42

Now as they went along their way they entered a village, and a woman named Martha invited Jesus into her house. She had a sister called Mary who sat at the feet of Jesus to listen to Him teach. But Martha was kept very busy serving everyone and went up to Jesus and said, "Teacher, do you not care that my sister has left me to serve alone? Tell her to help me."

But Jesus answered her, "Martha, Martha, you are anxious and troubled about many things. But only one thing is really needed, and Mary has chosen that good thing which will not be taken away from her."

It was a polite and selfless action of Martha to serve everyone food and drink while Jesus was serving Spiritual words to digest and understand that lead to Spiritual awakening, enlightenment and Eternal Life in the Heavenly Spiritual World. But while Martha was dealing with things of the flesh Mary was giving one hundred percent of her attention towards understanding the Spiritual words of Jesus that lead to Eternal Life in a Spiritual World of Love.

Mary was fully committed to the Spirit as the most important thing of all while Jesus was speaking, which He called the 'one good thing' while Martha placed earthly nourishment in front of Spiritual nourishment. Which is still however a manifestation of Love for others by serving them as Jesus also advised.

Know the Cost Before Committing

Luke 14:28-33

Jesus said, "Which of you intending to build a tower does not first sit down and calculate the cost to see if he has enough to complete it. So, just as you should not start something that you cannot finish, likewise unless you Spiritually separate yourself from all your Earthly possessions, you will not be able to become My student and follow My Way."

A student aspires to understand what the Teacher already knows and must follow the Teachings and implement them in the Way described. In the case of Jesus those of us who seriously wish to become a Spiritual child of our Loving Spiritual Creator as He was, need to have a good overview of all of the Teachings in the course and determine how far we can go with them.

We should all work at becoming like Him within our limits and life responsibilities and just do our best to go as far as we can with Him. We can always weave His Spiritual Way and Teachings somewhere in our daily life if we are awake to Spirit. Any amount of time spent with Jesus and His words is never wasted but the transformational aspects we must undergo to our character to become fully like Him requires a full Spiritual commitment.

Another particular point, which he gives numerous times, is about not being attached to the earthly material world, our possessions and body of flesh if you want to become fully Spiritual as He was and enter the Heavenly Spiritual world after passing through your death experience.

The Ultimate Commitment

Jesus gave us the ultimate example of what it means to be completely committed to being an Eternal Spiritual identity of Love instead of being a temporary body of flesh identity. He voluntarily allowed His body of flesh to be crucified by the followers of the two headed God of the Jews to show us all that we have another body, but it is Spiritual. He appeared briefly to the disciples in His Spiritual body after His body of flesh died to help them understand His Teachings. He laid His physical life down and took up His Spiritual Life for us to see the goal we must all aim for.

Only those who awaken to become at one with their Spiritual body of Love and live out of it while here on Earth can enter the Heavenly Spiritual World easily. All bodies of flesh die. Only our Spirit Lives on which is why Jesus taught the Spiritual Way of Love and Non-violence to awaken our Spirits and bring us to True Eternal Spiritual Life.

The greater the commitment each one of us has to Love, Forgiveness, Compassion Non-violence and Equanimity, the greater the chance of Peace spreading out upon the Earth for all of humanity. To be involved is to be Spiritual. To be Spiritual is to prepare yourself to Live in a Heavenly Spiritual World beyond all suffering and death. Everything to gain, nothing to lose as all material things are temporary anyway.

GOD IS LOVE LOVE IS LIFE
I am in your Love and your Love is in Me.

Chapter Twenty

Always Be Ready To Die and Live

John 3:6 Jesus taught, "Flesh only gives birth to flesh. Spirit only gives birth to Spirit. Marvel not that I tell you, you must be born again from above."

John 5:24 Jesus said, "He who hears My words and understands their meaning and lives by them will not be judged but pass through the death experience of their body of flesh into Eternal Spiritual Life."

Gospel of Thomas: Jesus taught, "Come into being as you pass away."

Always Be Ready to Leave

Luke 17:33-37

In these verses Jesus states that we have two different bodies with us right now and the death experience can occur at any time during the day or night while going about our usual daily activities. One person died in bed, one person died while grinding grain, one person died while standing in a field and another died while lying on a couch in the Gospel of Thomas. Jesus states that our Spiritual body goes to be in the presence of our Loving Spiritual Creator to reap as we have sown and the body of dead flesh is just food for the vultures. We must always be ready throughout every minute of every day to die to the flesh and rise in our Spiritual body to be in our Loving Creator's presence in the Heavenly Spiritual World by leading a Spiritual Life of Love.

Seek Heaven Within While Still Alive

Thomas Gospel: Jesus said, "Always look towards our Loving Creator as Her Spiritual child for as long as you live, so you may not die unprepared and then try to see her but be unable to see. The heavens and Earth will roll up before you when you die, but he who lives out of our Loving Creator's Spiritual Life-force will not taste death." And will enter the Heavenly Spiritual World.

Jesus is simply saying we must awaken to our inner Spiritual Life and live out of our Spiritual Body and Soul mind of Love every single day, that our Loving Creator gave to us to come to Heaven in. And we must never turn away from Her and Her Love and forget about Her for we do not want to die while that connection is broken and be unable to find it again. We connect to Heaven from within and we only have to think of Her every day to be with Her and Her Love and be ready to be in Her presence when called.

Becoming Spiritually Lazy

Luke 12:16-21

Jesus told them this parable, "The land of a certain wealthy man yielded plentiful crops. He thought to himself, 'What shall I do as I have nowhere to store my crops?' So, he decided to pull down his barns and build greater ones to store all his crops and his goods. And he said to his Soul, 'Soul, you have many goods laid up for many years, relax and have a rest, eat drink and be merry.'

However, the Loving Spiritual Creator said to him 'O Thoughtless one! This night your Spirit and Soul will be called back into My presence, then all those earthly material things you have stored up, to whom will they belong?' He had only laid up earthly treasure for his material life in the flesh but had stopped laying up Spiritual treasures for his Spiritual Life in Heaven."

This simple tale tells of a man who had so much material possessions stored up that he felt secure for the next few years in his body of flesh. So, he figured he could have a rest from Spiritual Ways and just enjoy the indulgences of the flesh for the next few years instead. But his body of flesh died that night and he had to leave his body of flesh and return in his Spiritual body and Soul to our Loving Spiritual Creator to see if he was ready to enter the Heavenly Spiritual World.

We all have to work and store up enough material possessions to live on for a healthy physical life. But it should be balanced out with a daily Spiritual Life as well that is always our primary identity. The temptation to shift into making our body of flesh the primary identity when we have an abundance of material wealth to enjoy can lead us to forget about our Spiritual Life.

And despite our body of flesh having an abundance to nourish it, our Spiritual practices may falter, weaken and stop, starving our Spiritual body and dimming our Spiritual Light which is the only body that leaves at death. Best to remain strong in our Spiritual body that leaves at death as all bodies of flesh grow weak and old and disintegrate back into the earth from which they were formed, and we take no material possessions with us.

The Lilies in the Field

Luke 12:22-34

Jesus said, "Do not worry about your life regarding what you shall eat; nor about your body about what you shall wear. For your Spiritual Life is greater than food rations and the body more than clothing. Observe the ravens for they cannot sow nor reap and have no storehouse or barn, yet our Loving Creator feeds them. How much more will our Loving Creator take care of you than these birds?

And which of you by worrying could increase his stature by even a small amount? If you are unable to do the least important of things, why are you worried about the rest? Observe the lilies in the field how they grow yet they neither work nor spin yet I say to you not even Solomon in all his glory was clothed like one of these. If such vegetation in the field today is then thrown tomorrow into the oven, how much more will our Loving Creator clothe you? You children of little Spiritual faith.

Do not waste time seeking after what you should eat or what you should drink nor have a doubtful mind about getting them. For all these things the nations of the world seek after, and our Loving Creator knows you all have need of these Earthly things. But seek the Spiritual Heavenly World of our Loving Creator first and all these things will be just additional to you.

Do not fear little flock for our Loving Creator is pleased to give you Her Heavenly Spiritual World to live in. Sell what you have and give to those in need, make yourselves pouches which do not wear out to contain a Spiritual treasure that does not fail in the Heavenly World. Do not store up treasures on Earth for yourselves where moth and rust can destroy and where thieves break through and steal. But store up treasures for your Heavenly Spiritual Life where no thief can come or moth or rust destroy. For where your treasure is there also will be your heart and Soul. So, do not worry about tomorrow today for tomorrow will have its own challenges to deal with."

Here Jesus is providing a general description of our daily earthly lives in our bodies of flesh and their needs. While not denying we all need these things to support our body of flesh He continually reminds us we have another Spiritual body which will be far more beautiful in the Heavenly Eternal Spiritual World.

And as that is our primary goal then all these material needs are just short-term additions, and we shouldn't over worry about them. And He reminds us not to waste our time storing up Earthly treasures that all eventually decay over time anyway.

The main thing Jesus teaches is to move into our Spiritual body and Soul mind of Love first as this is Eternal. Then by living a Spiritual Life on Earth and sharing the Loving Life-force from Heaven in us with other children, we will be preparing to receive that same Love in Heaven when out short time here on Earth is over. In this way we are ready to die and then Live again in Spirit.

Prepare to Have an Angel's Body

Matthew 22:29-33

Some Sadducees asked Jesus about a woman who had married seven times, and which husband would she be with after her dead body of flesh resurrected from the dead. Jesus replied, "You are mistaken, for you do not know the Teachings nor the power of our Loving Spiritual Creator. For when their Spirits and Souls rise from the death of their body of flesh, they neither marry nor are given in marriage for they are like Spiritual Angels in the Heavenly Spiritual World and can die no more.

And as for the dead body of flesh rising, have you not read what our Loving Spiritual Creator said to you in the past, 'I am the Creator of Abraham, Isaac and Jacob' who have all died. Our Loving Creator is not a God of dead bodies of flesh but of those who have come alive to their Spirit."

Jesus is giving us an incentive and glimpse of our new Spiritual body after we leave our body of flesh behind by describing them as being like Angel's Spiritual bodies that are Eternal unlike our bodies of flesh. But to have our Spiritual Angel-like body we must be living out of it now and be ready to die to the body of flesh and leave it behind. Always be ready to die and Live by leading a Spiritual Life now on Earth. Caterpillar becomes the butterfly.

Stay Spiritually Awake

Luke 12:35-40

Jesus said, "Be in readiness with your Spiritual Light always shining. Then you will be like those who wait to return to be with their master after his wedding. And when he calls them to come to him, they immediately open their door and leave to go to him. Blessed are those servants who stay awake and are watching to hear his call. And when he calls, he will be ready to receive them himself and have them sit down with him to eat and he will serve them their food.

If the master of the house knew what time the thief was coming, he would have stayed awake and not allowed his house to be broken into. Likewise, you must always be Spiritually ready to be in the presence of our Loving Spiritual Creator in the Heavenly Spiritual world when you are called."

Jesus is telling His followers to always be Spiritually alive and alert and not to forget that at any given moment in time you may be called out of your body of flesh at the time of your death experience. We also have to remain vigilant against the thief of temptation and not sin as this robs us of our Spiritual Life-force.

Then hopefully if we have remained Spiritually ready and well, we will come into the presence of our Loving Spiritual Creator and even meet our Spiritual Teacher Jesus and be able to sit with Him and thank Him for showing us the Way home. Always be ready for your body of flesh to die and leave it behind to Live in the Heavenly Spiritual World of Love in a perfect Spiritual body where Jesus is waiting to greet you. As Jesus said, "Follow Me to where I am going."

Don't Party Too Hard

Luke 21:34

Jesus taught, "Be careful in case at any time your Spirit and Soul become weighed down with partying, drunkenness, taking mind-altering substances and being overly distracted by the cares of this Earthly life. For the day your Spirit and Soul is called will come upon you unexpectedly and it comes to everyone on the face of the Earth. Therefore, always be alert and live out of the Spiritual Way of True Life. Then you will be ready to stand before our Loving Spiritual Creator in the Heavenly Spiritual World."

Jesus again warns us to be living out of our primary Spiritual body and Soul mind of Love and Non-violence here on Earth before we pass through the death experience of our body of flesh. And not to be indulgent in sensual gratification and all of the distractions of this material worldly existence that we can become preoccupied with at the expense of our Spiritual Life.

And no one knows for certain the hour of their death experience but every child on earth will have to pass through it and their Spiritual body and Soul will come into the presence of our Loving Spiritual Creator. Jesus is clearly stating that every child on Earth is a Spiritual child of our Loving Spiritual Creator whether they know it or not regardless of race, religion or no religion. But only those who have been awakened Spiritually and are Living out of their Spiritual identity of Love and the Spiritual Way of Life on Earth will be able to enter a Spiritual World of Love. Always be ready to die to the flesh, be reborn into your Spiritual body and enter into a Heavenly Spiritual World of Love.

Jesus was a realist and a Spiritualist as well. He was able to convey the importance of awakening to our ultimate Spiritual Life and identity while living a healthy earthly life in a body of flesh. He was very honest in his statements about the death experience of our bodies of flesh, but he does not want us to forget that the reality of physical death can lead to another reality of Spiritual Eternal Life providing we are Spiritually awakened to our True identity of Universal Spiritual Love before we leave.

GOD IS LOVE LOVE IS LIFE

Spread your butterfly wings.

Before your caterpillar stops and dies.

Open up your heart of Love and your Spiritual Eyes.

See the world around you through its material disguise.

Bring the Love of Heaven here beneath the Earth's blue skies.

Chapter Twenty-One

His Words Will Save You Not His Blood

Throughout the five Gospels Jesus clearly indicates what it is that will save you from suffering, awaken you into your Spiritual Body and Life and bring you into the Eternal Heavenly Spiritual World after the death of your body of flesh. It is His words not His blood as some Jewish/Christians teach. By listening to His words, understanding them and implementing them in your life you will become an awakened Spiritual child of our Loving Spiritual Creator in the Heavenly Spiritual World just as He did. This is the enlightenment that He and Buddha experienced and taught about to help us awaken also.

John 8:51 Jesus said, "Truly, I say to you if anyone keeps and practices My words, he shall never see death."

Luke 6:46 Jesus said, "Why do you call Me Teacher, Teacher but do not do the things I tell you?"

John 14:23-24 Jesus said, "If anyone loves Me, they will keep My words and live by them and our Loving Spiritual Creator will love them and will go to them and make a Spiritual home with them."

John 5:24 Jesus said, "He who listens to My words and understands their meaning and lives out of them and believes in our Loving Spiritual Creator who sent Me to teach them to you cannot be judged for they will do no wrong and will pass through the death experience into Spiritual Life."

John 6:63 Jesus said, "It is the Spirit who gives Life, the flesh profits nothing, the words that I have spoken to you are Spirit and they are Life."

John 8:31-32 Jesus said to the Jews who had believed Him, "If you live out of My words, you will truly be my disciples and you will know the Truth and the Truth will set you free."

John 3:11-12 Jesus said to Nicodemus, " Truly, I say to you we speak of what we know and testify of what we have seen, and you do not accept our testimony. If I told you of earthly things and you do not believe, how will you believe Me if I tell you of Heavenly things?"

Gospel of Thomas: Jesus said, "Whoever understands the meaning of these sayings will not taste death."

Gospel of Thomas: Jesus said, "Blessed is the one who came to Life before coming to Life. If you listen to my sayings and understand them, these stones will serve you."

John 4:13-14 Jesus said to the Samaritan woman, "Everyone who drinks of this Earthly water shall thirst again but whoever drinks from the Living Spiritual Water that I shall give them shall never thirst again. And that Water that I shall give them shall cause a flow of Spiritual Water to well up inside them, lifting them up into everlasting Life."

Gospel of Thomas: Jesus said, "Whoever drinks from My mouth will become like me, and I shall be like that person and what is hidden will be revealed to that one."

John 7:37-38 Jesus said, "If anyone is thirsty let them come to Me and drink. He who believes in Me, from his innermost Spiritual being will flow rivers of Living Spiritual Water."

Mark 4:1-13 Matthew 13:1-23 Sower of the Word Parable
In this parable Jesus uses seeds to represent His Spiritual words and Way of our Loving Spiritual Creator that He was trying to sow in the hearts, minds and Souls of the children. Some rejected the words outright and they never grew in Spirit, some only followed them for a while then abandoned them, others listened to them but spent their time enjoying material things and only the last group listened to the words, understood their transformational meaning and awakened to become fully Spiritual.

Mark 10:45 Jesus said, "For the child of our Loving Spiritual Creator did not come to be served but to serve others by Teaching many how to be set free from sin and dedicate His life to bring this about like a ransom paid to release someone from captivity."

John 15: 3 Jesus said, "You are already clean and free of sin because of the words which I have spoken to you."

John 15:7 Jesus said, "If you live in Spirit with Me and My Teachings and My words live in you ask whatever you desire, and it will be done for you."

Matthew 7:24-27 My Words are the Rock to build your Life on.
Jesus taught, "Everyone who comes to Me and hears My words, understands them and puts them into practice will be like a wise man who while building his home dug down deep and laid

the foundation on a rock. And the rain fell, and the floods came, and the winds blew and beat violently against that home but could not shift it and it did not fall because it had been founded on the rock.

But everyone who hears these words of mine and does not understand and practice them will be like a foolish man who built his home upon sand. And the rains came, the winds blew, and the floods came and beat upon that home, and it fell down. And great was its fall."

The home that cannot fall is our awakened Eternal Spiritual body and Soul mind of Love empowered only by the Loving Spiritual Life-force of our Loving Spiritual Creator that comes alive through understanding the words of Jesus. Jesus is saying we have to dig deep down beneath our body of flesh identity to find this hidden treasure of our True Eternal Spiritual Life identity. And it is His words and Spiritual Teachings that reveal our True Spiritual identity to us and how we can become at one with it and be saved. He is a rock we can rely on for support, guidance and Truth. His words awaken us and bring our Spirits alive.

Many things in this dangerous material Earth world can overcome and destroy our body of flesh but only our own sin, evil or wrong doings can damage our Spiritual Life. So, no matter what earthly storm or evil comes against Spiritual children during their life here on Earth in a body of flesh their awakened Spiritual body and Soul of Love they live out of can never really be overcome because it is formed not from the earth but from our Loving Spiritual Creator's Life-force of Love.

But a child who has built their identity or home based only on the flesh out of earthly and worldly material things will face a complete destruction of that identity at the time of the death experience of their body of flesh. And a life based only on sensual pleasures and material things can easily lead to dangerous developments that can harm your body and Soul. Flesh only gives birth to temporary flesh.

HIS WORDS WILL SAVE YOU NOT HIS BLOOD

While those children who have established a solid Spiritual Life and body based on the rock of His words will not be destroyed at the time of their death experience but be reborn as a full Spiritual child of our Loving Spiritual Creator in the Heavenly Spiritual World. Spirit only gives birth to Spirit.

We have just read seventeen independent sayings of Jesus that clearly state it is His words and Teachings that save your Spiritual Life if you just listen, understand their meanings, live out of them and are transformed by them. It is His words and Teachings that awaken you to who you really are. A Spiritual child of our Loving Spiritual Creator in the Heavenly Spiritual World of Love on Earth just like Him. Without them you would not know how to behave as a Spiritual child of our Loving Spiritual Creator so could not become Her Spiritual child.

His words and Teachings describe all the characteristics such as forgiveness, non-violence, compassion, generosity, equanimity and Love that must be present in us to bring our Spirit alive as our primary Eternal Spiritual identity that we need to become at one with to be able to enter the Heavenly Spiritual World. If Jesus just died on the cross and shed His blood but said nothing, we would have no way of knowing how to get to the Heavenly Spiritual world or who we really are as Spiritual children of Love.

Why Did He Shed His Blood?

The first and primary reason Jesus allowed His temporary body of flesh to be killed and shed His blood was to show us that we all have a Spiritual body and Life after the death of the body of flesh. He had to shed His blood in this way to set His Spiritual body free from His body of flesh. He couldn't commit suicide, and He didn't want to wait until old age or sickness ended His physical life. He knew the Jews were trying to stone Him to death for blasphemy any chance they could get, and it would get harder to avoid it the more He spoke the Truth about the false two headed God of the Jews. He was in a growing precarious situation.

He may have felt the threat was urgent enough and the time was right to reveal the actual reality of what He had been trying to teach the disciples all along. That we all have two very different bodies with us right now but only one lives on to reap as it has sown and is only Spiritual. The body of flesh returns to the earth and is no more than food for the vultures as Jesus said.

That is why His Teachings concentrate on us becoming at one with Love as our Spiritual Creator is perfect Love and so if we really want to be Her Spiritual children and enter the Heavenly Spiritual World, we must also become perfect Love. To achieve this in a dangerous dualistic world of Love and hate we need a Spiritual guide like Jesus or Buddha to show us the Way. They give us valuable words to guide us to awaken our Spirit.

And we only need the Loving Spiritual Life-force of our Spiritual Creator to empower our Spiritual bodies not potatoes and beans, water and gases which belong to the material world. And that is why He let His body of flesh die on the cross so He could appear to the disciples briefly in His Spiritual body, not His body of flesh, so they could literally see what He was talking about and then teach others this Spiritual Truth about our two different bodies.

This is what He meant when He said at the last supper, "Take this bread this is My body of flesh given up for you. Take this cup and drink for this is My blood of the New Covenant which will be poured out for many. Do this in memory of Me." Jesus is literally telling them He is about to let the Jews kill His body of flesh to show them something. In spilling His blood by the death of His body of flesh it will set His Spiritual body free. He will then be able to appear to them in just His Spiritual body which is the New Covenant or more correctly our New disposition or character as born-again Spiritual children freed from the flesh.

This saying about the blood is the same in Mark and Luke but Matthew deliberately distorts it by adding extra words to transform it into a Jewish overlay by saying, "This is the blood of the covenant which is poured out for many (for forgiveness of sins.)" Making Jesus a sacrificial lamb diverting attention away from what Jesus really meant. Only Luke has the correct word, 'New' Covenant with Jesus referring to His New Spiritual body.

John's main reference to Jesus talking about His flesh and blood is when Jesus says we must consume His flesh and drink His blood to become like Him and have Eternal Spiritual Life. Our flesh is consumed in death, and our blood is spilled out of our body just as His was in death and our Spirit will also be released from our flesh just as His was to hopefully enter the Eternal Spiritual Heavenly World just as He did.

Another general meaning of eating His flesh and drinking His blood is that we must become just like Him as Spiritual children of Heaven on Earth now by consuming His words that come forth from His body of flesh and blood.

This fits in with other similar sayings of Jesus about having to drink from His mouth to become like Him. He is using different ways to explain we must take into ourselves what He is saying and wake up to our Spiritual Life and become like Him.

The 'New Covenant' is a bad translation of the Greek and should be written in all Gospels as the 'New Disposition'. The definition of the word 'Disposition' means the natural qualities of a person's character. So, He is pouring out His blood from His body of flesh to reveal a New Spiritual Identity and Life with new characteristics and clearly states this is why He is sacrificing His body of flesh for them.

The 'New Identity' is different to the one they were familiar with in the body of the dualistic flesh. They were used to their old identity of love your neighbour but hate your enemy. Jesus tells them about the New identity characteristics of Love for all even the enemy, compassion, forgiveness, non-violence, equanimity and other Spiritual qualities. These are the natural characteristics of a Living Spiritual child of our Loving Spiritual Creator with a born-again Spiritual body and Soul mind of Love.

Flesh only gives birth to flesh. Spirit only gives birth to Spirit. So, He could only reveal the two different bodies to them if they witnessed the one that died, the body of flesh, and then soon after saw the one released from the body of flesh that lived on, the Spiritual body. That is why He could shed His body of flesh and its blood because He knew He had another Spiritual body that lives on.

He was indeed extremely courageous and totally selfless to do this for all of us to help guide us out of this dualistic, material world of Love and hate, pleasure and pain, Life and death to enter the Eternal Heavenly Spiritual World of Love in our Spiritual body of Love. His last Teaching was this extraordinary manifestation and culmination of all of His words to reveal the ultimate Truth about our life on earth and its purpose and how to become just like Him and follow Him to Heaven. As He said, "If you understand my words, the Truth will set you Free."

Jewish Overlays

John 15: 3 Jesus said, "You are already clean and free of sin because of the words which I have spoken to you." Jesus clearly states it is His words that clean us of sin not His blood.

The original authors of the Gospels were heavily focused on trying to bring the Jewish children out from worshiping the Jewish two headed God of Love and War to follow the One True Loving Spiritual Creator that Jesus was at one with as Her child. So, they used Jewish overlays to describe Jesus in a way that would resonate with Jews seeing Him through a Jewish lens in the hope they would follow Him and His New Spiritual Way of Love and see Him as the promised Jewish Messiah.

HIS WORDS WILL SAVE YOU NOT HIS BLOOD

The strong emphasis by many Jewish/Christians still to this day that only His blood on the cross washes our sins away comes from the regular Jewish sacrifices of animals made at the two-headed God temple to wash their sins away. And in the Old Jewish Testament book of Numbers 1-9 is the ritual of killing and sacrificing an unblemished red heifer in which no defect can be found. After killing it, they burn it and gather the ashes and place them in a clean place and they use the ashes to purify themselves of all sin. This is overlayed directly onto Jesus by Judeo/Christians who say He was perfect, unblemished and free of sin and the death of His body sacrificed on the cross purifies them of sin in the same way the red heifer purified the Jews of sin. This is a Jewish belief not Christian and not what Jesus Himself taught.

Instead, He spoke many times about His words are what save you from sin and a Spiritual death by sin, if you listen, understand them and practice them. If we do commit wrong doings or evil, we must feel the remorse and regret for doing so first and then come to our Loving Creator and apologise to Her and ask Her to forgive us and not do it again. And we may also have to apologise to anyone we hurt. And She always does forgive us if we are sincere and truthful. And our sins are only forgiven by our Loving Creator if we forgive others their sins against us anyway, which we find in the Teachings of Jesus not His blood. We must take reasonability for our own actions and Jesus will always be there to support us by washing ourselves clean with His Living waters of True Life that are His words and Spiritual Way of Love, Forgiveness and Non-violence.

And this is exactly what Jesus Himself taught in the prodigal son parable and with the woman caught in adultery. The prodigal son regrets and feels remorseful for his wrong doings; asks his father to forgive him which he does and welcomes him back home in joyous celebration where he stays and sins no more. The woman caught in adultery was sorry for her wrongdoing, Jesus says He forgives her and tells her to go on her way but sin no more. The words and Spiritual instructions that Jesus teaches us can cleanse us of all wrong doings and save us if we follow and practice them, not His blood.

And in Egypt the Jews were told to spread the blood of a sacrificed lamb over their doors so death will not come upon them. The term 'the lamb of God' comes straight out of these sacrificial offerings that go back to Abraham. Jesus was a shepherd, not a lamb. However, the symbolism of calling Jesus by this name would not be lost on the Jews, although it would be meaningless to others.

His blood on the cross of His dead body of flesh does help save us from death by revealing we have another more beautiful Spiritual body to join with before our flesh dies. His self-sacrifice was extremely important and inspiring to us all but not because He died for our sins but to reveal our True Eternal Spiritual body and identity which we all have within us that does not die but lives on reaping as it has sown.

Jesus Himself seems to have deliberately chosen the Passover feast timing for His death to reinforce the sacrificial lamb idea in the hope it would influence the Jews to follow Him. This would have made it easier for the Gospel writers to weave that Jewish theme in to see Jesus through a Jewish lens and make Him more acceptable to the Jews.

The Messiah overlays are another attempt by the Gospel authors to legitimise Jesus more to the Jews. They searched through the Old Jewish Testaments to find any pertinent references about the Messiah they could use to match the life of Jesus and say they are all prophesies about Him. They may or may not be, but they were an unnecessary addition along with the lamb symbolism because it is all about His transformational words and His Spiritual Way of Love, Non-violence and Forgiveness.

It would still be fair to call Him a Messiah or Anointed One of the Jews, but He was a Spiritual Messiah not the military Messiah they were praying, waiting and hoping for to come and make them great and powerful again. The great and powerful thing He brought for them was Universal Love but they rejected it.

All these Jewish overlays about Jesus held great significance to the Jews and may have swayed some to leave the two-headed God and follow Jesus and our Loving Spiritual Creator. Unfortunately, they can become a serious distraction and have led to distortions about Jesus and our Loving Spiritual Creator amongst modern Jewish/Christians who would rather focus on these Jewish overlays than His words.

And while these Jewish overlays would have only had a localised effect on the Jews His words of Love and the Spiritual Way to the Heavenly Spiritual World are Universal. His words and His Spiritual Way of Love, Non-violence and Forgiveness as a child of our Loving Spiritual Creator are the most important thing and will save you and me to Heaven if we just listen to His words, are transformed by them and follow His Way to the Heavenly Spiritual world of Love.

GOD IS LOVE LOVE IS LIFE

I will lay down My life for you.

Then I will take it back up again anew.

Then you will be able to understand just who

you really are beneath your body of temporary flesh.

Chapter Twenty-Two

The Kingdom of Heaven is Within

The reason Jesus said the Kingdom of the Heavenly Spiritual World is within you is because you have an Eternal Spiritual body and Soul mind of Love within your temporary body of flesh which you need to become at one with and live out of as only this Spiritual body can take you to Heaven. Buddha would say your mind or consciousness travels on after the death of your body of flesh. And both of these Spiritual Teachers taught our Spirit, or mind must be clean to enter a higher Spiritual state of existence called Heaven or Nirvana and we will all reap as we sow.

All bodies of flesh, including the earthly body of Jesus, eventually die and breakdown into the various material constituents they are made of and return to the earth from which they were formed. Our Spiritual body and Soul mind of Love are formed from a Spiritual source. Jesus calls this source an Eternal Spiritual Creator and Being of perfect Love. And it is Her Loving Spiritual Life-force that empowers and gives Life to our Spiritual bodies and Souls, and they need nothing else to have Life. And as the source of their creation is Eternal and perfect Love, so will our Spiritual bodies and Souls be Eternal and perfect in Love. He calls this knowing the 'Truth that will set you free.' Free from being only a temporary body of flesh that dies by awakening into your Spiritual body and Soul mind of Love that is Eternal.

Hearing His Spiritual Teachings can be the catalyst that ignites us to seek for this Truth within our physical lives. As Jesus says in Luke 12:49, "I have come to ignite a fire on the earth and how I wish it were already ablaze." And in the Thomas Gospel: "Whoever is close to Me is close to the fire and whoever is far from Me is far from the Heavenly Spiritual World." The term fire here represents Spiritual enlightenment or awakening. He spoke of this in different ways often using common daily activities to help lead the children into understanding the deeper meaning of something that was very foreign to them.

A simple metaphor or analogy using common symbols can often penetrate more easily into a child's mind and convey the meaning of theological explanations more clearly. Since most of the children Jesus taught were from a simple rural society and culture His parables were often crafted in this way especially for them. In Matthew 13:10-12 the disciples asked Jesus why He spoke in parables to the crowds. Jesus said, "To you it has been granted to be told the deeper mysteries of the Heavenly Spiritual World, but it has not been granted to them. For whoever has some understanding to him more shall be given and he will have an abundance of understanding but whoever does not have any understanding then what he currently has must first be taken away from him."

Jesus is very aware that to learn His New Spiritual Way of understanding, the old understanding they had must be replaced through a gradual transition of letting go of the old and adopting the new. That is not an easy task when old wrong beliefs are so heavily entrenched. While His disciples were privileged to be guided and slowly build up a deeper Spiritual understanding through the Teachings He personally gave them, the crowds had no basic understandings to build on. That is why He had to initially use symbolic parables to help them slowly transition into the deeper understandings of His Spiritual Teachings. It is often overlooked that He also had to use parables to avoid being stoned to death by the Jewish leaders for openly blaspheming their two headed God Yahweh.

The Kingdom of Heaven is Within You

Luke 17:20-21

The Pharisees asked Jesus when the Kingdom of our Loving Creator was coming. He said, "The Heavenly Spiritual World of our Loving Spiritual Creator does not come through visual observation, nor will they say, 'Look it is here!' or 'Look it is over there!' Realise this, the Heavenly Spiritual World of our Loving Creator is within you." Jesus is referring to the Spiritual connection with Heaven we can all have within our body of flesh by becoming at one with our inner Spiritual body and Soul mind of Love now.

Thomas Gospel: His disciples said to Him, "When will the Kingdom of the Loving Creator come? Jesus said, "It will not come by looking outwards. They will not say, 'Behold it is over there,' or 'It is over here.' But rather the Kingdom of the Loving Spiritual Creator is spread out upon the Earth, but men do not see it." Jesus states we will not find the Heavenly Spiritual World by simply looking outwards at the material World. We must look inside ourselves. If we only see this world through the eyes of our body of flesh with its dualistic mind it is a material vision only. But if we see this whole world through the eye of Love of our inner Spiritual body and Soul, then Heaven's presence has come to Earth through us. And if enough of us woke up to being Spiritual then Heaven would indeed be spread out across the Earth.

Thomas Gospel: Jesus said, "If your leaders say to you, 'Look the Kingdom is in the sky,' then the birds of the air will get there before you. If they say, 'It is under the sea' then the fish of the sea will get there before you. Rather, the Kingdom of our Loving Spiritual Creator is inside of you and outside of you. When you know yourselves then you will be known, and you will understand that you are Spiritual children of our Loving Spiritual Creator. But if you do not know your True Spiritual identity, you will live in poverty, and it is you who are that poverty."

Again, Jesus draws us to look inside ourselves for the Heavenly Spiritual World connection rather than search for it as an Earthly Kingdom we can see with our physical eyes. He says the Heavenly Spiritual Kingdom is both inside and outside of us. If we are an awakened Spiritual child of our Loving Creator on Earth as Jesus was, then the Loving Life-force of Heaven will empower our inner Spiritual body and Soul, and we will manifest Heaven's Love in the outside material world that is all around us.

But this can only happen if we fully realise we are Spiritual children first. This is what He means when He says we must get to know our True selves and become at one with our Spiritual identities and then we will be known by our Loving Creator as Her Spiritual children on Earth. But to remain in the flesh identity only, devoid of Spirit is to remain in poverty.

Thomas Gospel: Jesus said, "Whoever finds their True self is worth more than the material world. Whoever knows everything but lacks within, lacks everything."

Treasure Hidden in a Field

Matthew 13:44

Jesus said, "The Heavenly Spiritual World of our Loving Creator is like a treasure hidden in a field which a man found and in great joy at finding it he sells all his Earthly possessions and buys that field making it his own."

Thomas Gospel Jesus said, "The Heavenly Spiritual World of our Loving Creator is like a man who had a treasure hidden in his field but did not know it. And after his death he left it to his son. His son inherited the field but did not know it was there either so gave it away. Whoever bought it came and plowed the field and found the treasure. And he began to share it with those he loved."

Our dualistic body of flesh is the field, and our Eternal Spiritual body and Soul mind of Love is the treasure hidden within our earthly body that we must search for to find, like plowing into the earth to reveal what is beneath it. We need to plow through and break up our old dualistic ways of thinking and judging others that cover the singularity of Love that lies beneath them waiting for us to be at one with. It is by living out of this Spiritual Love now on Earth that we are preparing ourselves to enter the Heavenly Spiritual World of Love.

Once we discover it, we can let go of our material life of the flesh or possessions and center ourselves into our Spiritual Life empowered by this Loving Life-force with great joy at finding out who we really are. Eternal Spiritual children of our Loving Spiritual Creator in the Heavenly Spiritual World. But those who do not know about it or search for it cannot point it out to their children who do not look for it either. This is why we must be a Light to others in the darkness of this material world to help them find this Spiritual awakening too.

The One Great Pearl

Matthew 13-45

Jesus said, "The Heavenly Spiritual World of our Loving Creator is like a merchant seeking good and beautiful pearls and when he finally finds such a pearl, extremely valuable, he goes and sells all his Earthly possessions to buy that pearl."

Thomas Gospel Jesus said, "The Heavenly Spiritual World of our Loving Creator is like a merchant who had a supply of merchandise and then found a pearl. Now the merchant was wise; and he sold all his merchandise and bought the single pearl for himself. So also with you; seek after the treasure that is unfailing, that is abiding, where no moth comes to consume and no worm destroys."

In the day of Jesus pearls were rare and very valuable. Jesus again points out that we must go looking for the Spiritual pearl within ourselves and when we find it place that above all of our Earthly possessions and make that our primary identity. He also states in Thomas that our Spiritual body and Life is Eternal, and we will live out of it in the Heavenly Spiritual World beyond all forms of corruption. And the one who seeks it and becomes at one with it is wise because our Spiritual Life is Eternal, but our material life and body of the flesh is only temporary.

Thomas Gospel: Jesus said, "If you do not fast from the world, you will not find the Spiritual Kingdom."

The One Great Fish

Thomas Gospel Jesus said, "A person is like a wise fisherman who cast his net in the sea and drew it up full of little fish from below. Among them he found one good and great fish. The wise fisherman threw all the little fish back into the sea and without any hesitation he chose to keep the greatest fish. Whoever has ears to hear, let him hear."

This is the original and correct version spoken by Jesus which aligns with all of these sayings and is about personal Spiritual development and awakening. Again, the fisherman had to search among all the fish to find the one great and good one and being wise does not hesitate to keep the greatest fish of all, his Eternal Spiritual body and Soul and throws the other insignificant little ones back into the sea, which represent his temporary earthly identities made up of his possessions and position in society.

Matthew 13:45 Distortion of the Original Teaching

Jesus said, "The Heavenly Spiritual World of our Loving Creator is like a fishing net that was cast into the sea and gathered some of every kind. And when it was full they drew it up to the shore and sat down and collected the good into vessels but the bad they cast out." Matthew follows this with these words supposedly attributed to Jesus, "So it will be at the end of the age; the Angels will come forth and separate the wicked from amongst the righteous and will cast them into the furnace of fire. There will be wailing and gnashing of teeth." This version is false. It is not about personal Spiritual development and awakening but about the Jewish two headed God destroying evil children in an Apocalypse. And it does not match the preceding two sayings of Jesus in Matthew about the Kingdom of Heaven.

This altered version in Matthew could by itself possibly represent reaping what we sow but it has been linked to a distortion. Matthew has altered the original to turn it into an Apocalyptic account and destroy the True meaning of the words of Jesus. This is a serious distortion that runs throughout the Gospels to distract and take followers away from understanding the words of Jesus and become personally transformed and awoken into our Spiritual body and True identity by them to become the same as He was. A Spiritual child of Love of our Loving Spiritual Creator in the Heavenly Spiritual World. Instead, this represents the two headed God of the Jews in Daniel who destroys its children who do wrong and slanders Jesus and our Loving Creator by putting these words in His mouth.

In the original the fish rejected were just little and not cast out or destroyed for being little but put back in the sea to still exist. Even when we awaken to our True Spiritual identity, we still need material possessions and a profession, but we do not worship them anymore or base our identity on them. Matthew paints some fish as being evil children who are destroyed by the God of Jesus in an Apocalypse. The old wine of Daniel mixed into the new wine and poisoning it. Jesus said in the lost sheep parable, "It is the will of our Loving Creator that not the littlest or least of these lost sheep should be destroyed."

The 'end of the age' is the day on which we all die. Not an Apocalyptic event for the whole world. Although the way mankind is destroying this Earth world and treating each other we may bring an Apocalypse upon ourselves. But our Loving Creator and Jesus can never hurt anyone and will not be involved in such a monstrous action for they are perfect Love. The Divine Spiritual Law of Reaping as We Sow returns to us whatever we have created during our life. The original and correct fish parable in Thomas is to encourage us to all search for and find that perfect Loving Spiritual identity inside us and not to worship trivial, material, temporary things or empty egotistical identities.

Heaven is Like a Mustard Seed

Matthew 13:31-32 Jesus said, "The Kingdom of the Heavenly Spiritual World is like a mustard seed, which a man took and sowed in his garden. It is the smallest of seeds on Earth but when it has finally grown it becomes the greatest of all herbs and puts forth large branches. And the birds of the air can make their nests in its branches under its protection."

Jesus tells us the Spiritual seed of Heaven is planted in our own garden in the prepared soil of our physical identity and Earthly life. And if we are ready or prepared to receive the small seed which represents the Spiritual Words and Way of Love of Jesus then it will grow into a large Spiritual plant, the greatest of all plants and birds of the air will build their homes in it and be protected by it.

The 'birds of the air' means children who have awoken to their True Spiritual identity as the Greek word, 'air' also means Spirit. And once the seed of their Spiritual identity has fully grown or awakened it becomes the greatest part of their life, and they become the Spiritual children who will enter the Heavenly Spiritual World of Love to build their nests or homes in and be forever protected from suffering.

Our physical Earthly life is like the roots of a plant in the soil that provides nourishment and water for the trunk and stems to grow towards the Light. The Light provides a reaction within the leaves that produces sweet sugars and further nourishment for growth. Finally, a flower bud appears, and it opens to form a beautiful perfect shape producing the Heavenly perfume of Spiritual Love that fills the air. Likewise, from within the base of a body of earth our Life rises up to open into a Heavenly Spiritual body guided by the Light and Love of our Loving Spiritual Creator always shining upon us from Heaven.

Heaven is Like Yeast in Bread Flour

Matthew 13:33

Jesus said, "The Spiritual Kingdom of our Loving Creator is like a woman who took yeast and concealed it in three measures of flour until it had all risen."

Jesus is again pointing out that our Spiritual Life is found inside us. Flour dough by itself remains flat and will not rise. Just as our body of flesh remains flat when it dies and only our Spiritual body rises. The yeast placed in amongst the flat bread dough represents the Spiritual Teachings and words of Jesus that are mixed into our material life of the flesh. They are what cause us to rise into our Spiritual body and Soul mind of Love and get ready to enter the Heavenly Spiritual World of Love just as yeast makes bread dough to rise.

Yeast must have moisture and warmth to flourish and then the yeast cells grow and produce pockets of air that fill the flat bread and make it rise up. Interestingly the Greek word for 'air' can also mean Spirit. Likewise, the Teachings and words of Jesus will flourish in us if we have the warmth of Love in our hearts and Souls and the Living Water from Heaven bubbling up within us that Jesus gives us. Then they will cause our Spiritual body and Soul mind of Love to rise up and come alive, just as yeast causes flat bread to rise. But if the flour dough is cold the yeast will not flourish and make the bread rise and be soft. Likewise, if we are cold-hearted with no warmth of Love towards others the words of Love that Jesus gives us will not make our Spirits rise up. We will remain hard and never be soft.

Heaven is Like an Empty Jar of Flour

Thomas Gospel: Jesus said, "The Kingdom of our Loving Spiritual Creator is like a woman who was carrying a jar full of flour. While she was walking on a road far from home, the handle of the jar broke, and the flour spilled behind her on the road. She did not know it; she had not noticed the problem. When she reached her home, she put the jar down and discovered it was empty."

Jesus is saying that the material substances and Earthly life-force that support our physical journey as we walk along the road of life in the body of the flesh are always slowly running out. When we are born, we start our journey from Earth to Heaven and are at the farthest point from our Spiritual Heavenly Home but as time goes by, we can draw closer. And just like the woman carrying the jar of flour, we must carry our body of flesh with us until we get home to the Heavenly Spiritual World. Then one day our body of flesh will run right out of its life-force and lay down upon the earth empty of all life like the woman's jar was empty of flour when she finally reached her Heavenly home.

Then, if we have used our temporary physical life and its life-force to become Spiritually alive with Love and are ready, we will enter the Spiritual Heavenly World in a Spiritual body full of Life and leave behind our body of flesh now empty of life. The woman in this Teaching of Jesus who hopefully lived a good life only discovered she now had another Spiritual body to live out of when she left her dead body of flesh at the time of its death. Which is now just food for the vultures as Jesus said in His Teaching about two women grinding at one millstone. One dies and is food for vultures. And one is taken to be near to our Loving Spiritual Creator in the Heavenly Spiritual World of Love.

Saved by What is Within You

Thomas Gospel: Jesus said, "If you are born into the one within yourselves that one you now have will save you. If you do not have that one within yourself, what you do not have within you will cause you to have no True Life."

Jesus is saying we must be born again into our inner Spiritual body and Soul mind of Love identity for us to be saved to the Heavenly Spiritual World. This is the ultimate goal that Jesus gives us to aim for. And without being born into it and bringing it alive through listening to and understanding His Teachings we will have no real True Spiritual Life.

These Teachings of Jesus are powerful reminders that our True Spiritual identity is inside us and we are responsible for our own transformation into Spiritual children of our Loving Creator as a free will choice. But He has left us the instructions to follow, and He and our Loving Creator in the Heavenly World can always see us and will do all they can to help us succeed. We can talk to them any time about anything and ask for guidance and help and it is surprising how coincidental, unexpected and quirky their responses can be to encourage us and let us know we are not alone in this battle. They can always see us.

GOD IS LOVE LOVE IS LIFE
Look through the body of your flesh.
The Nexus to Heaven is within you.
Flesh gives birth only to flesh.
Spirit gives birth only to Spirit.
Marvel not that I tell you. You must be born again.

Chapter Twenty-Three

Our Characteristics as Spiritual Children

Jesus said if we are to become True Spiritual children of our Loving Spiritual Creator in the Heavenly Spiritual world we must become at one with Her perfect Love. This is quite logical as She has created our Spiritual Body and Life from Her own Loving Creative powers which are all perfect and pure so we must align our inner selves with this Spiritual perfection while here on Earth to be called Her True Spiritual children of Love.

Jesus provides us with the Spiritual characteristics we must have to bring our Spirit to Life filled with Light and Love empowered by our Loving Spiritual Creator's Life-force. This is what is called enlightenment. He gives them to us through His words and His actions. The following are some of the Spiritual characteristics we must believe in and practice every single day of our life. The more we practice the more we will be like a Spiritual child of our Loving Creator in the Heavenly Spiritual World.

Jesus had all the Spiritual characteristics and practiced them in perfect harmony and so entered the Heavenly Spiritual World after His body of flesh died and returned to the earth. All we have to do is follow His Spiritual Way to Heaven as He was the trailblazer who went before us to show us the Way of Spiritual Love that leads us safely through this dangerous material world to our Eternal Spiritual home.

The Heavenly Spiritual World Really Exists

Just because we are born into a body of flesh restricted by our physical senses does not mean another whole world and universe exists that is formed from a different Spiritual Life-force of Love. Which is why Jesus said we must awaken into our Spiritual body now to connect with it and enter into it after our body of flesh dies.

Always have faith that Heaven can see you and they know everything you are going through, even though you may feel alone they will help you in any way they can. For if you believe in them, all we have to do is ask and stay connected to them to receive their support. How we receive it is best known to them for they can see further ahead in our life than we can. We must just remember they are with us in our joy and with us in our suffering and will only Love us and never harm us.

Our Loving Spiritual Creator Really Exists

Have faith in the existence of our Loving Spiritual Creator in the Heavenly Spiritual World of Love even though we cannot see Her with our eyes of flesh but must feel Her presence in the Spiritual Way of Love that Jesus taught us to live out of. Be fully aware that She can see you all the time and will support and guide you on your journey through this dangerous material world of suffering to reach the Heavenly Spiritual World of Love.

Understand She is only Love and is not the two headed God Yahweh of the Jewish religion. Believe our Spiritual body and Soul mind of Love is perfect and has come forth from Her pure Love for us to have True Life in Heaven if we wish to accept it.

Without a deep belief in the Heavenly Spiritual World, our Loving Spiritual Creator and Spiritual life after death of our body of flesh we will not be able to follow the full Spiritual Way of Love that Jesus taught. They help us to stay on course, receive support from Heaven and help us cross over to reach the yonder shore of Heaven when our body of flesh dies.

The Spiritual Way to Heaven Really Exists

Jesus teaches a powerful, intelligent and logical Spiritual Way of Life to follow and live out of that transforms us, awakening our Spiritual body and Soul mind of Love that leads us out of this temporary, dangerous material world to the Heavenly Spiritual World of Love that is Eternal.

Pacifist Child of Our Loving Creator

"You have heard it said of old, 'An eye for an eye and a tooth for a tooth.' But I say to you, you must resist retaliating evil with evil. But instead, whoever strikes you on your right cheek, turn the other to him also. You have been taught you shall Love your neighbour but hate your enemy. I say to you, Love your enemies, bless them that curse you, do good to those who hate you, pray for those who spitefully use you and persecute you.

For our Loving Creator makes Her sun to rise on the evil and the good and sends rain on the just and the unjust and is kind to the ungrateful and the evil. Love your enemies, do good and lend hoping for nothing in return and your Spiritual reward shall be great. Therefore, if you wish to be True Spiritual children of our Loving Spiritual Creator in the Heavenly Spiritual World your Love must be as perfect as Her Love. Blessed are the peacemakers, pacifists in a violent world."

This is the highest practice we can attain to as Spiritual children on Earth, and we must lead the way against all the evil warmongers and armies of the world who teach children to kill other children of our Loving Creator. It is time for a pacifist revolution where young people must become Spiritual and stand against all governments who support the armaments industry by creating armies to use their filthy, murdering, satanic weapons.

I encourage all children in the world to never join armies. Without robot soldiers who are trained not to think for themselves and just be cannon fodder, the pathetic, demented, insane, warmonger leaders could never create a war. Soldiers hold the power to stop wars by not being soldiers anymore. Instead, they should do something else that is Loving with their short life.

Instead of ships loaded with satanic weapons and children trained to kill we need government ships loaded with aid, building materials for the homeless, food for the starving, machinery to dig wells, build hospitals, bridges or disaster relief, whatever may be needed and medical supplies all for free. And instead of paying for an army of children trained to murder, pay for an army of children trained in all these fields of expertise. I wish my country Australia, or some other nation would have the guts to lead the way but without Spiritual Love it will never happen. They will all continue the military madness.

If the corrupt governments of the world can spend an annual $2.718 trillion dollars on filthy evil weapons of war threatening other nations and starting wars which is insanity in a confined world, why can't they just spend it on helping everyone in need instead. Surely this is the only way for this little Earth world to grow in trust, Peace and Love for all.

What a disgusting waste of life, resources and taxpayers' money to create things that worship satan and pervert the Loving Spiritual minds of children instead of creating Loving things to help those in need empowered by the Loving Life-force of our Loving Spiritual Creator in Heaven.

We must demonstrate against all wars and the armaments industry in all nations as Spiritual children of our Loving Creator and followers of Jesus. Do not support any armies of war in your own country or elsewhere. Jesus gave His physical life to establish the pacifist Christian Spiritual Way to Heaven. Now Christian countries have army chaplains who bless the troops before they go and kill other children of our Loving Creator doing what Jesus said not to do.

This perversion of His Spiritual Way of Love and Non-violence must stop. Jesus said, "Put your sword or gun back into its holster. All who live by the sword or gun will perish Spiritually by the sword or gun." No follower of Jesus can ever be a soldier of death. We can only give Life, we can never give death. We must be fully committed to Love and Peace while we have the chance to do so. As we sow, so shall we reap.

No man or government in this world has the right to force you into joining their military satanic armies. If you do join, they will want you to give up your free will power to choose what is right or wrong for yourself. Then you just become a brain-dead robot doing what some murdering General, Government or President tells you to do. Never sell your soul to the Devil for a gun, some money and medals. Keep your own Soul alive filled with Love.

How to Help in War

If a war engulfs our homeland, we can only partake in it as medical assistants or care givers and we must treat those wounded on both sides equally. We have come to save and be Lights in the dark not to condemn and kill like the children who become beasts of the flesh, false shadow identities of darkness out of which all evil and wars comes forth. Mahatma Ghandi took this avenue of approach during any wars he was involved in by organising medical assistants and stretcher bearers to help the suffering wounded. That is the Way of Jesus as well.

We are All Her Children

All human children on earth have a Spiritual body like yours as all our Spiritual bodies are formed by the same Loving Spiritual

Creator and Her Life-force to be Her Spiritual children. She Loves us all equally whether saint or sinner. Remember this when you meet someone for the first time to help reduce a false ego identity of arrogance from arising in you. Greet all children as friends and no one as a stranger for if you only greet your own brethren as friends and only Love those who Love you what a limited and constricted Spiritual practice that would be as Jesus Himself taught. Love flows freely into you from the Heavenly Spiritual World so let it flow freely to all.

Perfect Love flows through perfect equanimity and enables us to be a friend to all in whatever way they may need help. Some may need strong confronting Love to stop their evil ways, and some may need gentle supportive Love to comfort them in times of suffering. Warn those who are committing obvious evil to others or themselves, like the warmongers, they are in grave danger of destroying their physical life and their Spiritual Life and try to convince them in any way you can to stop their evil and change their ways.

Even if we fail to change them, we are still obliged to speak the Truth to them to try and save them even if it is dangerous for us to do so. It is not our fault if they will not listen to our warnings. They are still a child of our Loving Creator but lost in darkness and Heaven works through us to help them come out of it.

In other cases, where a child of our Loving Spiritual Creator may be homeless, a person who is ill and needs care, someone who has lost a loved one to death or just a little child who needs to be loved we provide gentle, supportive, comforting Love to them. Each individual we help will need a certain type of Love suited to their personal current situation and experience.

And the wisdom from Heaven that comes with Love will assist us in doing the best thing we can for them. We must bring Heaven's Love to all because that is the only answer to reduce all suffering in this world. All good things come forth from Love.

Do not Fear Death of the Body of Flesh

Jesus taught, "Do not worry about anyone who can kill your temporary body of flesh that must die one day anyway but can do no more to you. Rather be concerned that your Spiritual body and Soul are always filled and alive with the Loving Spiritual Life-force placed in them by our Loving Spiritual Creator in the Heavenly Spiritual World. For that body is Eternal and can take you to Heaven so do not let it wither and waste away while in the body of flesh and protect it above all else."

Jesus taught, " Do not over worry about your temporary Earthly life, earthly possessions, food or money and your body of flesh which must all come to an end one day anyway. But rather focus your attention on your Eternal Spiritual body and Soul mind of Love and becoming at one with it now by awakening and living out of it while you have the chance. For this will lead you to Heaven. Then bring Heaven's Love to other children in need while you wait to enter the Heavenly Spiritual World."

Jesus is always reminding us to move into and live out of our True Eternal Spiritual body and Soul mind of Love that does not die. This is an extremely important instruction so we may see this temporary material world for what it really is and interact with it every day of our life through our Eternal Spirit.

Without this approach we may become entangled in the body of flesh, through greed, self-indulgence and ego powers and forget about our Spiritual body and Life of Love. Fully commit to leading a Spiritual Life while here on Earth.

He even gave up His body of flesh voluntarily to show us we all have another more important Spiritual body with us right now that lives on in the Heavenly Spiritual World. As Spiritual children of Heaven on Earth we must all be prepared to do the same. There is no greater Way to shine the Light of the Spiritual Way of Love and belief in Heaven than making our body of flesh a secondary body that we can let go of and our Spiritual body our primary body that we hold onto. We must not be afraid to die to the temporary flesh but be more concerned that we may not have the Spiritual faith and courage to Live by the Spirit. But as Jesus said, "I have overcome this material world, and you can too."

Always be Ready to Leave

Always be ready for the body of flesh to die and come into the presence of our Loving Creator who is pure Love by always living out of Her Loving Life-force so you may awaken into a new Life in your Spiritual body and Soul mind of Love in the Heavenly Spiritual World.

As spiritual children we must look constantly towards the Heavenly Spiritual World every day of our life on Earth drawing inspiration, guidance, strength and the Loving Life-force we need to exist as True Spiritual children of our Loving Spiritual Creator in Heaven on Earth.

At any second, any hour, any day, any month of any year our body of flesh could drop dead, and we have to leave it behind. Jesus was always reminding us to stay in connection with the Heavenly Spiritual World and our Loving Spiritual Creator to be ready for when the death experience occurs and we come into the presence of Heaven and our Loving Spiritual Creator.

Jesus taught, "The land of a certain wealthy man yielded plentiful crops. He thought to himself, 'What shall I do as I have nowhere to store my crops?' So, he decided to pull down his barns and build greater ones to store all his crops and his goods. And he said to his Soul, 'Soul, you have many goods laid up for many years, relax and have a rest, eat drink and be merry.' But that very night his Spirit was called out of his body of flesh to be in the presence of our Loving Spiritual Creator." We never know the hour, or the day so always be filled with Love and share it with everyone and stay clean in Spirit. The more we are connected and infused with the Loving Spiritual Life-force from Heaven the more we have to give to others around us.

Some Children Will Condemn You

Jesus warned His spiritual followers of Love and Non-violence that we will be hated by many who oppose the Spiritual Way of Life. He taught, "In this material world of Love and hate, peace and war, selfishness and greed, you will be like sheep amongst wolves, and many will reject you and persecute you because of your Spiritual Way of Love, Forgiveness and Non-violence that I have taught you. Do not be concerned for Heaven can see you and your place there is safe even though your life here on Earth may not be."

True followers of great pacifist Spiritual Teachers like Jesus and Buddha can expect to be hated by followers of War Gods and Gods of Greed in this temporary material world. And what they really hate is you shining the Light of Love and Spiritual Truth upon them exposing their stinking, evil filth of war, greed and hatred by simply being a believer in the Way of Love that leads to the Heavenly Spiritual World which they have no belief in.

We must stand firm and strong in Spirit against those who are weaklings in Love and Spiritual Truth lost in the darkness of their own making. How else can we save them except by showing them the Way out of their darkness. But Jesus was also practical in His advice by teaching that if you are being persecuted for your Spiritual Way of Love in one place it is fine to move away from those children to a safer place if they are not willing to change.

We saw this persecution take place during the Vietnam war in Australia and the U.S.A. where children who refused to be drafted into their satanic armies were called draft dodgers and thrown into jail for refusing to take part in killing other children. Many American children who were called up to be drafted fled to Canada for protection from persecution for refusing to go and kill other children. Wonderful, Spiritual action in the face of evil.

The Rich Hardly Ever Enter Heaven

Jesus warned us many times, "Those children on Earth who worship money and amass fortunes of material wealth at the expense of Love are the poorest of all. Those who are rich and greedy hardly ever enter the Heavenly Spiritual World after their body of flesh dies. For what profit is it to a man if he gains the whole material world but loses his own Spirit and Soul."

As Spiritual children we do not spend our short life gaining and worshiping money or material possessions that will not go with us when our body of flesh dies. They are all just dust in the end. Instead, we gain all the Spiritual Love we can by sharing our own Love with others every day.

The more selfless we become and the more Love we spend on others the more we shall receive from Heaven. That is the best investment to make with our lives on Earth because that is all we need to enter the Eternal Heavenly Spiritual World of our Loving Creator after our body of flesh dies.

However, if we are blessed with having a large amount of money it is extremely important to share it with those who have none and those who are in need. There are many charities that need to be supported financially for many good causes. Just like our Spiritual Love must be a flowing river we give to others for it to be alive and well used, so also extra money or wealth we have accumulated must flow from us to others in need for it to be used in a healthy Spiritual Way also.

Then our material life and Spiritual Life are at one in purpose and in perfect harmony with the Loving Life-force in us that gives us True Life. This can only arise in a child who has awoken to their Spiritual identity and makes that their primary identity on Earth to live out of. As Jesus taught, "Give to him who asks of you and from him who wants to borrow from you turn not away."

Give of Yourself

If we are selfish and greedy this will block the Spiritual Loving Life-force flowing into us that comes from the Heavenly Spiritual World into our Spiritual bodies and Souls to share with other children. This greed is not just about money but also refusing to give compassion, support, comfort, kindness, sympathy and good advice to really let that child know they are not alone in this world. To hold them in your arms and let them know from your own mouth and words that you care about them whether you can help them financially or not.

The most valuable thing you can give someone are your heartbeats because you only have so many to spend. Eat and drink with the homeless on the streets or anyone who needs your help and give them your companionship and support no matter how poorly off they are or lost in sin they may be for those who are well have no need of a doctor or friend but those who are ill or alone do.

Always be generous in giving and sharing with others in need whether it is material things or your time. No matter how much Love flows out of you the Spiritual wellspring of Heavenly Love inside you connected to Heaven just fills you up again. If we have an excess of money share it with those who have none. If we have an excess of free time share it with those in need of companionship or volunteer to help in a Loving charity. Enrich your Spiritual Life by sharing your Love with others. Give of yourself because in the end that is all you really have.

We must be impartial and without prejudice and give the same quality of Love to all. As Jesus said, "If your eye or mind is single and sees all things with Love your whole body will be filled with Light. But if you are divided within between Love and hate, acceptance and rejection, us and them, you will be filled with darkness, and your own Spiritual Light will dim." If you see someone in distress never pass them by thinking someone else will take care of them, for our Loving Creator maybe calling you to do it for Her by drawing your attention to them.

Heaven will give us all opportunities to grow in Spiritual Love and strength. Usually, it is just through family commitments but often it is the challenge of seeing a stranger in trouble and being tempted to pass them by, not get involved and let someone else help them. But this is no coincidence, it is a direct gift offered to you from Heaven to open you up to experience more deeply the Universal enlightenment of Love within yourself that Jesus and Buddha experienced by letting go of your divided dualistic Love and just becoming at one with Love.

Don't Live in an Ivory Tower

Don't be tempted to create a false shadow identity to live out of made from Ego to dominate others and feel powerful. Never let the poisonous, stinking weed of arrogance grow in your garden and smother the flowers of Love. Living in an ivory tower built from your ego high above others is of little help to those in need on the ground.

Arrogance can send you deaf by not respecting the one talking to you and looking down on them as inferior, so you disregard everything they say to you. This can leave you stuck in ignorance by refusing to acknowledge even truthful, intelligent, logical things they may say to you to help you.

Never let your Love grow cold. Never exclude someone from your Love always try to include them. And if someone rejects your Love then pray that they receive it from someone else and keep on Loving those near you. Always stay True to your natural Spiritual self and Love others equally. For Love is the Greatest power of all.

Jesus said, "If you want to be Truly great become like a little humble child free of Ego, selfless and full of Love and be of service to all in need. For the Heavenly Spiritual world is made up of children like these."

Care Equally for Both of Your Bodies

Our Spiritual body and Soul come from a pure source of Love and being at one with our body of flesh while here on Earth we must maintain a decent and natural good life for it to remain clean. As Jesus taught, "Your body of dead flesh is just food for the vultures. Your Spiritual body will leave and be taken to be near to our Loving Spiritual Creator in Heaven." We must be ready.

Treat your body of flesh with respect and feed it healthy foods and drinks, give it exercise and rest. Never put dangerous substances into it that can hurt its structures or forcibly alter your mind. Without a healthy body of flesh our Spiritual body of Love cannot manifest our Love easily in this material world for other children. We are Spiritual riders on an Earthly horse, and we must take care of it and always hold on to the reigns to direct our horse's actions to be only actions of Love and Non-violence.

Jesus taught, "Do not be good on the outside but rotten on the inside. It is the dirt inside the cup that needs cleaning." Before we can truly help other children, who may be lost in selfish or evil ways we ourselves must be washed clean of such things.

Jesus taught, "Do not be a hypocrite and point out the speck in your brother's eye while you have a beam in your own eye. First remove the fault from your own life and then you may see clearly in Truth and Love to help remove the fault from your brother's life." Do not judge the child only the action. He who is without sin can cast the first stone.

It is our own inner cleansing of our Spirits that allows us to receive the Loving Spiritual Life-force from Heaven to share with others in need. We must remove any rubbish or filth that we may have dumped on the inner wellspring of Love blocking its flow before it can run clean to be fit to share with other children in need. Spiritual children keep their Spirits and Souls clean.

Jesus taught, "It is not what goes into our mouths that defiles our Spirits but what may come out of them. Control your thoughts and you will control your speech and your actions and if you follow My words, you will remain clean."

Buddha taught the same Teaching as Jesus when He said we must all remove the inner adventitious negativities from our minds otherwise we will never become Spiritually enlightened and free from the ignorance of not knowing who we really are.

As Jesus taught, "Always live out of Heavenly Spiritual Love, be compassionate, be merciful, do not condemn, do not judge, forgive, do no violence to other children and be pure in heart and you will become children of our Loving Spiritual Creator in the Heavenly Spiritual World."

Beware of Temptations that Lead you Astray

Jesus taught, "Enter the Heavenly Spiritual World through the narrow gate. For wide is the gate and broad is the way that leads to destruction, and many enter in through it. But small is the gate and narrow the Way that leads to Spiritual Life and few there are that find it. Woe to this world because it contains things that cause children to stumble. And woe to the one who brings them into existence."

We are all born into a dangerous dualistic material world and we must always be on our guard both physically and Spiritually. But our Spiritual Life can only be damaged by ourselves if we open the door to the robber called sin or wrongdoing and let it come into our life and control us. As Jesus said, "Whoever commits sin and wrong doings is a slave to sin and wrong doings."

We must stay in control of our own Life and be responsible for it. Wrongdoings can act like parasites draining us of all the good Loving Life-force we have accumulated through selfless Love. They can steal all the Spiritual merit and Spiritual strength we have stored up making our Spirits anemic and weak unable to fight against sin anymore. Our body of flesh is like a vase holding the Spirit of our Living waters and with each wrongdoing, we are punching a whole in the vase, and more water leaks out until there is none left to live out of as a Spiritual child of Heaven.

Keep your Spiritual Life healthy and strong by only doing good things and only letting good things come into your Spirit. Stand guard at the inner door to your Spiritual Life and Soul mind of Love and refuse entry to any darkness or evil that can poison or feed off your Spirit weakening your Spiritual Life-force of Love.

Just follow the words and Spiritual Way of Love and Non-violence that Jesus taught and they will be your protection and the Way that leads us through this dangerous, dualistic material world to our Eternal Heavenly Spiritual home. For the sheep are many and easily misled but we have the shepherd Jesus and His Teachings to guide and guard us and lead us to greener pastures.

Always say Sorry and Ask to be Forgiven

If you do something that offends another child and our Loving Spiritual Creator, say sorry to the other child and ask our Loving Creator to forgive you for abusing the precious gift of Spiritual Life She has offered you. Feel sincere remorse and the sin is washed clean. It is usually our false ego identity and arrogance that prevents us from saying the word 'sorry' when we need to say it to someone. We must let go of our ego, overcome embarrassment and speak truthfully as a child of Love to restore our Spirits to good health.

But no matter how far we may have gone into the dark by turning your back on the Love and Light of our Loving Creator shining upon us, we only have to turn around to face Her again to feel Her Love still waiting to embrace us once more. She will never hurt us but guide us patiently back with Her Light and Love as She never sees us as a lost cause because we are Her children and She only Loves us.

Her Light and Love can reach into the darkest places and bring us home to Heaven. So, we as Her children must also see no one we meet as a lost cause and keep Loving them and act as the Light that guides them home. Never abandon someone in need and do your best to stay alongside them as your circumstances permit. One day you may need someone like they do.

Remember We All Reap as We Have Sown

What you give out to others in this life is what you will receive in your next life. The Divine Spiritual Law of Reaping What We Sow is like a river between Earth and Heaven we have to cross. Spiritual children who have lived a life of Love just walk across on top of the water. Children weighed down by the selfish evil they have committed sink like a stone and have to be cleansed in accordance with the degree of evil they have committed. This Spiritual reality is perfect justice and like a mirror will reflect back to us whatever we have done. We must always try to do good and be Loving as it is the best way to benefit others and ourselves at the same time.

Do Not Run Away from Suffering

It is better to stay on the cross of suffering than to run away into sin. We must not try to avoid the Truth of suffering of our Earthly life by turning to something that is bad for us but look towards Heaven for strength to help us carry the weight of our cross. While it can be a very difficult challenge to confront, we must try to remember that one day all our Earthly crosses of suffering will be lifted from our shoulders when we enter the Heavenly Spiritual World in our Spiritual body. Also, serious sufferings we undergo in this world can generate a strong belief in a better Heavenly World and inspire us to push on towards it despite our current situation of pain or suffering in this material world.

Share the Spiritual Way of Love with Others

Demonstrate the Spiritual Way of Love and Non-violence to reach Heaven to all other children you meet by your own living example of Love as a child of our Loving Spiritual Creator in the Heavenly Spiritual World on Earth. And share the Spiritual Teachings and Way of Love if they are interested but never force them onto anyone or threaten anyone who is not interested by telling them they will not be saved. That would be evil and against the Teachings of Jesus when He said, "If anyone hears My words but does not do them, I do not judge that person. For I did not come to judge but only to save."

When sharing the Spiritual Teachings and Way of Love, Forgiveness and Non-violence to any other child try to gauge their ability to understand them and deliver the Teachings in a way to suit each child's capacity to receive them without being overwhelmed by them.

Learn about other Spiritual faiths and search for the Love, Forgiveness and Non-violence in them to find the common ground and avoid becoming exclusive and condemning of all other Spiritual Ways. However, if their Spiritual Teachings are dualistic coming from a source that is both Loving and caring and violent and murderous then be aware that it is a dualistic Way and not yet fully evolved into the Way of Light and Love and do not join with them.

But continue to stand up for the Way of Spiritual Love and Non-violence and never be intimidated by those who follow faulty Teachings and are still in the dark about this Spiritual Truth. And always forgive them if they abuse you for your Spiritual belief in only the Way of Love and Non-violence for this is the True source of our Spiritual Life. Just continue to Love those close to you no matter where you may find yourself on your journey through this material dualistic world.

Jesus Wants Us to be Just Like Him

Jesus did not want to be put on a pedestal high above the rest of us beyond our reach but rather He sat beside us, ate with us, drank with us, cried with us and explained how we can achieve exactly what He did by following His Spiritual Way of Love and Non-violence to get out of this world and enter the Heavenly Spiritual World.

Every teacher wants their students to have the same understanding as they have and become like them to teach others. Jesus wants us to have the same Spiritual understanding of Love that He had and wants us to teach others the same. At first, we are all His sheep but must become a shepherd to whatever degree we can just like Him and help guide others home through our Love. Jesus said, "I no longer call you my disciples but friends."

Jesus said, " He who believes in My Spiritual Way of Love and Non-violence and Lives out of it will not only be able to do the works I do but even greater than these." He never said He was the only child of our Loving Creator, that was a Jewish overlay put onto Him to distort His message. He actually said we can all equally be Children of our Loving Spiritual Creator, become enlightened and follow Him to the Heavenly Spiritual World after we pass through the death experience of our body of flesh.

Jesus said He was the Spiritual Way, the Spiritual Truth and the Spiritual Life and He wants us to follow Him and become awakened to our True Spiritual identity like Him so we can also enter the Heavenly Spiritual world beyond all suffering and join Him there.

His Spiritual Way of Love, Compassion, Forgiveness, Equanimity, Non-violence, Generosity and caring for those who have fallen down are the foundational Rocks we build our Spiritual Life on and as long as we have those in us, we will be a Spiritual child of Heaven on Earth. Loving our Spiritual Teacher Jesus with all your heart and Soul but not doing what He said to do, is like loving the tree but never tasting the fruit.

We All Have Two Families

We all have two families. One is our biological Earthly family, and the other is our Spiritual family made up of all children on Earth regardless of race, religion or no religion who live a Spiritual Life of Love, Compassion, Forgiveness, Equanimity and Non-violence. They are our Spiritual brothers and sisters who Live out of Spiritual Love within their biological families, towns and countries. This is the only way this Earth world can become Spiritual.

All children on earth are potentially Spiritual children of our Loving Spiritual Creator in the Heavenly Spiritual World but not everyone knows who they really are or how to be one. And many are lost in the darkness of their own making. We must show them who they really are and can be through our own Spiritual Life and the Way we live and treat others. The above are just some of the main Spiritual characteristics we must have to help us all become Spiritual children of our Loving Spiritual Creator in the Heavenly Spiritual World. Jesus said His words are what save us providing we follow them and live out of them. They can transform who we are and awaken our Spiritual body and Soul mind of Love to have Life Eternal in the Heavenly Spiritual World. And it is the only way I know of to bring Peace on Earth.

GOD IS LOVE LOVE IS LIFE

Chapter Twenty-Four

Jesus Rose from the Dead Yes and No

Whether Jesus rose from the dead after His crucifixion in His physical body of flesh, that was now immortal or whether His body of flesh decomposed like all our bodies do and He rose in a Spiritual body, we must still become at one with Divine Love now. This was His main message, to arise and awaken into a Spiritual Love for all, like the perfect Love of our Loving Spiritual Creator and become Spiritual children of our Loving Creator in the Heavenly Spiritual World and be able to live there after life on Earth. It is all about Love.

Unless we live a life of Loving others in the Spiritual Way He taught, no matter what type of body we may have after our body of flesh dies and returns to the earth, we will not be prepared to enter the Heavenly Spiritual World.

The resurrection accounts describe two different types of bodies attributed to Jesus after He rose from the dead body of flesh. Some accounts say He had the same body of flesh that died on the cross but was now immortal, while other descriptions clearly show He had a Spiritual body. Based on His own Teachings, I believe that His physical body of flesh died and decomposed after death, but He rose in His Spiritual Eternal Heavenly body. This would seem to be the logical Spiritual conclusion, being more in keeping with His actual Teachings as we will see in the following dialogue.

The General Teaching of Jesus

If we look closely at the Teachings of Jesus, we can see He leaves us with a consistent message from the Heavenly Spiritual World. Jesus said, "That which is born of the flesh is flesh. That which is born of the Spirit is Spirit. Marvel not that I tell you, you must be born again from above. Our Creator is Spirit and perfect Love therefore to be Her Spiritual children you must become perfected through Love."

Jesus became fully aware that we have two bodies with us right now on Earth. One we can see, the body of flesh, and one we cannot see, the body of the Spirit and Soul. The body of flesh dies and returns to the Earth from which it was formed, while the Spiritual body and Soul return to the source of their origin, the Divine Loving Spiritual Creator in a Heavenly Spiritual World.

But we must have lived out of the Loving Life-force in our Spiritual bodies and Souls while on Earth, to be able to enter the Heavenly world. If we become beasts of the flesh, killing, taking part in wars, robbing, worshipping money and material Earthly possessions, being greedy, uncaring, dishonest, self-indulgent and generally manifest no Spiritual Love from our Loving Creator given to us to live out of, we will not be prepared to enter the Spiritual Heavenly World.

If we created and lived out of a false identity, a shadow figure replacing our True Spiritual identity based only on the flesh often driven by inflated egos, we cannot join with all the other Spiritual children who are in the Heavenly Spiritual World living in great joy and Love in their True Spiritual identities. Our Loving Spiritual Creator is Love, Light and Truth as Jesus said and we must be in a similar state to be with Her in the Heavenly Spiritual World.

As Jesus said, "It is the Spirit that gives Life. The flesh profits nothing. The dead body of flesh is just food for the vultures as it has no life in it anymore."

Our Body of Flesh is Dualistic

The flesh body is made of Earth elements, sustained by Earthly foods, water and gases, it operates with biological interactive functions of a chemical nature and provides our brain minds with a limited Earthly experience through the senses. These experiences can include various extremes such as great pleasure or pain from the same body of flesh and its biological functions and chemical reactions. It produces various dualistic experiences for us to engage with and to learn from.

Our body of flesh also has an inbuilt mind of duality producing judgmental beliefs. Love or hate, help or hinder, comfort or abandon, save or kill, us and them, all different types of thoughts that divide and separate children from each other, from the natural creation we are born into, and from the One True Loving Spiritual Creator. By itself, the human brain mind cannot reach a unified understanding or view, only the Soul mind of Love can achieve that by awakening our Spiritual body and becoming at one with the Loving Spiritual Life-force that gives us True Spiritual Life.

For most of us it is usually only partially awake, intermittently awake, stagnating or covered in various degrees of darkness produced by committing anti-Love, dark shadow actions. The children who fully awaken to their Spiritual body and Soul Mind of Love are called Spiritually enlightened; Jesus was one of these.

Our Spiritual Body and Soul Mind are Singular

The Spiritual body and Soul mind is singular. It is only empowered by the Loving Spiritual Life-force, or Holy Spirit, of our

Loving Spiritual Creator from whom we receive the offer of this extraordinarily beautiful gift of Spiritual life that lies within us to discover and become at one with. The Soul Mind, once awoken, cannot be disturbed by dualistic thinking anymore as it sees all things through the Life-force of Love, and only wishes to bring an end to suffering and the causes of suffering. Our Spiritual body fits with our flesh body like water in a vase. It perfectly fits whatever flesh shape it is poured into. But our Spirit is not the vase, not the biological temporary body of flesh.

The nourishment it draws from is the fountain of Living Water that wells up inside our Soul Mind of Love and Spirit, bringing us to Eternal Spiritual Life. This comes from the source of our Spiritual being, our Loving Spiritual Creator in the Heavenly Spiritual World. Once we join with it fully, we will be "born again into Spirit," for its source is the Eternal Loving Spiritual Creator. This is what Jesus was referring to when talking to the Samaritan woman at the well.

Jesus said to the Samaritan woman, "If you knew the gift the Loving Creator offers you and who I am who says to you, 'Give me to drink,' you would have asked Me, and I would have given you Her Living Water. For whoever drinks of this Earthly water shall thirst again; but whoever drinks of the water that I shall give him, shall never thirst, for the water that I will give him will become in him a fountain of water welling up into Eternal Spiritual Life."

The words of Jesus when taken into our Soul Mind and Spirit to immerse ourselves in the Truth that they reveal, will act as a catalyst to awaken our True identity as Spiritual children of our Loving Spiritual Creator. As Jesus said, "My words they are Spirit, and they are Life." Those who awaken to this Truth shall never thirst again for Spiritual Life for they have awoken or been resurrected into their True Spiritual identity from the flesh identity.

This is the True meaning of the resurrection Jesus spoke about. Our body of flesh then becomes like a crystal lens in a light house for a while until it shatters, magnifying the Light of Love awoken in our Spiritual bodies and Souls within us to shine for all to see. Jesus said, "No one lights a candle and places it under a basket or body of flesh, but they place it on a stand, to give light to all who come near it. I am the Light of the world; he who follows Me will not walk in darkness but have the Light of Life." Light dispels darkness, ignorance and reveals the Truth. Just as most plants die without sunlight, so we die Spiritually without the Love from Heaven in us.

Jesus had a massive spiritual awakening and realized He had both an Eternal Spiritual body with a Soul Mind of Love empowered only by the Loving Life-force of our Loving Spiritual Creator, and also a body of flesh empowered only by Earth foods and elements, with a dualistic brain mind. Jesus referred to this Loving Life-force being in His Spiritual body when He said, "I can do nothing of Myself but only what our Loving Creator shows Me to do. Believe that I am in the Loving Life-force of our Loving Creator and Her Loving Life-force is in Me. The words that I speak to you are not of Myself but come from the Spiritual Life-force of our Creator who dwells with Me, and She does the works."

Like all of us, Jesus was very limited with only a physical body of flesh to help anyone. But once He awoke to His True identity as a Spiritual child of our Loving Creator, with a Soul Mind of Love and an Eternal Spiritual body, He could do anything empowered by the Spiritual Life-force She placed in His Spiritual body. The Spiritual power of Pure Love is way beyond any physical powers. It is literally other-worldly. It was this Loving Life-force in Him that enabled Him to perform healings for children's sick physical bodies by letting it flow from His Spiritual body into them.

So, in the old Gospel translations the 'Father' was in Him and He was in the 'Father' as He said. And He wants us to be in the same relationship by awakening to our True Spiritual identity and living out of it now. This is how we find the Kingdom of Heaven within us; it is a direct Spiritual connection. But it cannot be seen by human eyes, we must see it through our Spiritual eyes of Love and manifest it through our actions and words. His body of flesh died, and He rose in a Spiritual body into the Heavenly Spiritual World.

Our True Life is About Our Spirit

Various Teachings of Jesus clearly show this was His main message, which leads us into becoming Spiritual children of the Divine Loving Spiritual Creator in the Heavenly Spiritual World, while here on Earth.

Jesus said, "You cannot worship and serve the Loving Spiritual Creator and material things at the same time."

Jesus said, "Flesh gives birth to flesh, Spirit gives birth to Spirit. Marvel not that I tell you, you must be born again from above."

Jesus said, "It is the Spirit that gives Life. The flesh profits nothing."

Jesus said, "Do not be afraid of (illnesses or) those who can kill your body of flesh but are unable to kill your Soul and Spirit."

Jesus said, "What shall it profit a man, if he should gain the whole world but lose his own Spirit and Soul."

Jesus said, "For in the Spiritual resurrection, they neither marry nor are given in marriage, and they cannot die anymore. For those who are considered ready to attain to Heavenly Spiritual Life, will be like Angels in Heaven." No longer biological but Spiritual bodies with a Soul Mind of Love to live out of as Spiritual children of our Loving Creator, who gives us these Spiritual bodies to have Eternal Life in the Heavenly Spiritual World, if we wish to accept them.

Jesus said, "The Loving Creator is Spirit, and those who wish to adore our Loving Creator must come to Her in Spirit and in Truth to be with our Loving Creator." The Loving Creator did not say to come in the flesh with a dualistic identity.

Jesus said, "The lamp of the body is the eye, if your eye is single and perfect, then your whole body shall be full of Light. But if your eye is imperfect, dualistic, then your body will be filled with darkness." We must understand our Loving Spiritual Creator correctly. Only the Soul Mind of Love is Singular, whole and perfect. In the sermon on the mount Jesus said the Love of our Spiritual Creator is perfect, so if we wish to be children of our Loving Creator, our Love also must be perfect. This is Spiritual Love, not a brain mind dualistic, biological love, given to some and withheld from others. It is commonly known as Agape.

Jesus said, "Lay not up for yourselves treasures on earth, where moth and rust does corrupt and decay, but lay up for yourselves treasures in the Heavenly Spiritual world, where neither moth nor rust can decay. For where your treasure is, there your Soul will be also." All things in the material world of temporary life decay, disintegrate and do not last including our bodies of flesh. Only the Spiritual World of Love and Truth is Eternal Life.

Jesus said, "Beware and be on your guard against every form of greed; for not even when one has a great abundance does your life consist of your possessions." Our True real Life is Spiritual and empowered by a Spiritual Loving Life-force, not money or material wealth.

Jesus said, "It is easier for a camel to pass through the eye of a needle, than it is for a man of material riches to enter the Heavenly Spiritual world." The only good purpose of having great wealth is to share it with those who have none otherwise it may drag your Spirit down into the quicksand of the material dirt.

Jesus said, "The Kingdom of the Heavenly Spiritual world does not come with signs to be observed, with the human eye so no one can say, 'Look here it is' or 'There it is'. For the Kingdom of the Heavenly Spiritual world is within you." Jesus is talking about our Spiritual body and Soul mind of Love within us that we must become at one with that connects us to Heaven.

Jesus said, "The Heavenly Spiritual World is like a treasure hidden in a field, which a man found and hid, and in great joy over finding it, he sells all that he has and buys that field." Here Jesus is referring to discovering you have a Spiritual body and Soul mind of Love empowered only by the Loving Spiritual Life-force of our Creator, in your own Earthly field of the body of flesh. And once you become at one with this True Spiritual Soul identity, you can let go of your flesh identity and material things.

Based on all of these Teachings and others that Jesus gave I believe the physical body of Jesus died on the cross, was buried and decayed returning to the Earth elements from which it was formed, as all our bodies of flesh do. I believe only His Soul Mind and Spiritual body rose to the Heavenly Spiritual World. After Jesus died, He appeared in His Spiritual body to the disciples, not flesh, and the disciples had to cover up what really happened in order to not frighten away the Jews from believing in Him and following His teachings and Spiritual Way of Love.

Why Cover Up the Truth

Firstly, we must establish why the disciples altered the facts. We can see the Jewish understanding of having a Spiritual body as well as a body of flesh, as Jesus taught, was very undeveloped as seen in this conversation Jesus had with Nicodemus.

Nicodemus, a Pharisee and ruler of the Jews came to speak with Jesus at night and said to Him, "Teacher, we know that you are a great Teacher come from God; for no man can do these miracles and signs that you are doing unless God is with him." Jesus answered, "Truly, truly I say to you, except a man be born again he cannot see the Kingdom of Heaven."

Nicodemus said to him, "How can a man be born when he is old? Can he enter a second time into his mother's womb and be born again?" Jesus replied, "Truly, truly I say to you, unless a man is born again of Water and the Spirit, he cannot enter into the

Heavenly Spiritual World of the Divine Loving Spiritual Creator. That which is born of the flesh is flesh. That which is born of the Spirit is Spirit. Marvel not that I said to you, you must be born again from above. The wind blows where it wishes and you hear the sound of it, but you know not where it comes from or where it goes. So, it is for everyone who is born of the Spirit." Nicodemus said, "How can this be.?" Jesus answered and said, "Are you a Teacher of Israel and do not understand these things? Truly, I say to you, we speak of what we know and testify of what we have seen, but you do not accept our testimony. If I told you of Earthly things and you do not believe, how will you believe if I tell you of Heavenly things?"

Clearly, even the Jewish Spiritual leaders had no idea of the Spiritual Truth that Jesus knew about. Nicodemus could not even conceive of having a body of anything but flesh, when he thought the only birth is a physical birth from a womb. He did not understand at all that we might have another Spiritual body and Soul mind of Love waiting for us to discover with us right now. He could not grasp what Jesus was saying. The concept was generally foreign to the Jewish children.

Jesus had awoken to this Spiritual reality and had two bodies alive in one. Most of us have a Spiritual body and Soul mind that is a bit drowsy at times or even totally asleep, but only a few have it fully awoken and live out of it on Earth. And that is the real problem for us. The entire world would change if this awakening occurred within us all. All war would cease, the armaments industry would be dismantled, children would no longer be trained to kill in armies, greed and violence would be unheard of, the wealth of the earth would be shared, we would live simple healthy lives of Love with minimal material possessions caring for the Earth and although natural physical suffering would still exist we would never make it worse, only help reduce it.

Jesus had spent years trying to teach the disciples how to awaken to this Spiritual Truth, experience it themselves, and then teach the good news to others. And to share the Loving Life-force of our Creator within their Souls and Spirit, by healing the sick and the lame of their physical infirmities. A temporary healing. But it was teaching the Spiritual Way of Love that brought those dead to their Spirit back to Life that was the main objective of Jesus to help children reach the Eternal Spiritual World of Heaven. But even the Jewish disciples with Jesus were still heavily influenced by the Old Testament Teaching of a dualistic God and could not grasp it easily, as seen in this episode.

While Jesus was on the way to Jerusalem, He had to pass through a village of the Samaritans and sent messages ahead to arrange overnight accommodation, but He could not stay longer with them. They did not want to provide accommodation as they were upset that He was not going to stay with them. When His disciples James and John saw Jesus being insulted like this they said to Jesus, "Lord, do you want us to command fire to come down from Heaven and consume them like Elijah did?" But Jesus turned and rebuked them saying, "You do not know what kind of Spirit you are of; for I do not destroy men's lives but save them."

Even though they were with Him constantly they still had no understanding of their True Spiritual identity that Jesus was trying to help them find within themselves to become Spiritual children of our Loving Creator. Other examples of the disciples not knowing our Loving Spiritual Creator and how to become Her Spiritual children of Love are found throughout the Gospels. The main point based on a learned Jewish leader like Nicodemus and His own disciples not understanding the inner Spiritual transformation and awakening that Jesus taught to become Spiritual children, explains the cover up by the disciples who said His body of flesh rose, not His Spiritual body and Soul. The Jews were simply not advanced enough in their Spiritual understanding of our Spiritual Life, our Loving Spiritual Creator and the Heavenly Spiritual World, for them to accept it.

Disciples Already Saw His Spiritual Body Twice

The disciples had already seen Jesus in His Spiritual body at least twice, while He was alive in the flesh. The first time was when He walked to them on the water in this account. 'And in the fourth watch of the night Jesus came walking to them, walking on the sea. When the disciples saw Him walking on the water, they were terrified, and said, "It is a ghost!" And they cried out in fear. But immediately Jesus spoke to them saying, "Take courage, it is I, do not be afraid."

And Peter answered Him saying, "Lord if it is you, bid me come to you on the water?" Jesus said, "Come." So, Peter got out of the boat and walked on the water and came towards Jesus; but when he saw the wind he became frightened and began sinking crying out, "Lord, save me!" Jesus immediately reached out His hand and caught him saying to him, "You of little faith, why did you doubt?" And they got back into the boat and the wind ceased and they were utterly astounded, for they did not understand about the loaves being multiplied either, for their hearts were still hardened.'

They had no real understanding of the Power of the Spiritual Loving Life-force and had yet to awaken Spiritually and be born again into their own Spiritual bodies and Soul minds of Love Jesus was trying to teach them about.

This is a really beautiful account of two things. Firstly, Jesus had become at one with the Spiritual Loving Life-force of our Loving Creator and was now able to have a full experience of His Spiritual body and Soul mind of Love, empowered only by the Loving Life-force of our Spiritual Creator. The Spiritual power of our Loving Creator can completely override any physical law or physical thing and remain unaffected by it.

Jesus simply moved fully into His Spiritual body and Soul Mind of Love, and because His Spiritual body was not affected by the laws of gravity, He could easily carry His physical body with it over the water. Just the thought from His Soul mind, empowered by Divine Love, made it happen. This is also how He healed sick physical bodies. He was able to do it with just a thought from His Soul mind of Love and the Loving Spiritual Life-force that was now sustaining His awakened Spiritual body and Soul flowed out of Him to whoever needed it and healed them.

Jesus describes this Spiritual Loving Life-force in Himself that we can all have in these words. "Of mine own self, I can do nothing. The words I speak are not my own but come from our Loving Spiritual Creator whose Life-force lives in Me, and whose Loving Spiritual Life-force in My Spirit enables Me to do these works and miracles. Truly, truly, I say to you, that whoever believes in Me and My Teachings, will also do these works that I do, and even greater works than these will he do."

Secondly, the walking on the water account also provides a good example of all of us through Peter. Encouraged by the sound of the voice of Jesus, coming from what he initially thought was a ghost or Spirit, Peter did walk on the water while he remained focused on Jesus. Peter had moved into his Soul Mind and Spiritual body without even knowing it. But then he took his eye off Jesus and noticed the physical waves and winds. This broke the Spiritual experience he was having through his own Soul Mind and Spiritual body empowered only by the Loving Spiritual Life-force of the Creator in him and he fell back into the physical mind of the mortal flesh.

He then became afraid of drowning and his body of flesh dying. He calls to Jesus for help, and of course Jesus grabs on to him as He grabs onto all of us who feel we are drowning and dying. But He acknowledges Peter's effort to move into his Spirit by telling him he was doing well, and he should have kept going and had no doubt about the Power of our Loving Creator's Life-force in his Spirit to carry him over the water.

Many times, throughout the Gospels Jesus tells us to never doubt the power of our Loving Spiritual Creator who is always with us and empowers our Soul and Spirit through Her Spiritual

Life-force She gives to us, if we only believe. I also wonder if the Spiritual body of Jesus, that would have been full of the Light of the Loving Creator, was glowing softly as He walked on the water. This would have added to their fear, but we do see this glowing effect of the Spiritual body in the following account.

The second time the disciples see Jesus move fully into His Spiritual body is at the transfiguration. 'Jesus took with Him, Peter, James and John and went up on a high mountain by themselves. And He was transfigured before them; and His face shone like the sun, and His garments became as white as Light. And two other figures appeared talking with Him. The disciples were amazed but fell face down on the ground and were terrified when they heard a voice speak from the sky. And Jesus came to them and said, "Get up, do not be afraid. Tell what you have seen to no one until I have risen from the dead (body of My flesh)." Here Jesus displays His Spiritual body that was now fully awakened within Him and deliberately shows it to the disciples with Him, but he tells the disciples not to mention it to the others as they were not yet ready to understand this.

It was obviously quite intentional on the part of Jesus, to select a few of His closest disciples to see His Full Spiritual body. And even though they saw His physical body walk up the hill and knew it was Him standing there they were still completely confused to see His Spiritual body suddenly appear to be glowing.

Again, this shows the enormous challenge that Jesus had to face to bring them out of the Old Testament dualistic God religion of the Jews, and into the singularity of the One True Loving Spiritual Creator. They still had no idea that they had this same Spiritual body within them as He did, with a Soul mind of Love empowered only by the Loving Spiritual Life-force of our Loving Creator in a Heavenly Spiritual World.

He knew He would appear to more of them in His Spiritual body after He died, so this incident is very important. He told them to wait until He had risen from His dead body before telling anyone of this so the three disciples can testify later that they also saw Him in His Spiritual body at the transfiguration before His body of flesh died.

This would help them all realise they must also have these Spiritual bodies with them now, but they are dormant as in most of us. And that is exactly what He is trying to get His disciples and us to all wake up to and realise. That we all have two different bodies, and we must awaken and become Eternal Spiritual children of our Loving Spiritual Creator in the Heavenly Spiritual World, while here in the temporary body of flesh.

And these Spiritual bodies do not die once they come alive by living out of them with the Loving Spiritual Life-force that empowers them here on Earth. This is the Spiritual body of Jesus that they saw after His physical death, to give them a great gift by appearing to them in this way. Life goes on in the Spirit after the flesh dies and returns to the Earth, so become at one with your True Spiritual identity now, and as Jesus said Himself, you will not really die at all.

But the disciples had a big problem after the resurrection when Jesus appeared to them in a Spiritual body only. We can see how terrified they were of seeing spiritual beings or ghosts in general. How were they going to convince anyone else of what they now knew about Jesus being resurrected in His Spiritual body from the dead body of flesh?

If we look at all the accounts following His burial, we can try to untangle the variations and additions that were placed in by the disciples, to cover up the Spiritual resurrection and replace it with a resurrection of the flesh. This would remove the fear that this would have caused for potential followers of the Way of Jesus, thinking He had become a Ghost or Spirit. Spirits were beings that Jews generally wanted nothing to do with in their culture. Instead, they were generally feared as we saw with the disciples who even knew Jesus for years yet were still frightened seeing Him in His Spiritual body.

I believe Peter and John hid the body on the Friday night after Jesus appeared to the eleven disciples, including Thomas, in His Spiritual body and they went and checked the tomb finding His dead physical body was still there. If they left it there for the Jews to find, the Jews would call them all liars and charlatans if they said they had seen Him alive and well and He spoke to them.

That would mean the end of His powerful Spiritual Teachings being passed on as everyone would leave the disciples and go back to following the two headed God of the Jews. So, Peter and John most likely hid the body and agreed on a secret cover story that His body of flesh came back to life and shared the Truth with no one. It may be possible that they told the other disciples, and Mary Magdalene may have had an important role but whoever knew they all agreed to cover up the Truth. But the less that knew the better the Truth would remain a secret.

The Gospel authors had a very difficult task to leave clues to lead you to the Truth that Jesus rose in a Spiritual body while planting false accounts that He had a body of flesh to cover it up at that time to make Jesus more acceptable to the Jews. The false flesh account stories for the Jews are simple and obvious, but they retained more subtle clues obvious only to those who understand the Teachings of Jesus. Such as His Spiritual body looking different after He rose and they did not easily recognize Him. And the most powerful one in John where Jesus tells Mary not to try and hold onto Him. John is obviously telling us Jesus was now in a Spiritual body no longer in a body of flesh like Mary's and she was not able to hold Him with her body of flesh. They couldn't openly teach it at the time but now it can be and should be to fully open up the Spiritual Way Jesus gave us to follow.

Different Gospel writers placed stronger Jewish overlays onto Jesus than others. Matthew was the worst and tried to have followers only see Jesus through a Jewish lens and corrupted some of the sayings to achieve this. John was at the other end and had some of the most Spiritually mystical sayings of Jesus about inner transformation like the Nicodemus and the Samaritan woman at the well dialogues.

Blind faith is dangerous; we all must do our best to seek the Spiritual Truth that Jesus taught by looking only at the words of Jesus ourselves and not the overlays of the Old Testament put onto Him. Never mix the Old Wine of War and Limited Love with the New Wine of Universal Divine Love or you will taint it, and it will no longer be pure.

Jesus said, "Do not try to tear a piece of the new understanding of our Loving Spiritual Creator and try to sew it onto the old understanding of the two headed God of the Jews as they do not match and it will lift off. The new from the old."

Possibilities of How the Resurrection Story Unfolded

1: Jesus dies in agony on Friday as His body of flesh is tortured to death on the cross.

2: Jesus' physical body died on the cross, but His Spiritual body and Soul immediately rose and left it behind. Neither His Spiritual Body and Soul nor physical body rose three days later. We see this in a statement He made while being crucified. One of the criminals being crucified alongside him said, "Jesus, remember me when you go into the Spiritual Heavenly World." Jesus replied to him, "Truly I say to you, today you will be with Me in the Heavenly Spiritual World." He did not say, "In three days' time, when My dead body of flesh comes alive again, you will be with Me in the Heavenly Spiritual World."

Jesus also taught this Spiritual Truth applies to all of us as well as Himself when He spoke about the two in a field, two women at the millstone, two in a single bed and two on a couch. Their body of flesh died and is of no use anymore and can be fed to the vultures and immediately their Spiritual body and Soul are taken to be near to the one who created them, our Loving Spiritual Creator to reap as we have sown.

He did not say their bodies of flesh will be raised from the dead three days later to be near our Loving Creator because they had already left their body of flesh in their Spiritual body just as He did. And He did not say there is an apocalyptic last day of judgement at some distant time when their disintegrated body of flesh rises back up from the earth because the day we die is our judgement day and we better be ready now because that is what Jesus is Teaching and saying.

3: Joseph of Arimathea and Nicodemus take down the body of Jesus that Friday evening, and place it in a tomb nearby, as it was getting late for the Jewish day of preparation for the Sabbath day which was upon them. They bring a mixture of Myrrh and Aloes to place around the body of Jesus, as is the burial custom, and they wrap it in a linen cloth. They rolled a stone against the door of the tomb and departed.

4: Mary Magdalene alone or possibly with Mary the mother of Joses, saw where they placed His body, then went home. They also would have seen them carrying the spices that they took with them to prepare His dead body with.

5: Friday night all of the followers of Jesus were in shock, panicked and were frightened that they might also be killed for being followers of Jesus. We see this clearly when even Peter denied knowing Him three times. Two followers fled the city probably that afternoon or Saturday evening on the road to Emmaus to get away to a safer place. They were talking together about what had happened to Jesus on the road, when Jesus came up to them and asked what they were talking about.

Importantly we are told, their eyes were kept from recognizing Him. He was in His Spiritual body and clearly it is different to His body of flesh but still in human form. Later when He was sitting down to eat with them Jesus took the bread, blessed it and broke it and gave it to them. And then they realized it was Jesus when He spoke the familiar words to them, then He just vanished out of sight. A body of flesh cannot do that. A Spiritual body can.

That hour, they rose and returned to Jerusalem and found the eleven disciples gathered together. Thomas was also there as correctly recorded in Luke 24:33 and they told them what had happened on the road, and how they realized it was Jesus they saw and spoke with. The long infill about what Jesus supposedly said to them in Luke's Gospel is a Jewish overlay added by the author to present Jesus as the promised Messiah of the Jews.

Only John's Gospel mentions an account of Thomas not being present and goes to great trouble to establish Jesus had a body of flesh not a Spiritual body to help cover up the Truth. It also maligned Thomas to cast dispersion on the Thomas Gospel that was also in wide circulation and had some original sayings of Jesus that were being deliberately altered and distorted.

This was because the dominant belief taking hold of the early Jewish followers of Jesus wanted to view Him through the Old Testament Jewish lens, as being a Jewish Messiah and sacrificial lamb for our sins. This was shifting the emphasis of His Teachings from practicing what He taught to awaken Spiritually and become just like Him, to worshiping Him and placing Him on an ivory tower above us all and no one can be like Him. Falsely teaching He is the only child of our Loving Spiritual Creator. Exactly the opposite of what He intended and clearly taught.

This seriously undermines His main message of seeing Him standing beside us, supporting us like the great Teacher and loyal friend that He is even when we fall down, to guide us to follow His Teachings and help us awaken to Our True Spiritual identity as well, as children of our Loving Spiritual Creator in the Heavenly World the same as He now was. Jesus saw this problem developing while He was still alive, so He clearly warned His followers saying, "You call Me Lord, Lord but do not do the things I command you to do." If we only praise Him, it can become an easy-out clause not to practice what He actually said to do.

The Gospel of Thomas records sayings of Jesus that concentrate more on personal inner transformation, rather than on worshipping Him as a sacrificial lamb for our sins. Instead of making Him unique and on a level that is unattainable to the rest of us, as seen in Matthew, Mark, Luke and some of John's Jewish overlays, the Thomas Gospel encourages us to become just like Him, equal to Him as a Spiritual child of our Loving Creator.

This was the true intention of Jesus as He said in John 15:15. "No longer do I call you servants for the servant does not know what the master is doing, but I call you friends for all things that I know I have made known to you." We still rely on Him to show us the Way, so He is still our lifesaver, and we openly acknowledge this and thank Him for what He did for us. But I believe He would rather we walk beside Him in Spirit, than stay bowed down before Him just praising Him and calling out His name.

The Thomas Gospel was most likely banned at the meeting held in Carthage in 397 A.D. by early church leaders, and no one was allowed to have a copy under threat of punishment, along with other books about Jesus also banned at the time. Thankfully, a nearly fully intact copy was found buried in a jar in 1945 near Nag Hammadi in Egypt.

6: The two followers on the way to Emmaus rush back to the disciples in Jerusalem that Friday or Saturday night and meet with them and those with them, probably including Mary Magdelene, in the locked room where they had gathered. And while they were telling them about seeing Jesus alive, Jesus suddenly appears amongst them.

Jesus said, "Peace be with you." But they were all startled and frightened and thought they were seeing a Spirit. (Correct. He was in His Spiritual body.) Jesus said, "Why are you so troubled, and why do questions arise in your hearts? See, it is I. As our Loving Spiritual Creator sent Me, even so I now send you." And when He said this, He breathed on them and said, "Receive the Holy Spirit." And then He suddenly vanished. I believe this is the correct version, all the other things were added to make children believe He had a body of flesh by the Gospel authors or others.

These added words are contradictory to the words Jesus spoke to Mary when He appeared to her in His Spiritual body. Luke adds Jesus saying, "See My hands and feet, handle Me and see; for a Spirit has no flesh and bones as you see that I have. Have you anything here to eat?" They gave Him a piece of broiled fish, and He ate it before them. These words are too specific and clearly contrived by Luke to directly counteract the very thing that was the Truth. Here we see Jesus saying to touch Him to prove He has a body of flesh and give Him earthly food to eat but He says to Mary in John's Gospel not to try and touch Him because He now only had a Spiritual body not physical and John intentionally includes this clue for those who can see. The Luke additions are false and part of a deliberate cover up to not mention He really had a Spiritual body to protect His Teachings from dying out and not frighten the Jews away from following Him.

7: I believe this is what likely followed. The disciples would have been in total amazement and bewildered at what just happened. They all know it was Jesus, but they all know He was not in a body of flesh but a Spiritual or ghost body that just appears and disappears. But He was clearly alive and well and spoke to them. They were still not aware we have Spiritual bodies as well as physical bodies. They must have had a very intense discussion about what they just saw after witnessing His physical death on the cross earlier that day. How could they tell people they saw Jesus alive and well but now He was a Spirit. Souls or Spirits have no form in Sheol where the dead go according to Jewish beliefs at the time. No Jewish person would want to follow a dead Spirit without form from the underworld of Sheol.

The only way to verify they really did see Jesus, was for someone to go to the tomb and see if His physical body was still there. If it was then they would know for certain that He appeared to them in His Spiritual body that He had been teaching them all about for the last three years. But it was Sabbath time and to go out they would have to go in secret. I believe Peter and John agreed to quietly sneak out later that night either Friday or Saturday after Jesus appeared to them to check the tomb for themselves.

8 : Although we do not have enough definite information as to what really happened, we can see possibilities based on the accounts. I believe just Peter and John went to the tomb secretly Friday or Saturday night after Jesus appeared to them in His Spiritual body. They were two of His closest disciples who also saw He had a Spiritual body at the transfiguration and when He walked on the water. So, they were in a better position to believe.

9: If Mary Magdelene was in the room with them, they would have needed her to show them where the tomb of Jesus was so would have taken her with them. If she was not there, they would have gone and gotten her. She was a devoted follower of Jesus. When they got to the tomb, Mary either stayed or was sent home by them. They rolled the stone back, went in and found His dead physical body still laying there. But to make sure it was Jesus and they had the correct tomb they had to remove some of the linen bandages and put them aside. And then they saw it was Jesus. If Mary was there, she saw it too. If not, only they knew. So, at this stage the Truth is only known by two or three followers.

10 : This was now a serious dilemma for Peter and John as disciples of Jesus who were entrusted by Jesus to spread the Spiritual Word, the Truth and the Spiritual Way to Heaven. The truth was that they all saw Jesus alive and well, but after now finding His dead body of flesh, He was obviously in a Spiritual body when He appeared to them. How could they deal with this and still tell people the Truth. If they told everyone they saw Jesus was alive and well any Jewish religious authority, who hated them and Jesus, could just go to the tomb and find His dead body and accuse them of being liars, and charlatans. And that could bring an end to people believing them anymore when they shared His Teachings. And that would risk the total collapse and destruction

of all His Spiritual Teachings and the Spiritual Way of Love that leads us to Heaven, and they would be lost forever.

And if they say He had a Spiritual body it will turn people away from following the Spiritual Way of Jesus because of the belief in Sheol and the formless underworld where all dead Souls go. So, how could He appear to them if He is formless. The Jews were not ready for this Truth. So, they covered up the one thing that could threaten to end the Spiritual Way of Jesus and destroy His Spiritual Teachings that lead us all to the Heavenly Spiritual World by hiding His dead body of flesh.

11: John and Peter either returned and told the disciples the dead body of Jesus was still there, and they must have seen His Spiritual body or did not go back and tell them but kept it to themselves and possibly Mary if she also saw His dead body.

12: At some point in the discussions about what to do and say, either between the disciples or just John and Peter and possibly Mary, someone must have suggested a compromise of the Truth. They can tell everyone they saw Him after He died on the cross and He was alive and well, which is the Truth. They can say this with great conviction and honesty. But then if they say He still had a physical body of flesh, by just adding some fictitious details to the story as in Luke, it will cover up the Truth that He was actually in a Spiritual body.

Then this might remove any fears about following Jesus for the Jews and save His Teachings and Spiritual Way from being lost. For the Jews were familiar with an Old Testament story about Elijah in 2 Kings 2:11 where they say he was just walking along when a chariot and horses swept down from Heaven and carried him to Heaven while still in a body of flesh.

So, it was possible for them to say a similar thing must have happened to Jesus to cover the Truth that He actually rose in a Spiritual body while His body of flesh was dead and lifeless just as He taught them it would be. That would mean they would have to move the body and hide it so the Jews can't find it. But it was a serious compromise of the Truth in a very difficult situation to save His Teachings.

13: A secret is best kept by the fewest number, so I believe Peter and John decided not to tell the other disciples. And so, after searching for a secret place where no one would ever find it, they took the dead body of Jesus during Friday or Saturday night and sealed it in a secret location. They left the original tomb door open, along with leaving the linen cloths they removed to make sure it was Jesus, for someone else to discover the body was missing. This would take any suspicion off them, and they can act as surprised as everyone else. Then once they hid the body of Jesus they went back and told the disciples nothing about what they did and only Mary may have known and they waited for the empty tomb to be discovered.

14: The other possibility is they went back and told all the disciples who were in agreement with what Peter and John did and why it was so important to hide His dead body of flesh to preserve the Spiritual Teachings and Way of Jesus. They were all loyal followers of Jesus and knew the Spiritual Teachings and Way of Jesus were under threat, along with themselves, so may have gone along with the plan. But I feel only Peter and John with or without Mary were actually involved in the coverup.

15: Mary had an important role in all of this, but it is uncertain to what extent. If she was with John and Peter and saw the dead body of Jesus, then she would be bound to keep it a secret if Peter and John directed her to do so. And she would have understood why they were going to hide it to help protect the Teachings of her master Jesus whom she dearly loved. It is quite reasonable to imagine her loyalty and love for Him would inspire her to do anything for Him to help protect the legacy of His Teachings. We can recall how Mary sat at the feet of Jesus listening to Him teach when He visited Her house while Martha was busy serving drinks and food. If that is the case then they may have agreed that Mary could come to the open tomb on Sunday morning, find it open and come and tell only them but act surprised to everyone else. If they sent Mary home after she led them to the tomb, then her involvement was accidental.

16: If it is Peter, John and Mary, they would have had to do this under cover of dark while not being noticed by any Jewish authorities. But great things can be achieved and fear overcome when Love and loyalty is the driving force. If we follow the real possibility that only these three know the Truth, then on Sunday morning Mary goes to the opened tomb by herself as planned or accidentally and the tomb is open, and no one else has discovered it yet being frightened now to be seen as a follower of Jesus.

17: It is now very interesting that in John's account after Mary finds the tomb empty, she goes to only tell Peter and John of the empty tomb, none of the other disciples. A perfect execution of a secret clandestine action by three of the most dedicated followers of Jesus to protect His Teachings and Spiritual Way from destruction, if it works and everyone believes the cover story. And since John is writing the Gospel he can adjust anything in anyway he wants to fit the desired outcome.

18: Peter and John go with Mary to the tomb all knowing it is empty and then Peter and John just go home but can now tell everyone that Mary found the tomb empty and they went and checked, and the body of Jesus was not there. If all the remaining disciples saw Jesus in His Spiritual body on Friday or Saturday night but did not know what Peter, John and Mary did then it would be easy to convince them that Jesus must have appeared to them in His body of flesh because of the empty tomb.

19: Mary stays at the tomb after Peter and John leave and then John records this powerful encounter between Mary and Jesus where he is clearly describing the body of Jesus is a fully Spiritual body that Mary cannot hold. But later he adds the very strong doubting Thomas story saying the opposite, that Jesus was in a body of flesh to throw in the red herring and help with the coverup that he and Peter set up. He did not want to destroy the

Spiritual Truth about Jesus rising in a Spiritual body so made that reference more subtle and the false flesh references far more obvious. As Jesus said, "He who has ears to hear, let him hear."

20: They had to wait until Sunday to start telling people that He appeared to them and they saw Him alive and well to give them time to hide His body of flesh. And since the tomb was not technically discovered empty until Sunday that fed into saying Jesus rose on the third day instead of the day He actually died. Jews also believed it took three days for your Soul or Spirit to leave your body and go to Sheol so they just had to switch from saying His Spirit left on the third day to His body left on the third day. It was easy for the Jewish Gospel authors to just add the words 'in three days' in the right place or search through the Old Testament to find references of being raised from the dead after dying with some specifically saying on the third day to help the cover story.

21: The main purpose of the Teachings of Jesus was to raise those dead to their Spirit back to True Spiritual Life. The dead flesh profits nothing. Feed it to the vultures. He constantly taught not to worry too much about your body of flesh as it is only food for the vultures at the end but rather be concerned about the state of your Spiritual body and Soul mind of Love which need to be alive and healthy to enter the Heavenly Spiritual World.

22: There are only three accounts in the Gospels, repeated in Mark, Luke and Matthew of Jesus actually saying Himself that He will be killed and rise again 'on the third day.' It would be easy for the writers to insert the words, 'in three days.' He was certainly predicting His upcoming fate and death and resurrection but based on His own Teachings He more likely said, "I will be killed but (in three days) will rise again." As He said, "I lay down My (physical) life in order to take My (Spiritual) Life up again. I have power to lay it (physical) down and power to take it (Spiritual) up again." He now had His Living Spiritual body as well as His body of flesh as He taught that we all have if we only searched for it.

"Flesh only gives birth to Flesh. Spirit only gives birth to Spirit. Marvel not that I tell you. You must be born again from above."

There are two other sayings inferring He will rise in three days. One in John where He refers to rebuilding the Temple in three days, saying, "Destroy this temple and (in three days) I will raise it up." Jesus is referring to His Spiritual body but it would be easy to insert the 'in three days' words here also to help reinforce the cover up story.

One of the other major Jewish overlays to cover up the truth is using Jonah 1:17 'And the Lord appointed a fish to swallow Jonah and Jonah was in the stomach of the fish for three days and nights before coming out.' In Matthew 12:40 the Gospel writer has Jesus saying this about Himself, "An evil and adulterous generation craves after a sign and no sign will be given to it but the sign of Jonah the prophet; for just as Jonah was three days and three nights in the belly of a whale so will the Son of Man be three days and three nights in the heart of the earth." But Jesus was not in the earth for three days as He said on the cross to the one crucified beside Him, He was leaving to enter the Heavenly Spiritual World that day. I believe Matthew has written these words himself to help with the cover story and even gone so far as to have Jesus say them to make them sound more authentic.

23: Although not in the Gospels Hosea 6:1-2 is a favourite of Jewish/Christians to show He rose on the third day. 'Come let us return to the Lord, for He has torn us, but He will heal us, He has wounded us, but He will bandage us. He will revive us after two days; He will raise us up on the third day that we may live before Him.' They place this Jewish saying as a false overlay onto Jesus.

24: Jesus said He was leaving the earth immediately, not in three days' time, to the thief beside Him the day He died on the cross. They are the words I trust and believe as being correct because He taught throughout the Gospels that we have two different bodies with us right now. One stays and is food for the vultures and one leaves and hopefully enters the Heavenly

Spiritual World at the time of our death. It is a logical, intelligent yet totally Spiritual Way of understanding the words of Jesus and what our Life on earth is all about.

The Added Cover Up Words

The Gospel writers of Matthew, Luke and John have all placed in additional words to make it appear that the dead body of flesh and blood of Jesus after being killed by the Jews came back to life and was still a body of flesh and blood. Mark and the Thomas Gospels do not say that. The writers left clues about the Truth that Jesus actually had a Spiritual body and not a body of flesh anymore amongst the fabrications for those who read the Teachings of Jesus and understand what He was really saying. "Flesh only gives birth to flesh. Spirit only gives birth to Spirit. Marvel not that I tell you, you must be born again from above."

Matthew's Fabricated Cover Up Words.

1: Matthew 27:62-66 On the next day after the preparation, the chief priests and the Pharisees gathered together with Pilate and said, "Sir, we remember that when he was still alive that deceiver said, 'After three days I rise again.' (Here Matthew consolidates the three-day cover story) Therefore, give orders for the grave to be made secure until the third day, otherwise His disciples may come and steal His dead body away and say to the people, 'He has risen bodily from the dead, ' and the last deception will be worse than the first." Pilate said to them, "You can have a guard; go make it as secure as you know how." And they went and made the grave secure and along with the guard they set a seal on the stone.

Even the disciples had little idea He was actually going to rise from the dead. John even says this, "Then the other disciple, who reached the tomb first, also went in and believed for as yet they did not know the scripture that He must rise from the dead." Why would the Pharisees who believed nothing Jesus said or taught be worried about it. It is easy to see how Matthew is attempting to cover up the Truth front on by writing exactly what really happened, that the disciples did hide His dead body, and then providing this storyline to counteract and deny it. Setting up the Truth and then knocking it down with a fabricated story. It is also very hard to believe Pilate would bother with such a request. He crucified Jesus as the Jews wanted and then he washed his hands of the whole affair. When these Gospels were written fifty to seventy years after the death of Jesus no witnesses were alive to deny these fabrications.

2: Matthew 28:1-15 Now after the Sabbath Mary Magdelene and the other Mary came to look at the grave. And behold, a severe earthquake had occurred, and an Angel of the Lord descended from Heaven and rolled away the stone and sat upon it. And his appearance was like lightening and his clothing as white as snow.

The guards shook for fear of him and fell as if dead. The Angel tells the two women Jesus is not in the tomb but has risen and they must go and tell the disciples He will meet them in Galilee. And they left the tomb to run and tell the disciples. And behold, Jesus met them and greeted them and they came and held onto His feet and worshipped Him. Jesus said, "Do not be afraid but go and tell My brethren to leave for Galilee and there they will see Me."

Here Matthew consolidates the cover up that Jesus had a body of flesh by saying the two women held Jesus by His feet, one being Mary Magdelene. This must have been put in to try to override the True account in John of Mary meeting Jesus in His Spiritual body and Jesus clearly saying, "You cannot touch Me now Mary," because He had a Spiritual body not flesh.

Supposedly the guards of Pilate are witnesses to this event of an Angel miraculously rolling back the stone not Peter and John as I believe is what really happened. So, Matthew manages to provide an Angelic being as the one who rolled back the stone, not the disciples, as another fabricated piece of the cover up story to divert people from believing it actually was the disciples.

'Now, while the women were on their way to tell the disciples, some of the guard came into the city and reported to the chief priests all that had happened. And when they had assembled with the elders and consulted together, they gave a large sum of money to the soldiers and said, "You are to say, 'His disciples came by night and stole Him away while we were asleep.' And if Pilate hears about this do not worry, we will talk to him and take care of it and keep you out of trouble." And they took the money and did as they had been instructed, and this story was widely spread among the Jews and is to this day.'

Here Matthew continues to use his fabricated Roman guard's story to further the cover up. Firstly, why would Roman soldiers go to the Jewish chief priest to report what supposedly happened instead of to Pilate. Secondly it would be worth more than their life if Pilate found out they fell asleep at their posts and they took a bribe from the Jews to lie than rather just tell Pilate what happened. And it would be highly unlikely Pilate could care less about what the Jewish priests said to defend his Roman soldiers who fell asleep at their posts. None of this makes any sense.

In Matthew's account of the risen Jesus, He only appears to the two women and later at Galilee to the eleven disciples.

Luke's Fabricated Cover Up Words

Luke 24: 26-49 While they were telling them these things, Jesus stood in their midst and said to them, "Peace be to you." But they were startled and thought they were seeing a Spirit. (Which they were.) And He said to them, "Why are you troubled, and why do doubts arise in your hearts?"

These are the only accurate words recorded by Luke of the Spiritual appearance of Jesus to the disciples. Other words extending from these words are found in John and must be added to form a more accurate and complete statement of Jesus. All that follows is fabricated to help the cover up story that He rose in a body of flesh and blood not a Spiritual body. We even see Luke go so far as to put these words in the mouth of Jesus Himself denying He was in a Spiritual body. A very powerful and simple way to get people to believe the cover up story who do not understand the Teachings of Jesus correctly.

Jesus said, "See My hands and feet, that it is I Myself, touch Me and see for a Spirit does not have flesh and bones as you see that I have." And when He said this, He showed them His hands and feet. While they still could not believe it because of their joy and amazement He said to them, "Have you anything to eat?" And they gave Him a piece of broiled fish, and He took it and ate it before them.

Here Luke also counteracts the truthful John account of Jesus telling Mary quite correctly, "Not to touch Me," by simply having Jesus say the opposite, "Go ahead touch Me." And he has Jesus Himself specifically saying He is not in a Spiritual body. Then he further consolidates the coverup story by getting Jesus to voluntarily eat some fish to prove He has a body of flesh just like theirs still. He also alludes that Jesus still has wounds in His hands and feet which goes directly against what Jesus said about all those who enter the Heavenly Spiritual World having perfect bodies like Angels. But He can appear and disappear and looks like a Spirit. No wonder they had to overwrite so many things to cover up the obvious Truth which they still had to include but then knock down with false fabrications.

Now Jesus said to them, "These are My words which I spoke to you that all things which are written about Me in the Law of Moses and the Prophets, and the psalms must be fulfilled." Then He opened their minds to understand the scriptures and said to them, "Thus it is written, that the Christ would suffer and rise again from the dead on the third day and repentance for forgiveness of sins would be proclaimed in His name to all the nations beginning from Jerusalem. You are witnesses of these things. And behold I am sending forth the promise of My father upon you, but you are to stay in the city until clothed with power on high."

Here, the rest of what Luke has Jesus saying is just a collection of prophetic promises about Jesus Himself and includes some Jewish overlays about Jesus rising on the third day and the sacrificial lamb idea that He died for our sins. These have all been fabricated by Luke to see Jesus through a Jewish lens as the sacrificial lamb, killed to cleanse us of our own sins and who rises back to life on the third day like Jonah. All Jewish overlays from the Old Testament religion of the Jews. In this version of events, they have to wait to receive the Holy Spirit but in John's more correct version Jesus Himself gives it to them when He appears in His Spiritual body which makes more sense.

John's Fabricated Cover Up words

John and Peter were the probable ones to hide the dead body of Jesus, possibly with Mary's help. So, John can easily craft a personal cover up story which is certainly the most comprehensive account of finding the supposed empty tomb by himself, Peter and Mary. But he also placed in the most powerful, accurate account of Jesus now being only in a Spiritual body when He appeared to Mary for those who could see through the cover up overlays. The overlays were deliberately placed in to protect the Teachings of Jesus being lost and so people would still follow the Teachings and Spiritual Way of Love and Non-violence of Jesus.

John's general dialogue is mostly accurate. Mary finds the tomb opened on the third day after Jesus was murdered. She goes and tells only John and Peter who go with her to the tomb. They have a look at the empty tomb and John says he and Peter just go back home while Mary stays. Then we have this powerful accurate account of Jesus appearing only in His Spiritual body which rose from His dead body of flesh to Mary. Obviously, Mary told John about this which only confirmed for John that Jesus was now alive in a new Spiritual body having already seen Him in His Spiritual body also on either Friday or Saturday night.

As with all the other appearances of Jesus after his body of flesh died, they do not easily recognise Him. Mary thinks He is the gardener. John also puts in cover ups like Luke when we read, 'On the evening of that day, the first day of the week (another third day cover up) the doors being shut where the disciples were for fear of the Jews, Jesus came and stood among them and said to them, "Peace be with you." When He had said this, He showed them His hands and His side. Then the disciples were glad when they saw it was the Lord.

Now Thomas, one of the twelve called the twin, was not with them when Jesus came. So, the other disciples told him, "We have seen the Lord." But he said to them, "Unless I see in His hands the print of the nails and place my finger in the mark of the nails and place my hand in His side, I will not believe." Eight days later, his disciples were again in the house and Thomas was with them. The doors were shut but Jesus came and stood among them and said, "Peace be with you."

Then He said to Thomas, "Put your finger here and see My hands and put your hand and place it in My side do not be faithless, but believing." Thomas answered saying, "My Lord and my God." Jesus said to him, "Because you have seen Me you have believed. Blessed are they who did not see Me but believe."

John crafts a very interesting contradiction. He gives the most powerful, graphic description using a fabricated Thomas dialogue of Jesus still having a body of flesh and blood with wounds and openings still in it from the crucifixion. So open that Thomas could stick his fingers in them. How long does it take for our perfect Angelic bodies to heal? But he also provides the most powerful description of Jesus really only having a Spiritual body when He appears to Mary. John now knew we have Spiritual bodies as well as a body of flesh as Jesus taught.

But he had to compromise that Truth to protect the Spiritual Way and Teachings of Love Jesus taught that brings our Spiritual bodies to Life. The Jews were not ready to understand or believe that we have two different bodies with us right now. One stays and returns to the Earth from which it was formed. One leaves to reap what it has sown and returns to the source from which it was formed. A Spiritual Being of perfect Love and a Creator of True Spiritual Life who placed our Spiritual bodies in our bodies of flesh to become at one with and leave this material world of suffering at the time of our death and enter the Heavenly Spiritual World. John seems to be the most aware of the two body Teachings of Jesus and faithfully passed it on in amongst the red herring distractions for those who truly understand the Teachings of Jesus to find. As Jesus often said Himself after a Teaching, "He who has ears to listen correctly, let him understand what I am really saying."

Mark's Gospel Has No Body of Spirit Cover Ups

The original ending of the Gospel of Mark has no account whatsoever of Jesus actually appearing to anyone in any form after His body of flesh was killed on the cross. It has Mary and two other women finding the tomb empty and an Angel appears telling them Jesus has risen and He is not here and tells them to go and tell the others He will see them later in Galilee. They are frightened and leave telling no one about it. Most scholars agree that an additional general ending was compiled by someone and added to Mark to bring it into alignment with the other three Gospels.

This is the same account found in Matthew regarding the Angel saying the same thing except after seeing the Angel they do go and tell the disciples. I feel John's account is the most revealing of the Truth about His body rising in Spirit not the flesh.

Thomas Gospel Does Not Mention the Resurrection

The Thomas Gospel, while not mentioning the classic resurrection of Jesus from a tomb, concentrates more on Jesus Teaching throughout the Gospel about us all having two different bodies with us right now. And we must become at one with our Spiritual body filled only with Light and the Loving Spiritual Life-force of our Loving Creator to have real Eternal Life after our body of temporary flesh dies. In the Gospel of Thomas, the overriding theme is to follow the Spiritual Way of Jesus and become like Jesus and awaken into our Spiritual body before the flesh dies and returns to the earth. Then we will find ourselves in the Heavenly Spiritual World beyond all suffering. Which I believe is exactly what Jesus intended in giving us His beautiful words of Spirit.

Children who follow the Spiritual Way of Jesus and believe in a Heavenly World of Love and One True Source of Spiritual Life, are prepared to leave their dead body of flesh behind. For as long as they just Live out of their Spirit of Love while here on Earth they will be ready to enter the Heavenly Spiritual World. Then we will see what an Angel's body really looks like because we will all have one. But if you believe you only have a body of flesh, you may not search for your inner Spiritual body and Soul Mind of Love now to become at one with and be ready to leave in at the time of your physical death. Whereas Jesus clearly advised us all, "The Kingdom of Heaven is within you. Seek and you will find."

The last words of the Beatles last official song on their last studio album titled 'The End' are, "And in the end. The Love you take is equal to the Love you make." And that is all Jesus was really saying too. And His last words of advice to us all in the Gospel of John are, "Follow Me." Not, "I am coming back."

GOD IS LOVE LOVE IS LIFE

Jesus taught we all have two bodies.

One is made of earth and returns to the Earth.

One is formed from a Spiritual Life-force

and returns to the source of that Spiritual Life-force.

Our Loving Spiritual Creator

in the Heavenly Spiritual World.

One lives on and one dies.

Jesus brings those dead to their Spirit

back to Life.

Chapter Twenty-Five

The Revelation Ruse

Definition of the word Ruse. Something done to deceive or trick someone. The book of Revelation is an extremely well-crafted, cunning and false entry placed at the end of the new Spiritual Loving Way of Jesus and the One Loving Spiritual Creator to detour followers of Jesus to go back and worship the two headed God of the Jews of War and Limited Love and destroy the connection with our True Loving Spiritual Creator in the Heavenly Spiritual World of Love. It slanders Jesus and the Divine pure source of Love He was at one with and wants us all to be at one with also, as Her Spiritual children of Love on Earth. I always advise every single Christian and follower of Jesus to rip it out and burn it. Its intent is evil.

Historically

Most theological scholars agree that the Greek style of writing seen in the Revelation Ruse is not the same style used in the Gospel of John. They also point out that Revelation focuses on judgement and Divine wrath of a God and Jesus destroying children's lives, which is the opposite of the Jesus Teaching of forgiveness and Love, and the description Jesus gave of our Loving Spiritual Creator of perfect Love He was at one with.

They are two completely different authors. You can't even compare the mystical beauty of some of the dialogues written about Jesus in John on Love with this load of dark, judgmental, revengeful and violent evil associated with the Jewish War God Yahweh 1, not the Loving Spiritual Creator of Jesus.

Alexandrian Bishop Dionisius said, "By the phraseology we can easily see the difference between the Gospels and Epistle and Revelation. The first two are written without any blunders in the use of the Greek and with remarkable skill regarding diction, logical thought and orderly expression. Revelation is not."

Gaius in the third century believed Revelation to be a fabrication by Cerinthus who, "By means of revelations which he pretends were written by a great apostle, brings before us marvelous things which he falsely claims were shown to him by Angels, and he says that after the resurrection the Kingdom of Christ will be set up on Earth."

Marcion was a Christian theologian in the late first and early second century. He completely rejected the Revelation book as being a book representing the jealous Old Testament Jewish God Yahweh 1 who demanded obedience and punishes mankind for disobeying his laws through causing them to suffer and die. Whereas Marcion correctly saw the Loving Spiritual Creator of Jesus as being a completely different universal Divine being of compassion and Love who looks upon mankind with benevolence and mercy.

Eusebius, an early Christian leader in the second to third century, labelled the book as questionable most likely not written by the Gospel of John author but did not condemn it outright.

Other early church leaders influenced by the Constantine factor who killed in the name of Jesus and our Loving Creator caused them to become corrupted converting pacifist Christians into Jewish/Christians. They wrongly led them back into worshiping the Jewish two headed God Yahweh again instead of the Loving Spiritual Creator that Jesus taught about. Then they agreed to include the evil Revelation book in the New Testament which obviously boosted their corruption converting pacifist Christians back into dualistic Jewish/Christians who can kill their enemies like the Jews instead of Loving their enemies like Jesus taught us to do. It is a very corrupting and evil book.

The Revelation Ruse was reluctantly accepted into the biblical canon around 397 A.D. at the Council of Carthage. It was reluctantly included in the eastern Christian churches around 680 A.D. Skepticism and rejection was always still present amongst True followers of Jesus as it is today. Predominantly by the Eastern churches, some of whom still refuse to acknowledge it as a biblical New Testament book as it is the Jewish Old Testament book of Daniel revised to slander Jesus and our Loving Creator.

Martin Luther called Revelation, "Neither apostolic nor prophetic," but under the pressure of opposition he revised his opinion later to accept it but could still, "Not see Christ in it." He was right. Jesus and our Loving Creator are not there but a distorted Jesus and the two headed God of the Jews is well and truly present. Especially Yahweh 1 the brutal, murdering War god of the Jews. No Christian should ever read this book.

Origins of Apocalyptic Revelation.

In general, it seems the author of Revelation is a Palestinian Jew with some Christian knowledge. He displays a strong affinity and familiarity with the Jewish Scriptures, especially Daniel, that few converts would have. Sholars say the book alludes to the Old Testament around 500 times, more than any other New Testament book. The extreme Jewishness of the author can also be seen in the many uses of Jewish terminology and poor Greek grammar that a Greek writer on such a topic would never produce.

The apocalyptic belief of the Jews originated around the third to first centuries B.C often mixed in with a Jewish expectation of a mighty warrior Messiah who will make Israel great again. It seems to have been heavily influenced by Zoroastrianism which teaches dualism and a cosmic battle between good and evil culminating in a final battle where all evil is vanquished and all of creation will be reunited with the Creator in perfection.

They also believe in a final resurrection of the dead and a final judgement for all based on their earthly lives and actions. A great prophet or Saviour figure also plays a significant role in the final Apocalypse. Modern scholars say the book of Daniel was written by a Jew exiled in Babylon around the second century B.C where he was likely influenced by Zoroastrian beliefs.

The book is often cryptic and uses symbolic terminology of beasts with multiple horns, wars between opposing forces and other such fanciful images and a Son of Man coming on the clouds of Heaven. He will be given dominion over all of mankind and all children will serve him and his Kingdom will never end. The Revelation Ruse is almost a Jewish carbon copy of Zoroastrian beliefs with a combination of some Christian dialogues, Jesus as the Saviour or Messiah figure and the two-headed God of the Jews being the creator. And they bring destruction upon mankind.

And that is the exact intention of this corrupt Jewish book planted at the end of the Spiritual Teachings and Way of Love of Jesus who leads you out of the two headed God of the Jews only to be duped and taken back by this cunning detour sign to worship the two headed God Yahweh of the Jews again. Instead of following Jesus to where He has gone by becoming Spiritually awakened to your True Spiritual identity as a Spiritual child of our Loving Creator in a Heavenly Spiritual World of Love. Very devious and cunning indeed.

Jewish/Christians place this Jewish dialogue as a powerful overlay onto Jesus and combine this Son of Man in Daniel with the Revelation Ruse where Jesus is depicted in this way at the end of the world. The term Son of Man was used in other Old Testament books as a general term to describe someone who is a simple human being. Which is why Jesus used it, as He was just an ordinary human being like all of us, but He underwent a Spiritual awakening and realised He had another identity of a Spiritual body and Soul mind of Love that is Eternal. And then taught us how to find and awaken into it as well and go to where He is. As His last words in the Gospel of John state, "Follow Me." He is not coming back on the clouds.

The Purpose of the Revelation Ruse

I call the Revelation Ruse one of the most cunning, evil and slanderous attacks ever thought up to deceive the followers of Jesus and take them away from becoming like Him through just reading His Spiritual Way of Love to follow Him to the Heavenly Spiritual World. It copies Daniel's cryptic symbolic imagery and takes it to new heights of unintelligible, irrelevant, mesmerizing puzzles to spend your whole life trying to figure out and decode. Wasting your precious time by distracting and taking you away from looking only at the transformational Spiritual Teachings and words of Jesus that can lead you to our Loving Spiritual Creator in the Eternal Heavenly Spiritual World of Love.

Jesus Himself said it is His words that save you, instead you are sucked into waiting for Him to come back one day and save you during an horrific Apocalypse that He and our Loving Creator supposedly cause, while they slaughter all the bad children, the lost sheep. This doesn't quite match the story of the Loving Shepherd who saves the lost sheep that Jesus taught about Himself and our Loving Creator, does it?

And the most insidious thing it does of all is to destroy your Spiritual Mind or eye from being single and full of Light and the Loving Life-force of your Loving Creator that gives your Spirit True Life by Loving all children both good and evil. As Jesus taught both He and our Loving Creator are perfect Love, and we must be also to enter Heaven. But the corruptor who wrote this Revelation Ruse is telling you that they are actually both dualistic and divided within themselves between Loving some and hating and destroying some. And Jesus warned us all that if we are divided within ourselves, we will be filled with darkness. The exact Way of the two headed God of the Jews that Jesus tried to bring them out of.

Someone who hated Jesus and the Christian Spiritual Way of Love, Non-violence and Peace has cleverly dropped Jesus, the Prince of Peace and our Loving Creator, into the middle of a version of the book of Daniel from the Jewish religion. Obviously, it must have been an apocalyptic Jew who did it. Jesus and our Loving Creator have then been covered over in a cryptic, convoluted load of lies and dark distortions that are all associated with the violent, murdering Godhead of War Yahweh 1 of the Jews.

He did this deliberately to convert Christians back into being Jewish/Christians and shift their Spiritual connection from our Loving Spiritual Creator back to the two headed God of the Jews of War and Limited Love. If they could fool Christians into believing that Jesus and our Loving Spiritual Creator are going to slaughter the bad, evil children at the end of some mythical time but save the chosen good children, then Jesus and our Loving Creator are revengeful killers and murderers.

Just like the perverted War God of the Jews that Jesus gave His life to bring the Jews away from and into the One True Loving Spiritual Creator. And of course, it leads Christians to fall into the trap of murdering again in wars just like the Jews destroying their connection with our Loving Spiritual Creator and Her Loving Life-force in their Spiritual bodies.

The writer has some knowledge of seven Mediterranean Christian groups and makes out Jesus is telling him what to say to the seven churches. He describes Jesus in two different ways. Firstly, as a 'son of man' so we know it is Jesus. The first description says He is clothed in a robe with a golden sash across his chest, His head and hair were like wool and as white as snow. His voice sounded like many waters, and His face was like the sun shining in its strength. But there is another cunning description running inside it. His eyes were like a flame of fire, and his feet were like burnished bronze when it has been made to glow in a furnace and out of his mouth came a sharp two-edged sword and He has the keys to death and hades.

The first description is very nice and Loving and clearly refers to Jesus as a lamb of God by mentioning the word wool. But take a close look at the second description cleverly mixed in to the first. His eyes are flaming; He has a dualistic sword; His feet are glowing like feet found in a furnace of fire and He holds the keys to death and Hell. The second description is of Satan the War God Yahweh of the Jews. It is Satan who holds the keys to temptation, death and Hell not Jesus and our Loving Spiritual Creator who hold the keys to Heaven. This person is a Jew who wants Christians to worship the War god of the Jews and sets Jesus up as the bait to convert you back into being Jewish and destroy the Loving Way of Jesus and our Loving Creator that you were at one with.

The general dialogues to the seven churches involve warning them against going astray or they will suffer in various ways and make some legitimate Spiritual points. However, at one point Jesus supposedly says to the church at Thyatira, "I gave Jezebel time to repent, and she does not want to repent of her immorality. Behold, I will throw her on a bed of sickness, and those who commit adultery with her into great tribulation, unless they repent. And I will kill her children with pestilence."

This is the revengeful satanic War God of the Jews not Jesus speaking. Although this Jezabel is a symbolic leader of immoral conduct we only have to recall the story of how Jesus treated the actual woman caught in immoral adultery with forgiveness and compassion. We must also remember that Jesus only healed the sick He did not cause sickness to clearly see this particular Revelation account of Jesus is a pile of dog droppings.

In the message to Laodicea Jesus says, "Because you are neither cold nor hot but are only lukewarm, I will spit you out of my mouth." Jesus never abandons anyone and neither does our Loving Spiritual Creator. We may be Spiritually lazy and stagnating, but they still shine their everlasting Love upon us patiently waiting for us to come alive in Spirit and be saved.

It then goes into a bazar dream sequence where a Heavenly book with seven seals on it needs to be opened by someone, but no one could be found worthy enough to open it. But hang on, a lamb standing as if slain with seven horns and seven eyes came and took the book out of the right hand of He who sits on the throne of Heaven. And all praised the lamb and fell down and worshiped Him who saved men with His blood. This is a misleading Jewish overlay put onto Jesus as a sacrificial lamb whose blood saves you when Jesus said Himself it is His words that will save you. And to describe Jesus having seven horns and seven eyes is a very Jewish overlayed symbolism and almost makes Him out to look like a monster instead of a lamb.

Then these cunning dialogues move into the insidious culmination of destroying who Jesus and our Loving Creator really are by Jesus personally being the one who opens each seal in the Heavenly World. By doing so He then supposedly instigates destruction, earthquakes, plagues and fires to kill many children and literally incites children to kill each other in war. (Jesus said Love your enemies, pray for those who persecute you.)

He then spreads a horrible sickness onto children's bodies. (Jesus healed the sick of all their illnesses.) He kills a third of all creatures in the sea. (Why would He even do that? Are fish evil? It makes no sense.) He poisons drinking water. (Jesus said He has the water of Life to give to everyone.) He causes famine to starve children to death. (He multiplied the loaves and fishes to feed the hungry.) He releases locusts like scorpions to torture children for five months. (Jesus expels all harmful things from our life including evil spirits to free us from being tortured.)

He then releases Angels from Heaven to murder a third of mankind and bring death upon the children of the world. (Angels are pure in Spiritual Love and can never harm any of us. They only protect us from harm. These sound more like demons.) These filthy Revelation evil acts are exactly the sort of things a Satanic Godhead of War does not Jesus or our Loving Spiritual Creator in the Heavenly Spiritual World of Love.

And after a mammoth battle set between good and evil children the temple of the Jewish God in Heaven was opened and there were flashes of lightening, sounds of thunder, an earthquake and a great hailstorm. Then there was a war in Heaven as well, (the place beyond all suffering that Jesus Teaches about where no evil can come.) Then there is a very cryptic, convoluted scenario involving all sorts of weird beasts that are symbolic of unknown various forces on earth and in Heaven. Angels (Demons) finally gather the evil children, and they are crushed to death in a wine press driven supposedly by our Loving Creator's anger, with blood coming out to the depth of a horse's bridal for two hundred miles. (Jesus said, "I have not come to judge the world but to save the world.)

Then a song of praise is sung by the good children praising the Lamb Jesus for being so righteous in causing these brutal, vicious actions towards the lost children of our Loving Creator. Then more destruction is given out by Jesus and supposedly the Loving Creator of Jesus when another Angel (Demon) from Heaven is sent to kill every living thing in the sea. Another Angel (Demon) from Heaven makes the sun so hot it burns people's skin. Another Angel (Demon) of Heaven dries up rivers. More hailstones about one hundred pounds each are sent down by Jesus and supposedly by our Loving Spiritual Creator to kill more of Her children who did not bow down and obey them.

Then after more killing and destruction supposedly caused directly by Jesus and our Loving Creator it says, 'From His mouth comes a sharp sword, so that with it He may strike down the nations and rule them with a rod of iron, and He treads the wine press of the fierce wrath of God the Almighty.' The War God Yahweh 1 of the Jews. This sounds more like Adolf Hitler than Jesus. Then it goes on in a dream sequence where finally satan and all the lost sheep are thrown into Hell forever by our Loving Creator and Jesus. Jesus the shepherd who came to save the lost sheep from Hell is now throwing them into Hell.

What a crock of dog droppings. What a disgraceful slandering of my Spiritual Teacher of Love and forgiveness and Great friend Jesus and of course what a disgusting, filthy portrayal of our Loving Spiritual Creator in the Heavenly Spiritual World of Love. This is all about the two headed perverted God of the Jews and their War God Yahweh 1 and trying to trick Christian followers of Jesus to follow it again. It is satanic through and through.

It perverts who Jesus was and still is and destroys the perfect Love of our Loving Spiritual Creator in the Heavenly Spiritual World who gives all our Spiritual bodies and Souls Her Loving Life-force to have Spiritual Life. There are no direct words of Jesus in this distorted, perverted book only a dream sequence someone supposedly had and then wrote about. You cannot distort something without adding some points of truth to then distort them. So, a few correct examples of things Jesus might say are added into the convoluted storyline to fool children into believing that all the rest of the rubbish and slander must be about Him and our Loving Creator as well.

Jesus is only Love. Our Loving Spiritual Creator is only Love. The Heavenly Spiritual World for us to enter is only Love. Guess how you have to be if you want to follow Jesus and enter Heaven? Only Love. Jesus was a pacifist in this sometimes violent, distorted world for this very reason. Only those who are single in Love will be filled with Her Light and Loving Life-force and will enter Heaven. Those who are divided within themselves into Loving and saving some children, while hating, condemning and murdering other children are lost in the darkness of their own making.

Jesus came to save, heal and restore the Spiritual Way of pure Love for us to follow and awaken us to our true Spiritual identities of Love and to become children of our Loving Spiritual Creator in a Heavenly Spiritual World. They can never harm anyone and are kind to the ungrateful and the evil and they shine Her Love always on all of Her children both lost and found.

GOD IS LOVE LOVE IS LIFE

Rip out the evil book of Revelation and burn it.

And stay in the Loving Spiritual Way that Jesus taught.

And become Spiritually alive and be a Loving Spiritual child

of our Loving Spiritual Creator in the Heavenly Spiritual World

here on Earth.

Chapter Twenty-Six

Apocalyptic Overlays Put Onto Jesus

The Book of Revelation is a cunning well-crafted, deceitful decoy or subterfuge and slanders Jesus and the pure Loving Spiritual source and Loving Life-force that empowers our Spiritual bodies and Souls to have True Spiritual Life that Jesus leads us all to. It leads unwary followers of Jesus away from our Loving Spiritual Creator who is only Love, and the Heavenly Spiritual World of Love, back into a Jewish trap to worship the two headed God of the Jews with a brutal Godhead Yahweh 1 of war, revenge, thieving and murder and a Godhead Yahweh 2 of Limited Love on one body called Yahweh. Two for the price of one. A divided God not at One with Love and Non-violence as Jesus taught the real Loving Spiritual Creator is.

We know the Gospel writers copied certain things from each other. It is difficult to know how many of the Gospel writers were initially involved in overlaying the apocalyptic sayings attributed to Jesus and then further overlaying the lie that Jesus was going to return at the Apocalypse and also cause it to happen. The reason these appear throughout the Gospels to varying degrees is to deliberately link Jesus and our Loving Creator to the Jewish book of Daniel and the false book of Revelation to consolidate the lying slander said about them.

And to distract followers from only focusing on becoming like Him and being transformed by His Spiritual Teachings and Way of Love to bring their Spirits alive. Instead, they get followers to keep waiting for Him to return and save them. But He said to follow Him to where He has gone by becoming a Spiritual child of Love on Earth now by awakening into your Spiritual body and Soul to be ready to enter the Heavenly Spiritual World. Jesus is not coming back but will always help us get to where He is if we just follow His words. We are not alone; Heaven will always help us but each one of us must choose by ourselves to become a Spiritual child of Love. Jesus can't do it for us.

Matthew Fabricating Apocalyptic Overlays

I do not believe Jesus ever talked about Himself in this apocalyptic, 'Son of Man coming in the clouds' way at the end of time to throw bad children into Hell and take the good children to Heaven with Him. Jesus in fact taught we must listen to and understand His words and Teachings become transformed by them and follow Him to where He has gone, the Heavenly Spiritual World of Love.

Matthew seems to be the ringleader in falsifying these Apocalyptic sayings attributed to Jesus. Whether it was done deliberately to distort who Jesus really was and destroy His Spiritual Way of perfect Love and the Loving Creator or whether Matthew thought his fanciful embellishments would help the Jews follow Jesus we will never know. Or maybe another writer has overwritten Matthew possibly the Apocalyptic Jew responsible for the Revelation slander if Matthew wasn't the author of it himself. But one thing is certain to me, they are all false and misleading.

We have a very revealing insight into the corruption of the words of Jesus at Matthew 13:47-50 that exposes how this Gospel writer or someone who overwrote Matthew took a saying of Jesus and deliberately distorted and perverted it to suit this apocalyptic overlay putting it directly into the mouth of Jesus. It is a fabrication and lie because by the grace of Heaven we have the original correct version in the Thomas Gospel to compare it with.

Thomas Gospel: Net Cast into the Sea

The original and correct saying of Jesus from the Thomas Gospel. Jesus said, "A person is like a wise fisherman who cast his net into the sea and drew it all up full of little fish from below. Among them he found one good and great fish. The wise fisherman threw all the little fish back into the sea and without any hesitation he chose to keep the greatest good fish. Whoever has ears to hear, let him hear."

Here Jesus is following on from finding the one great pearl saying and finding the great treasure hidden in the field saying and now finding the one great and good fish among many little ones saying. They match perfectly. The one great and good thing Jesus is referring to is our Spiritual body and Soul mind of Love within our body of flesh that we have to find and become at one with to have Eternal Heavenly Life.

We can recall Jesus actually talking about this one good thing to Martha when He said, "Martha you are worried about many things. But only one thing is necessary, and Mary has chosen that one good thing and it will not be taken away from her."

We must detach ourselves from all the worldly temporary material things which are worthless in comparison and let go of any little egotistical identities we may be living out of and move into and become at one with this one great and good thing we have found within ourselves. This is our primary True Spiritual Eternal identity and Life which we will have in the Heavenly Spiritual World of Love. This original and accurate saying is about our personal Spiritual awakening into our True ultimate Spiritual identity that Jesus says we must all find amongst our lesser earthly identities. Matthew's version distorts this saying.

Matthew 13:47 Net Cast into the Sea

Matthew or someone overwriting Matthew perverts this saying of Jesus in the following way. Matthew 13:47 Jesus said, "The Heavenly Spiritual World of our Loving Creator is like a fishing net that was cast into the sea and gathered some of every kind. And when it was full they drew it up to the shore and sat down and collected the good into vessels but the bad they cast out." Matthew altered the saying to set up the following false addition attributing it to Jesus.

Matthew 13:49 Jesus then supposedly says, "So it will be at the end of the age; the Angels will come forth and separate the wicked from amongst the righteous and will cast them into the furnace of fire. There will be wailing and gnashing of teeth." Matthew altered the focus and changed the parable ending to act as a segway into adding his own apocalyptic words and falsely attributed them to Jesus.

Matthew firstly replaces 'A person' with 'The Heavenly Kingdom'. This version is not about personal Spiritual development and awakening as Jesus originally intended but it has been deliberately changed and distorted to link Jesus with the Apocalypse where He destroys all evil children and saves the good children. This links Him back to the two headed God of the Jews again and the book of Revelation lies. And the correct 'end of the age' is the day we all die when we will all reap what we sow right then, not some distant apocalyptic time that comes from the Jewish Old Testament book of Daniel.

And it obviously does not match the preceding two sayings of Jesus in Matthew about the Kingdom of Heaven being like one great pearl and one great treasure. Matthew then deliberately alters the focus further by replacing the 'one wise fisherman' who represents all of us as individuals learning to become Spiritual with the pronoun 'they'. This convenient distortion allows Matthew to introduce Angels into the false storyline.

He alters the fish from being little unimportant ones and one great good one that represents our search for our Spiritual awakening and True identity into being bad fish cast out and good fish who are saved. Just as he altered the seeds in the tares and wheat parable. Then He introduces his false Apocalyptic end of time overlay attributing these fake words to Jesus where Jesus says Angels from Heaven will separate the good from the bad at the Apocalypse and throw the bad children into Hell.

Angels are pure in Spirit and only empowered by the Loving Life-force of our Loving Spiritual Creator whose Love shines on the good and on the evil. Angels only save us from harm and suffering like Jesus Himself. They cannot hurt us in any way. Matthew loves the Jewish book of Daniel and ties Jesus into it any chance he can get or create himself. These are dualistic Jewish overlays to replace the Loving Creator of Jesus with the two headed God of the Jews and destroy the Spiritual message and Way of Pure singular Love that Jesus gave for us to find within ourselves.

This is a serious Jewish Apocalyptic distortion that runs throughout the Gospels to pervert and take followers away from understanding and concentrating on the words of Jesus and become personally transformed and awoken into our Spiritual body and True identity to become the same as He was. A Spiritual child of Love of our Loving Spiritual Creator in the Heavenly Spiritual World of Love. Instead, this represents the two headed God of the Jews who destroys its children who do wrong and slanders Jesus and our Loving Creator by putting these words in His mouth. They are false, evil and should be destroyed.

Other False Apocalyptic Sayings

Matthew adds other false sayings throughout the Gospel about the Apocalypse and Jesus returning. At 10:23 he has Jesus saying,

"Truly you will not finish going through all the cities of Israel until the Son of Man comes," another reference to Daniel. At 11:20-24 Then Jesus began to denounce the cities in which most of His miracles were done because they did not repent. "Woe to you, Chorazin! Woe to you Bethsaida! For if the miracles had occurred in Tyre or Sidon which occurred in you, they would have repented long ago in sackcloth and ashes. Nevertheless, I say to you, it will be more tolerable for Tyre and Sidon in the day of judgement than for you. And you, Capernaum, will not be exalted to Heaven. You will descend into Hades for if the miracles had occurred in Sodom which occurred in you it would have remained to this day. I say it will be more tolerable for the land of Sodom in the day of judgement than for you."

Matthew has Jesus falsely referring to the day of judgement to come at the Apocalypse, another reference to Daniel and Revelation and has Jesus condemning whole townships of people to Hell which goes against who Jesus was and what He taught. Collective punishment is a hallmark of the revengeful Jewish Godhead of War of Yahweh 1. Matthew has contrived these words himself putting them into the mouth of Jesus to support his own agenda.

The Correct Sower of Seed Parable of Jesus

This is the True correct Sower of the Seed Parable. Jesus said, "Hear and understand the parable of the Sower of the Seed. When anyone hears the words of the Kingdom of the Heavenly Spiritual World and does not understand them, then other bad things can come into their life and rob them of the chance for the words to take root in their hearts and Souls. This is the one who receives the seed by the wayside.

He who received the seeds of the words on stony places, is he who hears the words and immediately receives them with joy; but he has not taken them deeply enough into his heart and Soul and fully committed to them so endures with them only for a while. For when tribulation or persecution arises against him because he is following the Spiritual Way of Love and Non-violence of Heaven, he weakens, stumbles and falls away from the words.

He who received seed among the thorns is he who hears the words, but the cares of this material world and the deceitfulness of riches overtake and choke the words in him, and he becomes Spiritually unfruitful.

He who receives the seeds of the words of the Heavenly Spiritual World on good ground, is the one who hears the words and understands their Spiritual meaning and bears Spiritual fruits; some a hundredfold, some thirty, some sixty."

This original correct parable of the Sower of the Seed has Jesus explaining that not everyone will listen to His words, follow them and be transformed by them. He then lists a few reasons why this happens so we can avoid them happening to us. It is a simple parable making us aware of the traps we can fall into that stifle our Spiritual awakening. Jesus never says those who do not listen to His words or do not follow them will be thrown into Hell. We must always remember Jesus actually said, "If anyone hears My words and does not keep them, I do not judge them."

Matthew 13:36-43 The False Wheat and Tares Saying.

This is a falsified version produced by Matthew of the correct preceding Sower of the seed parable that Jesus gave that has no mention of any child being thrown into Hell. Again, he has hijacked the theme of the original spoken by Jesus involving seeds that are sown that only represent His Spiritual words in the same way he took the original fish in the Net Cast into the Sea and has created his own perverted version by changing the seeds being the words of Jesus to now represent bad and good children.

Matthew creates a totally new false storyline to feed into his own Apocalyptic agenda painting Jesus as coming on the clouds at the Apocalypse to bring an end to the world, murdering the evil children and saving the good. This whole parable is made up by him or someone else to pervert the original meaning of the Sower parable just as Matthew perverted the Net in the Sea parable to feed his own Apocalyptic agenda. This is a false parable.

Matthew's False Altered Version

Jesus explained the Tares and Wheat parable to the disciples. Jesus said, "He who sows the good seed is the Son of Man. The field is the world, the good seeds are the sons of the Kingdom of Heaven, but the tares are the sons of evil. The enemy who sowed the tares is satan, the harvest is the end of the age, and the reapers are the Angels.

Therefore, as the tares are gathered and burned in the fire, so it will be at the end of this age. The Son of Man will send His Angels and they will gather out of His Kingdom all things that offend and those who practice lawlessness and will cast them into the furnace of fire. There will be wailing and gnashing of teeth. Then the righteous will shine forth as the sun in the Kingdom of Heaven. He who has ears. Let him hear."

Matthew again perverts a parable of Spiritual advice given to us by Jesus turning it into the Apocalyptic end of the world with Jesus at the controls changing the seeds that Jesus used to originally represent His Spiritual words from Heaven, into the bad seed and good seed children. Exactly what he also did with the fish parable. And he has Jesus instigating the murder of the lost sheep by sending Angels to throw them all into Hell just like his perverted version of the Net in the Sea parable. This is a lie.

Again, slandering Angels and Jesus who says He is a shepherd who saves lost sheep. I believe Matthew has deliberately distorted the words of Jesus and written this Himself with his own interpretation of the original Sower of the seed parable like that done with the one big fish parable or someone else has overwritten Matthew and added this false Apocalyptic version. This is all based on the Jewish book of Daniel and Revelation, two Jewish books about the two headed God Yahweh of the Jews.

Going Not Coming

At Matthew 16: 27 Jesus supposedly says, "For the Son of Man is going (to come) in the glory of His Father with His Angels and will then repay every man according to his deeds." Matthew is again linking Jesus to Daniel and the Apocalyptic Revelation Ruse book by simply adding the words 'to come' flipping the direction. Jesus actually said He was going in the Spiritual glory of our Loving Spiritual Creator which is His Spiritual body.

Matthew 16:28 Jesus said, "Truly I say to you, there are some of those who are standing here who shall not taste death until they see the Son of Man coming (going) into His Kingdom." The Greek word translated as 'coming' in the Gospels can legitimately also mean 'going'. Going, is the correct translation in this case. Jesus knew He would soon be killed by the Jews. Here He is simply telling them that some of them will still be alive when they see Him killed and ascend in Spirit or 'go' into Heaven.

Matthew has distorted the words of Jesus by changing going to coming and providing a way to link Jesus again to Revelation and Daniel by having Jesus say the word 'coming' to provide some credence for the false Revelation Ruse book to be believed as authentic by gullible followers.

I believe these words that Matthew wrote are deliberately distorted from the original words Jesus spoke. Matthew changed them to cast Jesus as the promised Messiah in the book of Daniel coming on the clouds of Heaven at the Revelation apocalypse to kill the bad children and save the good children. This Apocalyptic agenda of Matthew is seen throughout his Gospel. Pure slander and a very Jewish Old Testament two headed God idea and belief from the book of Daniel. Jesus simply said, "Follow Me and My Spiritual Way of Love and Non-violence to Heaven."

Distorted Wedding Invitation Parable

In the original invitation parable of Jesus, we are told that everyone is invited to follow the Spiritual Way of Jesus to the Heavenly Spiritual World, but the first group invited declined to come for various worldly reasons that Jesus lists. Just as He listed similar reasons in the Sower parable for not wanting to become Spiritual. So, others are invited to join Jesus in the Heavenly Spiritual World by following His Way. And anyone who prepares themselves Spiritually by following His Way of Love and Non-violence can enter. But those not robed in Love and non-violence cannot enter. Jesus does not kill anyone who rejects His invitation in this correct saying. As Jesus said, "If anyone hears My words and does not keep them, I do not judge them."

False Matthew 22:2-7 version. Jesus said, "The Kingdom of Heaven is like a King who sent out invitations for his son's wedding. But those who received them did not want to come for various worldly reasons. So, the King sent invitations again to them, but they all said they were too busy to come, and some mistreated his messengers and even killed some of them. (The King was enraged with anger and sent his armies and destroyed those murderers and set their city on fire.") He then invited others who were willing to come.

Matthew has made up this sentence about killing the children who killed some of the messengers and burning their city and puts the words in the mouth of Jesus which slander Him and our Loving Creator. It is not found in Luke's version of the same parable. This is the way of the two headed revengeful War God of the Jews Yahweh 1 not the Way of our Loving Spiritual Creator or Jesus. It is designed to deliberately muddy the waters of who Jesus really is and our Loving Spiritual Creator trying to lead all

Christians astray and back into worshiping the two headed God Yahweh of the Jews with a revengeful, violent Godhead of War and a Godhead of limited Love on the one body.

False Apocalyptic Words Pinned to Jesus

Matthew 24:3-39 Here we see another obviously contrived false account by Matthew added onto a probable correct short answer of Jesus. This starts by the disciples pointing out to Jesus how wonderful the Temple buildings look. Then Jesus simply replies by telling them that not one stone will be left standing on another as one day they will all be thrown down.

The disciples later supposedly ask Him, "Tell us when will this happen and what will be the sign of your coming and the end of the age?" This is clearly a contrived, false segway question made up by either Matthew or the over writer of Matthew to put words in the mouth of Jesus to again link Him to the Revelation Ruse book and the two headed God of the Jews. Jesus never even mentions in His comment anything about the end of the age or His coming again only that the Temple will one day be destroyed.

This false segway leads Jesus into supposedly making a rambling dialogue about the Apocalypse drawing from Revelations and Daniel again about the abomination of desolation from Daniel appearing, famines, wars, earthquakes, the moon no longer giving its light, stars falling from the sky, He will send out His Angels to gather the chosen ones and He will be seen returning on the clouds of Heaven like lightening. Total rubbish.

All of this is Revelations and Daniel regurgitated by Matthew or someone who wants the followers of Jesus to believe He is the Son of the Jewish two headed God Yahweh 1 of death, revenge and destruction. And it slanders the Loving Creator of Jesus and Jesus Himself to destroy the Spiritual Way and Teachings of Love that Jesus gave us to follow to help us all enter the Heavenly Spiritual World of Love after death. I do not believe this was said by Jesus but is a fake addition by Matthew or someone else. But based on the many heavy Jewish overlays throughout Matthew it would indicate Matthew is most likely the one who fabricated these sayings attributing them all to Jesus and distorting what Jesus actually said and taught slandering Him in the process.

Two Bodies Teaching Perverted

Matthew 24:40-41 Then at the end of the false apocalyptic rambling attributed to Jesus Matthew perverts the original message of one of the most important Spiritual Teachings that Jesus gave by attaching it to this apocalyptic made-up ramble. He hijacks the powerful two bodies in one Teaching of Jesus where He clearly states we all have two bodies with us right now. One is a body of flesh that dies and can be fed to the vultures, and one is a Spiritual body taken to be near to our Loving Spiritual Creator at the time of our death experience to reap as we have sown.

Matthew destroys its meaning by connecting it to Jesus returning at the end of this Apocalyptic ramble. Jesus supposedly says, "For the coming of the Son of Man will be just like the days of Noah. For in those days before the flood they were eating and drinking, marrying and giving in marriage until the day that Noah entered the ark, and they did not understand until the flood came and took them all away; so, will the coming of the Son of Man be. (There will be two men in a field; one will be taken, and one will be sent forth. Two women will be grinding at the millstone; one will be taken, and one will be sent forth.) Therefore, be on alert for you do not know which day your Lord is coming."

Here Matthew is seen hijacking and perverting the original Teaching of Jesus concerning our two different bodies that will separate out from one another at the time of our death for his own Apocalyptic agenda. He uses the original Teaching like a filling in a sandwich between two slices of Apocalyptic bread. He has used it to distort the description Jesus gave about one woman or man having two different bodies in one, perverting it into Jesus talking about two completely different men or women.

And the only place and time this event occurs is when Jesus returns on the clouds at the time of the Apocalypse. Whereas Jesus clearly taught it occurs at the time of our death. A serious distortion removing the importance of being ready to die at any time by having your Spiritual body alive and well empowered by the Loving Life-force of our Loving Spiritual Creator in Heaven.

Matthew Alters the Timeline

Matthew 15:31 Jesus supposedly said, "When the Son of Man comes in His glory and all the Angels with Him then He will sit on His glorious throne. And all the nations will be gathered before Him, and He will separate them one from another as the shepherd separates the sheep from the goats. He will put the sheep on His right and the goats on the left. Then the King will say to those on His right."

Then we have a beautiful dialogue that follows about how we must all be kind, helpful and compassionate to all those in need. And those who are Spiritual and filled with Light and Love will enter the Heavenly Spiritual World and those who are devoid of Spiritual Light and Love will have to enter into darkness to be cleansed.

This again is a Teaching with a typical and beautiful, compassionate dialogue of Jesus about the characteristics we must all have as Spiritual children of our Loving Spiritual Creator and a warning to children devoid of Love about reaping as we sow, that has been manipulated and used to say this event will only happen at the Apocalypse when Jesus returns with His Angels. Jesus taught it actually happens for all of us on the day we die so we must always be ready by following His Spiritual Way and Teachings of Love and Non-violence.

Matthew Adds False Words

Matthew 26:64 And the high priest said to Jesus, "I adjure you by the living God that you tell us whether you are the Anointed one the Son of God." Jesus said, "You have said it yourself; (nevertheless, I tell you hereafter you will see the Son of Man sitting at the right hand of power and coming on the clouds of Heaven.") The first part of the answer would be enough for the high priests to convict Him of blasphemy. The extra words are Matthew's additions using a quote from the book of Daniel and other Old Testament Jewish sayings. Again, the purpose is to link Jesus to the Apocalypse and the Revelation Ruse to mislead followers of Jesus and take them away from focusing on becoming like Him to be ready to enter the Heavenly Spiritual World when they die and instead wait for Him to come back to save them.

Matthew is well known as the Jewish Gospel for good reason as it is heavily loaded up with Old Testament references and prophecies and the Jewish account of the Apocalypse in Daniel. He wants everyone to only see Jesus through a Jewish lens as the only chosen child of the two headed God Yahweh who will return at the Apocalypse to kill some children and save some children. Instead of the Universal Spiritual child of our Loving Spiritual Creator in the Heavenly Spiritual World filled only with Love. And Jesus teaches we can all become just like Him in every way by following His Spiritual Way of Love and Non-violence.

Mark Fabricating Apocalyptic Overlays

In Mark's Gospel at 13:1-27 we see a near word for word account of what is written in Matthew's long Daniel and Revelation regurgitation at 24:3-39. I believe Matthew pasted it into Mark's Gospel while copying some of Mark for his own Gospel. Due to the very heavy Jewish overlays found throughout the Matthew Gospel and only one other found in Mark, it is reasonable to conclude it was Matthew who fabricated it first. Mark is generally believed to be the earliest Gospel, but it seems highly unlikely based on the rest of Mark's Gospel that he wrote this Apocalyptic ramble. He mainly concentrates more on the actual Teachings of Jesus than any Jewish prophecies of Jesus returning to save all the good children and throw the bad children into Hell one day.

The only other reference made in Mark, found also in Luke and Matthew, concerning Jesus coming again on the clouds of Heaven at the Apocalypse is at Mark 14: 62 where the High priest asks Jesus, "Are you the Anointed one, the Son of the Blessed One?" Jesus replies, "I am, (and you shall see the Son of Man sitting at the right hand of power and coming with the clouds of Heaven.") This is the same quote from Daniel that Matthew uses to make out Jesus said this Himself. When just saying, "I am," would be enough to have Him stoned to death for blasphemy. Again, this is to link Jesus to the Revelation apocalyptic false book to give the Jewish book credence as an authentic book about Jesus and our Loving Creator to slander them.

As we can see Mark barely mentions anything about Jesus being linked to the Apocalypse book of Revelation or Daniel compared to Matthew except for the similar account of Matthew's long rambling Apocalyptic dialogue that I believe someone else inserted into his Gospel. The Gospel of Mark is overwhelmingly more concerned with following the Teachings of Jesus that save us now instead of waiting for Him to return.

Luke Fabricating Apocalyptic Overlays

Luke in 10:12-15 copies the Matthew dialogue at 11:20-24 where Jesus apparently says that various towns where He performed miracles but did not repent will be brought down to Hell at the judgement day. Again, a probable reference to the Apocalyptic Daniel and Revelation books. It is likely to be a Matthew origination not Luke's.

Luke 12:35 and 40 Jesus said, "Be dressed in readiness and keep your lamps lit." This is a correct saying of Jesus. Luke adds later, "You too be ready for the Son of Man is coming at an hour you do not expect." Here Luke is adding a false link to a Teaching of Jesus about always keeping your inner Spiritual Light burning for you do not know when you will die. Luke distorts this by using it to infer Jesus is coming at the Apocalypse which links Him to the Jewish Revelation Ruse and Daniel books.

Luke Slanders Heaven and Jesus

Luke 17:22-36 Here Luke provides a shorter version of Matthew's 24:3-39 long Revelation and Daniel dialogue attributed to Jesus about the Apocalypse that he probably copied from Matthew or Mark after Matthew probably inserted it into Mark. Luke adds an account of Lot where Jesus apparently says, "On the day that Lot went out from Sodom it rained fire and brimstone from Heaven and destroyed them all. It will be just the same the day that the Son of Man is revealed."

These words put into the mouth of Jesus are straight out slander against who Jesus and our Loving Spiritual Creator are in the Heavenly Spiritual World of Love. What a load of filthy garbage to even say that the Heavenly Spiritual World of Love is going to rain down fire and brimstone upon children. These false words assassinate the True identity of Jesus as a Spiritual child of Love and Non-violence and turn Him into a military Messiah of the Jewish two headed God Yahweh. Who slaughters all the lost sheep who do not obey Him and only saves those who do obey Him. Just the sort of thing all war mongering dictators do. Not a Universal shepherd Loving all His sheep, whether found or lost as Jesus Himself said He was, and our Loving Spiritual Creator is.

We already saw Jesus rebuke His own disciples who wanted to call down fire from Heaven to kill the people in the Samaritan village who insulted Jesus. Jesus told them they had no idea who the True God really was. Fire and brimstone raining down from the sky would certainly be a satanic manifestation to harm and murder children just as the two headed War God Yahweh of the Jews does. And Luke is saying Jesus will return one day during the Apocalypse and bring this about. Again, this links Jesus to the false Revelation book to take children of our Loving Creator back to worshiping the two headed God of the Jews Yahweh.

Luke also Perverts the Two Bodies Teaching

Luke also copies and includes the same ploy in Matthew to link the ending of this Apocalyptic ramble to the parable of two in a field, two in one bed and two at a millstone implying when Jesus comes at the Apocalypse one person is taken and another person is left. By implying the two at the millstone, two in the field and two in the one bed are two completely different people they are destroying the True Teaching of Jesus which says we all have two different bodies in the one body with us right now.

Luke Perverts the Talents Parable

Luke 19:12- 27 In this dialogue Luke provides a version of the talents parable where each servant is given some money from their master to put to good use. Those that do and increase the money are rewarded but the one who did nothing with the money has it taken from him. This is a correct saying of Jesus.

But in the dialogue, we also read these very brutal, revengeful false words supposedly representing Jesus and His Loving Creator that are cleverly mixed in to the story. "A nobleman went to a distant country to receive a Kingdom for himself and then return. But his citizens hated him and sent a delegation after him saying, 'We do not want this man to reign over us.' The nobleman said on his return, 'These enemies of mine who did not want me to reign over them, bring them here and slay them in my presence.'"

Here Luke has a full-on description of the revengeful, murdering two headed War God of the Jews who slaughters anyone who does not obey him. Implying that Jesus and His Loving Spiritual Creator are the ones who are going to do this when Jesus comes again at the Apocalypse. A very cunning way to transform Jesus and our Loving Spiritual Creator in the Heavenly World of Love into the violent, revengeful, murdering two headed God of the Jews. And thereby take Christians back into being Jewish worshiping their God and not the Loving Spiritual Creator of Jesus. This is pure slander. If we choose to reject the Spiritual Way of Jesus and His words, He does not kill us nor does our Loving Spiritual Creator. They just keep on Loving us until we awaken to become Spiritual children, no matter how long or how many lifetimes that may take.

The Common Apocalyptic Ramble

Luke 21:10-28 Here we see another false version of Matthew 24:3-39 and Mark 13:1-27 regurgitating the books of Daniel and Revelation in a rambling dialogue of death and destruction about the Apocalypse and Jesus returning on the clouds of Heaven. Obviously the three accounts come from a shared source. So, they are really only one account with some variations added by the writers but with the same message that links Jesus the Prince of Peace and our Loving Creator to the false Revelation Ruse book.

And they are the ones who will bring death and destruction upon mankind for not obeying them but save those who do. Just like the two headed God of the Jews which is why these cunning Jewish overlays are scattered amongst the True Teachings of Jesus about Love, Non-violence and Forgiveness.

They are placed in amongst the True Teachings of Jesus to over-ride the Spiritual Truth about our Loving Spiritual Creator and Jesus that will set you free. Instead, they convert Christians back into being Jewish Christians worshiping the two headed

God of the Jews in the name of our Loving Creator. Total slander and deliberate corruption of what Jesus really taught about Her and the Spiritual Way of Love and Non-violence to reach Heaven.

John Fabricating Apocalyptic Overlays

John makes virtually no mention of an Apocalypse or Jesus coming back one day on the clouds at the time of an Apocalypse. His only points that wander a bit are that Jesus is a Jewish sacrificial Lamb of God and was the only Son of God who can save us and that God may judge and be wrathful at times. His Gospel is easily the best as it talks about the Loving Spiritual Way of Jesus that can transform us all from beings of flesh into being born again into beings of Spiritual Love. In John we find Jesus saying, "Flesh only gives birth to flesh. Spirit only gives birth to Spirit. Marvel not that I tell you, you must be born again from above."

Sacrificial Lamb of God

John 1:35-36 Here John has John the Baptist calling Jesus the Lamb of God as a Jewish overlay. 'And the next day John was standing with two of his disciples and he looked at Jesus as He walked by and said, "Behold, the Lamb of God."' This sees Jesus through a Jewish lens as a sacrifice to save us by taking our sins away by His death. Jesus said it is His words that save us not His physical death or blood on the cross.

Only Child of God Distortion

John 3:16 Here John makes Jesus out to be the only child of our Loving Spiritual Creator begotten by our Loving Creator. These words are not spoken by Jesus but by the writer of the Gospel after Jesus finishes His talk with Nicodemus. "For God so loved the world that He gave His only begotten Son that whosoever believes in Him shall not perish but have Eternal Life. He who believes in Him is not judged; he who does not believe in Him is judged already because he has not believed in the name of the only begotten Son of God."

Jesus is a Spiritual child of our Loving Spiritual Creator who awakened to His True Spiritual identity by seeking the Spiritual Truth and its source. He uncovered the Treasure of His Spiritual identity hidden in the field of His Earthly flesh and became at one with it. He then began Teaching us to find it also and become like Him. We can all become children of our Loving Spiritual Creator if we search to be born again in the Spirit of Heavenly Love from above as Jesus taught us to do.

However, it is True He was the first Jew we know of to awaken to this Spiritual Truth of Universal Love and a Spiritual Creator who is only Love. John also overlays the Jewish belief that only those who believe Jesus is the son of God will be saved, and all others will be judged. That is incorrect.

More correctly, all those who follow the Spiritual Way of Jesus will become Loving children so will be Spiritually safe and all those who follow a darker Way of evil will reap the suffering they have sown. It applies to all children on the Earth regardless of religion or no religion. The Spiritual Way of Jesus is a Universal Way of Love and Non-violence and can be found in many different belief systems to varying degrees.

John 5:21 and 12:47 has Jesus say, "For not even the Father judges anyone, but He has given all judgement to the Son. He who honours Me honours Him and he who does not honour Me does not honour Him. I did not come to judge the world but to save the world. If anyone hears my sayings and does not keep them, I do not judge them."

We reap as we sow, Jesus and our Loving Spiritual Creator have no need to judge us, we are our own judges and the Spiritual Law of Reaping What We Sow is always in existence. They just want us to awaken and become Loving Spiritual children and follow the Way of Love home to Heaven. They can never hurt us.

John Slanders Our Loving Creator

John 3: 36 Here we see another Jewish overlay of judgement put onto Jesus. "He who believes in the Son has Eternal Life but he who does not obey the Son will not see Life but the wrath of God." The first part is correct because it refers to following the words of Jesus that give us True Spiritual Life. But then we see the Loving Creator painted as a wrathful God of the Jews who punishes those who do not obey him. Slandering our Loving Creator whose Light and Love shines on the good and the evil until they awaken into their Spiritual Life. Any wrath we receive is of our own making.

Thomas Gospel No Apocalyptic Fabrications

There are no Apocalypse or Jesus coming back on the cloud's sayings in the Thomas Gospel at all. There are virtually no heavy Jewish overlays. It is all about His Universal Teachings and words of Love and understanding them to transform and become just like Him and follow Him to where He has gone. The Heavenly Spiritual World of Love beyond all pain and suffering. Which is exactly the intention of what His Teachings were all about.

His words can awaken our Spiritual Life while still in a temporary body of flesh and get ready to leave on our own judgement day. The day our body of flesh dies. Not some book of Daniel and Revelation Jewish death and destruction Apocalypse time in an unknown future with Jesus and our Loving Creator coming back to slaughter Her lost children and save those who were good.

This is why the Gospel of Thomas was banned by the strong contingent of Jewish writers who had another agenda. To make Jesus the only one who can become fully Spiritual, the Jewish Messiah and the only one who is a Spiritual child of our Loving

Spiritual Creator in the Heavenly Spiritual World of Love. And place Him on an ivory tower above us all and emphasise His death on the cross as a sacrificial Jewish Lamb to pay for our sins instead of focusing on His Universal words of Love and Non-violence that awaken us all to become the same as Him.

They allow you to worship Him but never believe you can be exactly like Him in every way. Only He is sin free, yet all His dialogues are about setting us all free from being slaves to sin by following His words and becoming like Him. They have undermined His Teachings to prevent us being fully empowered by the same Spiritual Life-force in our own Spiritual bodies that He found within Himself from our Loving Creator in Heaven. To set us free from the flesh and to Spiritually awaken just as He did.

Jesus Wants Us to Be Just Like Him

In Matthew 10:25 Jesus says, "It is sufficient for the pupil to become like his Teacher." And "Whoever believes in Me and My Teachings, you will be able to do these works I do and even greater ones than these."

His Teachings are not exclusive like the Jewish ones He tried to change. They are a Universal inclusive Spiritual Truth found in all of us throughout many religions and ways of life that can save us all to Heaven and bring Peace on Earth if we only follow His Spiritual Way of Love and Non-violence.

GOD IS LOVE LOVE IS LIFE
Love is all there really is. The rest is just confusion.
Love is all there really is. The rest is just delusion.

Chapter Twenty-Seven

Spiritual Analogies

The Bridge of Jesus is Our Bridge Too

I often spent time crossing a river on a foot bridge from one shore to the other while taking a walk and stopping halfway in the middle of the river wondering why I felt that I was stuck between two worlds. The Earth world behind me and the Heavenly shore in front of me but due to a physical attack on my body of flesh I was too ill to be of much use in the Earth world but was not yet fully alive in my Spiritual body to be in the Heavenly World. The bridge was a wonderful symbolic place to contemplate this.

Halfway across the bridge above the flowing river below I would talk to our Loving Creator and Jesus and wonder why I was unable to be healed. To either have a full life on Earth for a while or possibly be welcomed into the Eternal Heavenly Spiritual World if I was ready to enter, rather than being suspended between the two and feeling of little use to anyone.

Then one day I realised the answer they were giving me by getting me to stop in the middle of the bridge between the two shores of the Earth world and the Heavenly Spiritual World was right in front of me the whole time. They were trying to help me understand that I was the bridge itself between the two shores just as Jesus was and wanted us to be also. But at present I could only bring a little of Heaven's Love to Earth due to my illness.

I already knew I had two different bodies in one by listening to His words and Teachings and that my Spiritual body and Soul was now my primary body not my body of flesh. But my body of flesh was the only way I could manifest the Loving Spiritual Life-force that was now empowering my Spiritual body, given to us by our Loving Creator, to come into this world to help children in any small way that I could. I was just a small bridge now.

But I realised what being a Living bridge really meant even when we are ill. Half of my Living bridge was made out of my body of Earthly flesh with its feet firmly planted on the shoreline of the Earth world. While the other half of my Living bridge was made out of my Soul and Spiritual body with its feet slowly becoming more firmly planted on the shoreline of the Heavenly Spiritual World guided by the words of Jesus.

Two different bodies from two different worlds joined together above the middle of the river to form one complete arch that spanned the river from one shore to the other. A Spiritual child of Heaven connected to Earth. Just as Jesus realised that He was a bridge in this same Way once He became enlightened.

And although I was not yet as Spiritually awakened as my great friend and Teacher Jesus was, I knew that if I just kept following His words and Teachings they would gradually transform me also into an awakened Spiritual child of our Loving Spiritual Creator in the Heavenly Spiritual World. Just as they can transform everyone to become a Spiritual child of Love on Earth.

The Bridge of St. Christopher

We should all be striving to become a Living bridge between the two worlds to help other children by having one foot in Heaven and one foot on Earth. This is like the beautiful story of St. Christopher's Spiritual awakening to become a bridge. He wanted to serve the greatest being on Earth. So, he first found the greatest, most powerful and richest Earthly king and asked to serve him. The king said that he indeed was the greatest king on Earth, and no one was greater or richer than he was and welcomed Christopher's service. So, Christopher happily began serving him.

Then one day a messenger came to the king telling him that satan was approaching the city with his devils on the road about a day away from here. The king trembled with fear and cried out, "We are all doomed," and he crossed himself with the sign of the cross. Christopher said to the king, "You told me there was no one greater than you in this world. So, why are you so frightened of this person called satan?" The king replied, "I have not got the type of power needed to overcome him."

So, disappointed in the Earthly king, Christopher left him because he still wanted to serve the most powerful person on Earth so he went to ask satan if he could serve him. He went and met satan and his devils on the road and asked if he was the greatest most powerful being on Earth because he only wanted to serve the greatest one. Satan told him he was the greatest and could destroy the life of anyone he wanted to and welcomed Christopher to serve him.

But as they continued travelling along towards the city, they saw a shrine dedicated to Jesus up ahead on the side of the road. Satan said, "I am frightened to go near that shrine we will have to go the long way around it." Christoper said to Him, "I thought you said you can destroy the life of anyone in this world. Why are you so frightened of that shrine with the cross on it?"

Satan replied, "I am the Lord of Darkness dominating this material Earth world and I can destroy all children by inciting them to hatred, greed, murder and evil doings and finally put their mortal body to death but that cross belongs to Jesus. He is the only one who can destroy me because He is not of this world but of the Heavenly Spiritual World of Love, Light and Truth. And I am a shadow figure and His Loving Light and Truth shining on me will destroy me."

So, Christopher left satan and searched for this person called Jesus to serve Him. He travelled far and wide searching for Jesus until he came to a strong flowing river with rapids where an old Spiritual hermit was living in a hut by the river. He told the hermit that he wanted to serve a person called Jesus but could not find him anywhere. The hermit informed him that he could start serving Jesus by following His Spiritual Way and helping children who are in danger in this world. And Jesus would be very pleased if he did that for Him for that was the type of work He did Himself.

Christopher said, "But how do I serve Him. I would like to meet Him in person to thank Him for letting me serve Him." The hermit told him that if he was patient and just started serving him now by following His instructions which he will share with him, then there is no doubt he will eventually meet Him as time goes by. Christopher asked him what kind of work he could do for Jesus. The hermit told him that the main work Jesus did was to reduce and remove the sufferings of children and save them from a Spiritual death.

He said to Christopher, "Many children try to cross this dangerous river by themselves and are washed away by the current and seriously injured and some perish and die. You are tall and strong, and you're the sort of person that Jesus needs to serve Him and His work by helping to carry them across this dangerous river safely to yonder shore."

So, Christopher started happily doing just that and He saved many children of our Loving Creator from perishing in the dangerous river by helping them to cross over to the safety of the yonder shore. One day a small child came and asked him to carry him across the river. As Christopher was moving through the dangerous waters the child seemed to get heavier and heavier until He could barely keep standing but finally reached the yonder shore to put the child safely down.

Christopher asked the child, "Who are you, I could barely carry you across the river?" The child answered, "I am the child of our Loving Spiritual Creator, the one known as Jesus whom you now serve, and I have carried the weight of this suffering world on my shoulders and now you are helping Me by doing the same thing." Then the child just vanished.

Any Spiritual work we perform in this dangerous Earthly world of suffering brings the Love of Heaven and our Spiritual Loving Creator to Earth through our life on Earth. It does not matter how big or small that work is, or how few or many those works are for the Heavenly Love is always the same. As long as it Lives in us and flows through us to others, we are at one with it and have Eternal Spiritual Life.

The Two Plank Analogy

Our personal Spiritual / Earthly bridge to connect us to the Heavenly shore from the Earthly shore is like being born with two planks the same size that are exactly overlapping each other and stuck so close together that they appear as being just one. But the nature of the two planks and substance they are each made from is very different, but they are joined together at one end with a hinge made of Love. The hinge was created in the Heavenly Spiritual World and can only be opened through the power of the Spiritual Loving Life-force that Jesus teaches us about to become at one with.

There are instructions printed on every Earthly plank saying to use this to crossover the river to find a Treasure waiting for you there. Everyone can see and hold the first plank easily which is like an Earthly plank of wood made from earthly elements and material Life-forces, but not all can see the second plank that is overlapping the first that they are holding. That is because it is made of Heavenly elements and a Spiritual Life-force and is like crystal glass that is so pure and clean that you can look right through it at the wooden plank and not even know it was there.

Many children only saw the wooden plank and tried to push the wooden plank stuck together with the clear crystal plank of glass over the river to reach the yonder shore. But no matter how hard they tried it would only reach halfway and then just fall into the water, and they had to pull it out and try again. They often had meetings and discussed how they could make the plank longer to reach the promised land and treasure waiting there for them across the river, but it seemed they all had the same problem and same size of wood.

Many of them worshipped money and had accumulated large amounts of monetary and material wealth as it gave them great power to do almost anything they wanted to do or have anything they desired in the material world. So, believing in this power of money and material wealth some tied their fortune to the plank and tried to float across the river on it. They thought that they would be able to reach the yonder shore and Treasure waiting there for them through the power of their great Earthly wealth. But they barely left the shoreline when they all sank beneath the waters weighed down by their material wealth.

Many just gave up trying unable to figure out how to use the plank successfully to reach the yonder shore. Then one day while they sat around talking about whether the instructions and story about the Treasure waiting for them on the yonder shore was just a big hoax, a shepherd wandered by and asked them what they were all talking about so intently. And they explained the conundrum they all had of how to use this plank given to them to cross to the yonder shore where a Treasure was promised to be waiting for them to receive. And how they all failed no matter what they tried and were beginning to think it must be a joke.

The shepherd said, "I had the same plank as you, but I was inspired to look more closely and deeply at the plank and discovered how to make it reach the yonder shore and now I can go over and come back again any time I want." They were amazed that a simple shepherd had worked out such a complex, bewildering conundrum when they with all their material wealth and intellectual intelligence as leaders in this material world could not. "How did you do it?" they asked the shepherd.

He said, "I found another plank that is Spiritual and as clean as pure glass that is overlayed on the wooden plank which has a hinge made of Love at one end. And once I found that hinge and realised what it and the plank was made of, I just opened up the Spiritual plank of pure crystal glass and both of the planks then extended out as One and formed a safe bridge for me to reach the other shore easily."

And they asked the shepherd how was it that he could see the plank of Spiritual glass when they could not. And if He found the Treasure and what was it. And He replied, "The Spiritual plank attached to the wooden plank can only be seen and found by looking through the eye of Love of your Spiritual body and mind. You were looking through the eyes of your Earthly body and mind filled with the vision of greed within you which blinded your Spiritual Eye from seeing the Truth. The Treasure is Eternal Spiritual Life and Love."

This analogy concerning the Spiritual Teachings of Jesus is centered around some important Spiritual points He often taught. Firstly, we are all born with two different bodies. The wooden plank represents our body of earthly flesh and material mind and if we only live out of that body, we will not be able to reach the yonder Spiritual shore of Heaven. The clear plank made of pure crystal glass is our Spiritual body and Spiritual mind of Love but is invisible to our eyes of the flesh so we must search for it within ourselves by having a warm and Loving heart towards other children. When both bodies are fully alive, and at one in purpose they can connect us from the Earth world to the Heavenly world as if they were only one body made of Love, just like a bridge.

Children who worship money, material wealth and Earthly power can never cross into the Heavenly Spiritual World as they have only lived out of their body of temporary flesh. The river we must all cross is called, 'The Divine Spiritual River of Reaping What We Sow,' and it never stops flowing. Spiritually awakened children can cross easily but those weighed down with evil or wrong doings, greed or a cold selfish heart are swept away by the flowing waters and carried to another destination to be cleansed in accordance with the life they led.

Our Spiritual body and mind of singular Love can only be awakened through the power of the Spiritual Loving Life-force of our Loving Spiritual Creator in the Heavenly Spiritual World who gives us our True Life. So, we must connect to Heaven within us by living out of the Loving Life-force placed in our Spiritual bodies by our Loving Spiritual Creator. It is this Heavenly Love that we find within us that opens us up fully so we may reach the Heavenly World after passing through the death experience of our body of earthly flesh.

Once we are Spiritually awoken, we will see this material world and everyone in it through our Spiritual eye or mind of Love and we will bring our body and dualistic mind of the flesh into perfect alignment with our own Spiritual body and mind of Love. Our two bodies now fully awakened to span from Heaven to the Earth like a bridge empowered by the Loving Spiritual Life-force of our Loving Spiritual Creator flowing freely from the Heavenly World through both of our bodies to all children and all living things on Earth.

The Two Hands Analogy

Both of our bodies are strongly connected and overlay each other so they appear as one body. It is like placing your hands together palm to palm in perfect alignment with your fingers spread open but if you look at them from a distance you only see one hand. And at the time of passing through our death experience the connection between the hands is broken and as they slide apart it reveals there were two hands there all the time. One hand now falling to the ground and returning to the Earth from which it was formed. One hand waving goodbye as it leaves for the Heavenly Spiritual World beyond all suffering from which it was formed. If that hand is ready to enter.

Again, this simple Spiritual analogy about what Jesus was teaching is to clarify His words that we all have two very different bodies with us right now, but most children do not realise or believe this anymore. One is formed of temporary earthly flesh that will die and return to the earth while our Spiritual body is formed from a Spiritual Life-force. And if our Spiritual body is full of Spiritual Life and Love we will leave our body of flesh when it dies and enter the Heavenly Spiritual World of Love and Peace. And while here in the Earthly material world we can perform far more good works with two hands working in perfect harmony empowered by Heavenly Love than just one hand or body of flesh working without it.

But we must bring our Spiritual hand or body to Life ourselves by living out of it every day. Jesus can't do it for you but will always be there beside you to guide and hold on to you and help you to do it. As Jesus said, we only have to follow His instructions on how to bring our Spiritual body and mind of Love alive to have True Life and then live out of it as our primary identity while on Earth and we will never really die. Spirit is not flesh and flesh is not Spirit as Jesus so simply and correctly pointed out. They are two entirely different bodies in one here on Earth.

The Water in the Vase Analogy

A vase is often made of clay material from the earth. It is solid and made of many complex elements within the clay. Every vase can look different. Some are tall, some short, some narrow, some wide, some white, some black, some square, some round, and the possibilities are endless. Vases are unique like our bodies of earthly flesh. But each vase holds a form made only of water.

Water is a different substance to material clay and as a liquid it can flow and take the shape of any vase. When you pour the same water from a well into different shaped vases the water takes the form of each different vase perfectly. Our Spiritual bodies are all the same in our vases, just like the water. We have to look through the material vase of the other child to see the inner Spiritual child within is just like us. The Treasure hidden in the field of our clay vases is our Spiritual body and Soul mind of Love.

The Treasure Buried in the Field

This is the original analogy given by Jesus in Matthew 13:44 combined with the Thomas Gospel where He points to the inner Spiritual Treasure within us all.

Jesus said, "The Kingdom of Heaven is like a Treasure hidden in a field and a man who was ploughing that field found the Treasure and filled with joy covered it until he went and sold all his Earthly possessions to buy that field and own the Treasure." Jesus is simply saying that our Spiritual Life is hidden within our body of Earthly flesh, and we must search for it to uncover it, and it is more important than our whole physical, material life.

In Luke 9:62 Jesus refers to the plough again to teach that once you start looking for the Spiritual Treasure within you, you must not stop and give up and return to being just material, or you will not easily find your Spiritual body. Jesus said, "No one after putting his hand to the plough and looking back on the things he left behind is ready to enter the Heavenly Spiritual World of our Loving Creator."

The following is another version based on the original, 'Treasure buried in the field of our body of flesh', that Jesus gave to help open up His original short analogy and the message it contained while presenting it in the traditional style.

A kindhearted miner who knew where gold was buried went to the home of a man and said to him, "I am here to tell you that I know all about gold and where it can be found. And I am here to give you this good news that you have a rare, precious and pure type of gold buried in your own backyard. All you have to do is dig and search for it and uncover it from beneath the dirt that is concealing it from view. I have this book of instructions to follow so you can find it."

The man replied, "Well I have never seen it and I have lived in my home for 50 years. I don't believe you and I don't believe such a rare, precious gold like that even exists or that such a gold could be in the backyard of my own home. Stop bothering me and go away and take your instruction book with you you're wasting my time and interrupted me while I was checking my bank balance on the computer." So, the kind miner felt sad at what he was missing out on but took no offence and went on his way.

He then went on to another home that he also knew would have the same type of gold in their backyard. He called to the man and said, "I am here to tell you that I know all about gold and where it can be found in your home." He then told the man the same things as he did to the previous man informing him also that it was in his own backyard. And also offered him the instruction book to locate it.

This man was amazed to hear such good news and was filled with joy at his good fortune and was overwhelmed by the loving generosity and kindness of the miner to reveal this to him so he may claim the gold as his. He was really struggling in life and said to the miner, "You have saved my life by telling me about the gold, I love you more than anyone for telling me this." And he gladly accepted the book of instructions the miner offered to him and held it with great reverence.

He then said to the kindhearted miner, "Please stay here with me always as I wish to celebrate you every day for coming to me with this good news about the gold and giving me this book on how to find it. And I want to bring my friends to meet you so they can celebrate your name with me." The miner said, "I appreciate your gratitude, but I have others to tell about the gold and must move on. And anyway, you cannot see or own the gold that is yours until you uncover it from the earth yourself. That is the most important thing of all and why I came to tell you of this. It is vital you follow all of my instructions in this book I gave you on how to find the gold to enrich yourself as you only have a limited time to find it." And then the kindhearted miner left.

The man held the book lovingly in his hands that could change his life, and it was now the most valuable item he owned thanks to the kindhearted miner whom he now loved more than anyone in the world. So, he put it on his shelf in a very safe place of honour and sat and looked at it every day praising the kindhearted miner who gave it to him but never read it. Luke 6:46 Jesus said, "Why do you call Me, 'Lord, Lord' but do not do the things that I say?"

The Kindhearted miner came to another home and told the owner the same things he said to the others and then offered him the book of instructions also. The owner of that home was initially overjoyed and gratefully accepted the book and thanked the kind miner for the knowledge he had revealed to him about the hidden gold in his own backyard and the wonderful book of instructions he gave to him on how to find it. He told the miner he would start searching for it that very day. The kindhearted miner then went on his way.

He eagerly began reading the instructions and following them in great anticipation of finding the buried Treasure. But after a while he said to himself, "Some of these instructions in this book I understand and can do but others seem very difficult to me, and some seem unnecessary and others I totally disagree with, and I don't want to do them. If I have to follow all of these instructions to uncover the gold it seems to me to be more hard work than what the gold may be worth. So, I think I would rather just stay the way I am and give this a miss." Then he threw the book out and failed to tell his children anything about it.

He came to another home and again explained why he had come and offered that owner the book of instructions also. This person was amazed at such good news and gratefully accepted the book praising the kindhearted miner for thinking of him and bringing him this good news with the instruction book to follow. After the miner left, he immediately sat down to study the instructions and slowly gathered all the tools he needed to uncover the gold. Some he already had while others he had to go out and acquire in order that he had all the necessary tools the miner instructed him to have to uncover the golden Treasure.

He then began applying all the tools to the job of uncovering the Treasure hidden in his own backyard until it began appearing from within the field of earth that had been covering it up all the time. Following all of the instructions he finally set it free from the earth and lifted it up glistening in the sunlight and for the first time he beheld the beauty and the purity of this rare, precious gold that was buried in his own backyard, but never knew it was there. And he thought of the kindhearted miner who went to all that trouble to tell him about it and how to find it and was grateful to him. And now it was his to call his own thanks to the kindhearted miner who helped him find it.

Our True Spiritual Life and Spiritual body and Soul is hidden within our body of flesh. Some children do not believe it exists at all and so never look for it. Some children have immense love for the one who told them about it and treat the instruction book with great reverence but never read it so never look for the gold either but just love the one who gave them the book. Some children are very grateful to the one who gave them the book and start to read the instructions enthusiastically but soon find they involve too much hard work so decide to give up, never look for the gold either and throw the book away.

But some children are very grateful to the kindhearted miner and love him for giving them the knowledge and instruction book on how to uncover the gold. They immediately start reading all the instructions and gather together all the tools mentioned that are needed to uncover the gold by digging in the earth until the gold begins to be revealed to them just as he said it would be. Only then do they understand what the Treasure he spoke of really was, their own Eternal Spiritual Life filled only with Love, the richest most pure thing of all to have as your own.

And thanks to the kindhearted miner's Love for them and giving them his instructions they have now found this inner Spiritual Treasure and they have become at one with that Treasure and now are that Treasure.

Every child searching for the golden Spiritual Treasure within themselves firstly needs to have belief in the Treasure's existence, the source of the One who created it, and the Loving Teacher's Spiritual Way to understand and follow to find it. All children require the same tools but few children have the full set so they must acquire the ones they do not have.

These may include such things as the tool of forgiveness, the tool of generosity, the tool of kindness, the tool of compassion, the tool of non-violence, the tool of equanimity towards all children, the tool of not condemning, the tool of caring for those in need especially those who have fallen down, the tool of humility along with others mentioned in the instruction book.

But the most important tool of all from which all the others are made is Love. For Our Loving Spiritual Creator is only Love and it is She who created our Spiritual Life, Spiritual body and Soul out of Her Loving Spiritual Life-force for us to come out from this material world of suffering at the end of our journey and enter the Heavenly Spiritual World of Love. And since She is Spiritual and only Love, Eternal and True Life then all She creates is only Spiritual, Love, Eternal and True Life.

Soul Riders on an Earthly Horse

We are all like Spiritual riders on an Earthly horse. We are not the horse, and the horse is not us. But everything our horse feels we feel and experience also. And the Spiritual feelings we can experience can also be felt by our horse.

We have an obligation to care for our horse and make sure it eats healthy foods, give it only healthy drinks, avoid all dangerous substances that might hurt it, exercise it, don't work it too hard, give it rest when needed and tend to any injuries that may occur to it.

We have the same obligation to our Spiritual body and Soul and must always keep them healthy through being Loving, forgiving, compassionate, generous, kind, helpful and selfless. We must always be nourished by the Loving Spiritual Life-force flowing into us from our Loving Spiritual Creator in the Heavenly Spiritual World and never commit any wrongdoing that might block that flow entering into us. We can then share this Loving Life-force endlessly with other children as the more we share the more flows into us, and we are never empty of this Heavenly Love. Endless Love flowing from Heaven through us to all children.

Then we hold the reigns of our horse and together we act as one in purpose to bring Heaven's Love to all those in need until our horse's life ends and they return to the earth, and we dismount to return hopefully to the Heavenly Spiritual World.

GOD IS LOVE LOVE IS LIFE

Chapter Twenty-Eight

Conclusion

Jesus was as human as you and me with all the same challengers we all have to face born into a temporary physical body of flesh that one day dies. With all the same problems of trying to understand the purpose and meaning of our short life on Earth amongst so many different belief systems and opinions of other children. Blessed from Heaven He searched for the ultimate answer that made sense of all the dualities of this material world like Birth and Death, Pleasure and Pain, Peace and War, Evil and Good, Rich and Poor, Health and Sickness. Eventually He was able to find a singular Spiritual Way to view it all through, that not only made sense of it all but empowered Him to bring only Love and Non-violence into this complicated puzzle to help resolve all the needless man-made suffering. And He also realised there is another Spiritual World beyond all suffering that we can all go to after passing through our death experience if we know the Way.

He became Spiritually awakened through searching for and finding the source of the Loving Spiritual Life-force from the Heavenly Spiritual World and becoming at one with it. This was the Loving Spiritual Creator He taught us about who is only Love. He then realised we all have two different bodies with us right now. One body is Spiritual and Eternal empowered only by the Loving Spiritual Life-force of our Loving Creator and lives on after death to reap as it has sown. Our other body is a biological body of flesh made from and empowered only by earthly elements and dies and returns to the earth from which it was formed.

He understood the characteristics that we must all become at one with that brings our Spiritual body and True Life alive and how to live out of it here on Earth to be able to enter the Eternal Heavenly World. So, He dedicated His life to share this knowledge with everyone and taught us how to also awaken our Spiritual body and Soul mind of Love before our body of flesh dies. His Teachings are Universal and apply to all children and can transform anyone into becoming a Spiritual child of our Loving Spiritual Creator while still here on Earth.

But the choice to listen to His words, understand them, follow them and become transformed by them is a deeply personal free will decision and each one of us must make that decision alone for it to have True Spiritual strength and conviction. We must not allow coercion or blind belief in what someone else tells us to influence our decision. It must be a logical, intelligent understanding of the Spiritual Truth and Way of Love that Jesus taught that makes perfect Spiritual sense in this chaotic, dualistic and dangerous material world.

An answer that gives us the power we need by becoming at one with the Loving Spiritual Life-force from our Loving Spiritual Creator in the Heavenly World to be able to confront and deal with all the challenges we may meet on Earth through the eyes and Soul of our Spiritual identity of Love. I hope you may think more deeply about this and also become committed to being a pacifist Spiritual child of Heaven on Earth.

Many distortions and perversions have crept into the Spiritual Teachings and Way of Love and Non-violence that Jesus taught two thousand years ago. But anyone who can see Him as Love and Non-violence and our Loving Spiritual Creator as Love and Non-violence also, will be able to recognise the false overlays put onto Jesus and our Loving Creator and ignore them.

With Love from me to you. Christopher John Joseph

Chapter Twenty-Nine

GOD IS LOVE
LOVE IS LIFE

**Our Loving Spiritual Creator is Only Love.
Jesus is a Child of Our Loving Spiritual Creator
empowered only by Her Loving Spiritual Life-force.
May we all be Children of our Loving Spiritual Creator**

By Christopher John Joseph a pacifist follower of Jesus for 68 years who believes the core principles of the Teachings of Jesus are Love and Non-violence. They are Universal and available to all who choose to find them within the field of their own Earthly flesh. Flesh only gives birth to flesh. Spirit only gives birth to Spirit. Marvel not that you must be born again into your Spirit.

Contact: jcinfocus@gmail.com

www.ingramcontent.com/pod-product-compliance
Lightning Source LLC
Chambersburg PA
CBHW071950070526
44583CB00015B/1132